# THE VOICE
## OF MODERN
# HATRED

Nicholas Fraser was born in London and educated at
Oxford. He has worked in Paris, New York and London as
a reporter, columnist, producer and commissioning editor.

ALSO BY NICHOLAS FRASER

**CONTINENTAL DRIFTS: TRAVELS IN THE NEW EUROPE**

**EVITA: THE REAL LIFE OF EVA PERÓN**

# THE VOICE OF MODERN HATRED

**ENCOUNTERS
WITH EUROPE'S
NEW RIGHT**

**NICHOLAS FRASER**

PICADOR

**For Celal and Marie,**

**and for Isabelle and Joanne**

First published 2000 by Picador

This edition published 2001 by Picador
an imprint of Macmillan Publishers Ltd
25 Eccleston Place, London SW1W 9NF
Basingstoke and Oxford
Associated companies throughout the world
www.macmillan.com

ISBN 0 330 37213 0

1 3 5 7 9 8 6 4 2

A CIP catalogue record for this book is available from
the British Library.

Typeset by SetSystems Ltd, Saffron Walden, Essex
Printed and bound in Great Britain by
Mackays of Chatham plc, Chatham, Kent

# CONTENTS

# PERMISSIONS ACKNOWLEDGEMENTS

Every effort has been made to contact all copyright holders. The author would be happy to rectify any ommissions at the first opportunity. Grateful acknowledgement is made to the copyright holders for permission to reproduce extracts from the following:

*The Drowned and the Saved* by Primo Levi, translated by Raymond Rosenthal (Michael Joseph, 1988), copyright © Giulio Einandi editore s.p.a., 1986. Translation copyright © Simon & Schuster, Inc., 1988.

*Slouching Towards Gomorrah* by Robert H. Bork, copyright © Robert H. Bork, 1996, published by HarperCollins Publishers Inc.

*The Buddha of Suburbia* by Hanif Kureishi, published by Faber and Faber Ltd.

*The English Auden* by W. H. Auden, published by Faber and Faber Ltd.

*Beloved Chicago Man* by Simone de Beauvoir, published by Victor Gollancz.

*A Time of Gifts* by Patrick Leigh Fermor, published by John Murray (Publishers) Ltd.

*Pasolini* by Enzo Siciliano. Grateful acknowledgement is made to the author.

*Colour and Citizenship: A Report on British Race Relations* by F. J. B. Rose and others, copyright © Institute of Race Relations 1969, published by Oxford University Press.

*The Abbess of Crewe* by Muriel Spark, in *The Collected Fiction of Muriel Spark* vol. 2, published by Houghton Mifflin.

# ACKNOWLEDGEMENTS

Some of the research for this book was done in the course of a documentary film on the Far Right which was shown throughout Europe. My thanks go to Mark Thompson, Jane Root and Nicola Moody at the BBC; Hans-Robert Eisenhauer at ARTE, the Franco-German cultural channel; and Mette Hoffmann Meyer at TV2. The idea for the film (and much else) came from Celal Artunkal, and he shares the dedication. Gill Coleridge gave me confidence in the project and Richard Milner provided invaluable editorial support. The George Soros Open Society Foundation contributed not to this book, but to the finishing of the film. I hold a special debt to Jo Lapping. My less than fortunate family put up with many things, not least the long-term presence around the hearth of such unappetizing works as *Mein Kampf*; and they receive my heartfelt thanks. The following people helped me out: Yori Albrecht, Krishan Arora, Carole Bienaimé, Don and Hilly Boyd, Norman Davies, Frances de Souza, Bruno Funk, Naomi Gryn, Christian Harlang, Leonie Jameson, R. B. Kitaj, Séverine Labat, Colin MacCabe, John Marshall, Narinder Minhas, Patrick Moreau (though, alas, he will not agree with my conclusions), Christian and Tamsin Poveda, Heike Rebholz, Diane Weyerman, Paul Winstone, Leslie Woodhead, Inigo Thomas, Fred Tuten and Karen Marta, Rinke van den Brink, Iikka Venkalanti and Pierre Vidal-Naquet. From those whom space prevents me from acknowledging, I beg forgiveness. The errors in the book are my own.

# INTRODUCTION

'Love of humanity is easy. People only detest each other from nearby.'

Jacques Chardonne

The more I became acquainted with hatred, the faster it appeared to change character. There were isolated acts – violent pinpricks, one might say – to consider. Also, there was a type of organization that facilitated the coming together of large numbers of people, ostensibly in the name of solidarity but with the express aim of differentiating its adherents from their enemies. But I learnt, too, that so much variety in the expression of hostility was delusory. If you studied hatred – as I did – you might find yourself flipped around what appeared to be a giant, brightly coloured pinball machine. But you would end up helpless, in the same dark place at the bottom of the board. For it seemed that the essence of hatred, whatever its objects, was identical. Hatred appeared to be about to leave the field, vanquished at last, but in Europe it would always return. There appeared to be no end to the fomenting of bitter, pathological enmity, and no shortage of those ready to be perpetrators. As I finished this book, hatred appeared to be chasing me. In the European spring of 1999, close to a million ethnic Albanians were expelled from their homeland in Kosovo. Their Serb tormentors often tore in pieces the old Yugoslav passports, rendering these new deportees stateless. The Serbs wished to destroy an entire nation, and their actions reminded all Europeans of the horrifying recent past of genocide. Mass graves could be seen from the air near many villages, and it was in response to these atrocities that NATO began its campaign of airstrikes. Later, the Albanians took their revenge on the Serbs. But there was hatred to be found closer to home, too. During those same weeks, nail bombs were placed in three separate London sites, where they might be expected to harm as many people as possible. A shopping area frequented by blacks was targeted in Brixton, then an Asian market in East London's Brick Lane, and finally a pub frequented by gays in Soho. The man arrested and charged with these atrocities proved not to be a member of any existing right-wing group but a 23-year-old engineer from a suburban estate in Hampshire. It appeared that he was a solitary operator, acting from a deeply held if perverse sense of personal mission. A similar warped sense of outrage appeared, too, to have motivated the attack by Swedish far-right activists on a journalist who had been investigating their activities and whose car was blown up. The Swedes wondered exactly what they and their famed welfare system had done to deserve such hatred, posing a question by now familiar in circles where hatred was discussed. Were the rest of us perhaps at fault and in some sense to blame for the monsters in our midst? Would it be a good thing if, acting in its own defence, right-thinking society was less indulgent towards the liberties of those for whom freedom meant the liberty to spread hatred or maim?

For over two and a half months, beginning in January 2000, it was possible to sit in a room in London at which the question of whether the Holocaust had actually happened was argued over. Court 37, just off the Srand, was heavily attended each day. There were Jewish veterans and their wives and curious bystanders. Doggedly, reporters sat through the entire proceedings. The white wood tables, lit by neon, were each day more cluttered with documents. At one end of the courtroom sat the lawyers representing Penguin Books, and the historian Deborah Lipstadt. At the other was the burly pinstriped figure of David Irving. Because he was acting on his own behalf, Irving handled his own mass of paper. He moved from a table to a dais, depending on whether he was doing the questioning, or being cross-examined. Irving claimed that his own reputation had been irretrievably damaged by Deborah Lipstadt's book. He could no longer find publishers for his work. Because he was banned from libraries in many countries, it had become impossible for him to practise his historian's trade. Not always successfully, he attempted to distinguish himself from those with whom he had associated, and whom he now dismissed as fanatics. While he conceded that this case could only have been brought by him in Britain or the United States, he appeared to believe that within a society that prided itself on the existence of free speech lay another, more insidious form of censorship.

Day after day the proceedings wound through the darkest paths of twentieth-century history. We heard expert witnesses, not just on the quality of Irving's handling of historical evidence, but on the placing of ventilator shafts in the roofs of the Auschwitz crematoria. One afternoon was devoted to the question of whether the gassings at Auschwitz (those which Iriving alleged had not occurred) had been broadcast to the world as part of a wartime disinformation campaign sponsored by British Intelligence. The red-robed

Mr Justice Gray appeared to become impatient with Irving. Clearly, he didn't believe that this was how the British behaved.

Films of the hisorian's speeches and interviews were replayed in court (one of my own encounters made an appearance), and these took us away from wartime Poland to contemporary Britain. I watched James Rampton QC strive to make use of Irving's many indiscretions in an effort to establish whether the historian was indeed a racist. Irving had said that he didn't like having his passport checked at Heathrow airport by a Pakistani. Now he insisted that these words didn't make him a racist. Rampton was betraying unreasonable susceptibility to 'race' by raising the matter. But Irving was unsuccessful. The judge decided that he was a racist and anti-Semite, that he had kept company with neo-Fascists; and that, in so far as the term could be reliably applied, he was indeed a holocaust denier.

Throughout the trial, Irving had behaved like an actor. He played at being a historian, a military expert, a learned (and injured) polemicist. And yet the role which kept him happiest was that of a civilized Englishman unjustly deprived of his heritage:

Irving     What did you mean, where did the Irvings come from? How far back are we going to go?

Rampton   That is the point, is it not? How far back do you have to go? Does it matter, Mr Irving?

Irving     It does. You see, what I am saying in this entire paragraph is this. Someone born in England of 1938, all the values that I grew up in, grew to respect and admire and love, I regret what has happened now. Sometimes I wish I could go to Heathrow airport, get on a 747 and take a ten-hour flight and land back in England as it was . . . That is what this paragraph is saying.

Rampton   Yes, it is. It is saying that England has changed in a
          regrettable respect, now that we have all these black
          people.

Listening to Irving, I was forced to acknowledge the
degree to which such views had become wholly familiar to
me. I had spent more than two years chasing those whom I
had to call, for want of a better word, members of the Far
Right, interviewing them first for a documentary film, then
for this book. Before exposure to so many proponents of
hate, I might have been perplexed or shocked. Now they
seemed part of the scenery I had accumulated. But I still
puzzled over the nature of the enquiry which had taken
me all over Europe, beginning in France with a rally of Le
Pen's, passing through Italy, Belgium, Germany, Denmark,
Austria, Bosnia and back to Britain. I still needed to explain
to myself exactly why it was that I, a half-English, half-
French reporter, with no long-standing interest in the
ragged, semi-clandestine armies of the Right, now found
myself having groped through this darkness. Troubled I
was, certainly, by what I had found – but I wondered what
had proved so complicated about the assignment I had set
myself.

In the minds of many observers, a simple, easily discern-
ible pattern characterized the Far Right in Europe. For all
their apparent varieties, it was thought that the new fascists
bore a more than family resemblance. They represented
hatred in its simplest, purest form, just as they had done sixty
or seventy years previously. Begin to colour the map black,
and it was surprising for such interpreters of the fascist
condition just how much of present-day Europe, despite the
changes of the past fifty years, still came attached to its
squalid past. 'I see no real difference between the skinheads

and neo-Nazis of today and the Nazis of a generation earlier,' wrote the Italian semiologist Umberto Eco. 'There is the same kind of stupidity and determination to destroy; the same hatred of others and the will to destruction.'[1] In 1995 a report compiled by the anti-defamation league of B'nai B'rith suggested that there were over 70,000 racist, anti-Semitic activists in thirty countries throughout the world. The perpetrators communicated with each other by means of the Internet and were capable of mounting a threat to democracy. 'We still hear the deadly march of Nazi thugs,' said the league's national director, Abraham Foxman. 'We dare not ignore the first sounds of jackboots.'[2] Dormant for a decade or two, munching on old bones, the beast had reawakened – it was lurching from its fouled lair, drooling, with blood on its hands and a moronic expression.[3]

But things were not as simple as this recurrent image would suggest. The fascists did periodically return, and they appeared to score some successes, though they often failed, too. But they were also to be encountered in many different guises, not all of them sinister or moronic. I met many people who were prepared to call themselves fascists, or Nazis, for whom the idea of fascism wasn't unsympathetic. I was still amazed that they had the bad taste to exist. However, I also encountered a far larger group of people who adhered to what appeared to be some of the distinguishing features of fascism even while they earnestly, and not wholly convincingly, disdained any true connection. In Germany, France, Denmark, Italy and Belgium, in rain-washed marquees, at parades or in rundown bars, I went back again and again to these people. In the course of so many conversations I became convinced that they were indeed a threat to democracy in Europe – but that they differed in many important respects from the neo-Nazi thugs who dominated the popular imagination.

These half or no-longer fascists often spoke a coded language of euphemism, and it was therefore hard to tell whether they retained any real connection with the mid-century originals. Some of them preferred to be called populists, or even (for this was the decade, outside Britain, of the extinction of individual currencies, the abandonment of coherent frontiers) members of national parties. In France, Belgium and Austria, parties advocating the removal not just of foreigners but recently naturalized immigrants attained mass support. These parties polled consistently between 10 and 15 per cent of the vote, surviving even when they appeared to be threatened by their own self-directed enmities.

In my own country there had been such a racist movement, and its presence had caused much consternation, but it was now close to extinction. Britain was now apparently faced by what a judge, controversially, had called 'institutional racism'. This raised the question of whether 'racism' could survive the failure of its political expression, taking refuge in the fabric of society itself. It posed the embarrassing question of whether what the progressives called 'racism' wasn't something less sensational – people who saw each other as being different and didn't get on together. In Scandinavia support for the Far Right ebbed and flowed as part of a resentment of the way in which precious welfare resources went to foreigners, but it was also a symptom of the loss experienced as the familiar picture of ethnically unmixed societies slipped away. In Italy the picture was less clear because the old Far Right – greybeard fascists from the Mussolini era – had been hijacked by a new generation, ostensibly adopting the forms and practices of democracy. It was hard to know how seriously one should take this change of heart. In Germany, by contrast, censorship of the nationalist movement was practised extensively. Some sort of clandestine neo-Nazi underground survived police infiltration, but the Nazis had drifted towards respectability, joining such parties as the DVU, the Republikaner and the NPD. So much censorship had become first a national habit, then part of the way in which Germans saw themselves. These days it was difficult to establish how seriously Germans took their extremism.

I found myself ill at ease in such gatherings, in some respects more perplexed than I was with those who were able to identify themselves unrepentantly as racists. Like many people, I was uncertain what to make of Jörg Haider, the leisure-suited leader of the Austrian Freedom Party. He had lectured me on the similarities between his own worldview and that of Mrs Thatcher and Tony Blair; but I was not wholly convinced. However, some aspects of the international outcry that greeted the arrival to power of his party as part of a coalition in January 2000 also left me uneasy. To be sure, Haider's views were xenophobic, but he was not a Nazi. He hadn't broken any treaties, and there was nothing illegal about his views. As things currently stood, the European Union itself could not intervene in what was still an Austrian affair.

But it was possible for individual countries to act, and they did so, all fourteen of them, acting in rare concert. There were demonstrations against Haider throughout Europe. Prince Charles declined to represent an exhibition of British design in Vienna. In France the opposition to Haider was hailed, perhaps prematurely, as the first step in the creation of a 'political Europe'. Martine Aubry, France's Minister of Employment, joined her European colleagues in cold-shouldering Frau Elisabeth Sickl, her Austrian counterpart. At an EU summit she read out a passage from the autobiography of the Austrian novelist Stephan Zweig, *The World of Yesterday*, in which Zweig recalled how Hitler had proceeded against his enemies in one small dose of violence after another. Because it could be said that the violence was far away, 'on the other side of the frontier', the doses were increased, and Europe ultimately died of the poison. There were no more frontiers in Europe, which meant that whatever Haider did, it applied to all of us.

Haider was not much of a democrat, and he depended for his power on the acceptable expression of raw prejudice. He wished to stir up the quiet world of Austrian politics. But Haider was also opposed to the European Union. He disliked the cosmopolitanism of Brussels – with good reason, since the addition of member states to the east of Austria would accelerate the ethnic dilution which he and his supporters resisted. A new movement of the Far Right would probably take the shape prescribed by Haider. It would be well-spoken and fashionably-dressed. Among other things, it would certainly be skilled in the arts of euphemism. Without having recourse to violence, it would nonetheless end by reducing the scope of liberties in Europe. But how should Europe best respond to this threat?

The Far Right could be described as a collection of lost tribes, but they also shared a view of the world, however irrational this might seem. None of the convenient formulations fitted their condition or came near to describing their noxious combination of hatreds. In the sense in which the word was used in 1960s America, they had become a genuine counterculture, opposing what had become the placid centrism of the sluggish mainstream, and providing a frisson of interdiction. Their existence countered the boredom of contemporary Europe, even if it wasn't clear whether the alternative they offered could ever be said to lead anywhere. Although the Far Right did appear to hark back to the

European past, it was capable of equipping itself with modern means of propagating its ideas. Goebbels would have been proud of the many elegant web sites and the use of email to circumvent the many clumsy efforts at censorship. Far-right militants were able to point scathingly at the many petty repressive measures directed towards them. If this was the best that democracy could do, it proved, simply, that their antecedents were right and that the paraphernalia of elections and parliaments was a sham.

The quest for hatred in Europe, it was clear to me, was no longer a simple matter. It also placed special demands on a reporter, which I had not anticipated. I had in the past encountered what was superficial evidence of greater human depravity, but this was proving somewhat different, and in some respects worse. My reporter's mask of objectivity slipped rapidly. Each time I thought of returning to the fascists, while packing my things in comfortable London, I would be gripped by a sudden fear. I knew pretty much what I was likely to find, to be sure, and there was no chance of my being converted. But I was nonetheless influenced by these haphazard encounters. It was a question of my being forced to confront much that was unpleasant. I knew about these things from books or memory, but I had never (having been sheltered, like so many lucky, post-war Europeans) been exposed to them. And I found that my own beliefs were tested, severely in many instances. I was a somewhat different person when I finished the book.

Meanwhile my map of Europe was filling up with concentric blobs of varying shades of dark, pulsing or swelling. This is what I wrote after my first meeting with Le Pen:

They don't talk to me, they talk at me. Imagine an open wing of a lunatic asylum. Imagine an autistic society. I could do this for years and get nowhere ... I could be here for a century.

and later:

> People who aren't or can't be democrats ... I wonder why the notion of democracy isn't attractive to so many people? Liberals tend to think (patronizingly perhaps) that you have to be intelligent to be democratic. But perhaps democracy is more than intelligence. Perhaps sensibility counts, too.

and still later, after a weekend spent under the rain in Flemish Belgium:

> But *why* shouldn't I hate these people – and not just their ideas?

Who could look at an old piece of footage of Hitler or Mussolini these days without laughing? Who would think that the ancient clobber of shabby, medal-bedecked, over-braided uniforms and third-rate military music might once again stir European hearts? Alas, my own experience told a different story. There were real dictators in the Balkans who won elections and called themselves democrats. Closer to home, Le Pen's hatred appeared contagious; as I faced him, I could imagine myself catching a specially virulent form of rabies. In such moments the excess distance of irony which reporters were trained to adopt was no good. Entrapping, needling by asking the same questions over and over again, backing them into corners so they couldn't escape, I got those whom I interviewed to show their hatreds. It was my way of asking them to come clean about themselves, whether they were politicians or not. But I wondered about this, even as I got better at organizing my provocations. Very possibly what I was doing was merely re-enacting the old Guignol or Mr Punch plot for a mass audience, reducing the fascists to a spectacle. Was the existence of hatred so shockingly unacceptable? Was it even so unusual? Nightly, during the 1930s, displays of hatred were laid on for audiences and no one saw any need to complain about them then. In more than twenty years' reporting I had never encountered these ticklish problems. Again and again, I was brought up short by them.

Unlike many of the alarmists I met along the way, I didn't think the fascists would necessarily come to power. But I did know that they were capable of pervasive influence, even in their electoral weakness; and that in time this would come to seem their truly important function. When I suggested brutally, as a provocation, that his own career meant nothing and that he would ultimately end nowhere, as a failure, it was Le Pen who pointed this out to me. '*Vous autres*,' he shouted, waving his hands and for a brief moment sounding a little like his enemy de Gaulle. He wanted to tell me how stupid I and so many liberals were. I didn't understand modern politics, he told me, gesturing furiously. He meant that he and his ideas had more influence than any number of third-rate so-called democratic hacks whom the rules of the electoral game permitted to say they were in power. I should be looking not at the surfaces, but instead at deep loyalties. And I should examine hatred as if it were a religious movement or a real set of beliefs. Only then would I become capable of acknowledging the real challenge to democracy in Europe.

Le Pen helped me with this formulation. Even as I wished for us all to be done with such people, I felt that it was necessary to describe who they were and, if that proved to be possible, why they held the views they did. Somehow, I had to understand them – and here I was then, a latter-day *petit reporter* who had fetched up in the wrong album: *Tintin au pays des Fachos*. It was as if a black and white movie with which I was painfully familiar had been colorized for my exclusive benefit. As my predecessors had done – all those mackintoshed, hard-drinking, unshockable heavy-deadline types from the 1930s – I wanted to know the enemies of democracy. If I understood exactly how it was that so much hatred for foreigners existed, and so much contempt for the language of mildness, I felt I would know whether European civilization was indeed once again threatened. And I would also know what sort of Europe could best serve as a fence or moat to such implacable enemies. Lastly – and this became most important of all – I would understand what it should mean to be a European in our times.

# LOOKING FOR THE FASCISTS

> 'I don't want to dominate anyone
> I don't need money
> I don't need power
> Truly I need nothing.
> But here I am, at home where I should be – and all these
> Jews fuck me off . . .'
>
> Céline, *Bagatelles pour un massacre*[1]

It was in Argentina that I was first confronted by the true face of fascism. In the mid-1970s, I spent time in Buenos Aires exploring the ambiguous memory of Eva Perón. Flying from New York, it was the *mode rétro* of fascist Argentina that struck me most of all. The city seemed just like a portion of Europe, except that its crumbling facades and endless peeling posters gave it the air of decadence expensively sought after for the anti-fascist epics Bernardo Bertolucci was making at the time. But I wasn't prepared for the pervasive fear that seemed stamped on every face. Nothing in my own European past had prepared me for the muffled horror of a civil war in which enemies were daily carted off in anonymous cars, tortured, shot, or – it happened many times – dumped in the river from aircraft while still alive.

Nor, walking about empty streets and looking behind me,

was I familiar with the way in which everything could be tarnished by the exercise of political violence. It was clear to me that the military government was composed of fascists. But it took me a little longer to realize that the guerrillas, too, despite the Marxist-Leninist theology in which their actions were cloaked, were not democrats. The Montoneros (they were named after a brutal leader in the racist *gaucho* wars in which Argentina's Indians were exterminated) robbed banks, took hostages, executed an ex-president on the grounds that he had violated Eva Perón's body, and heedlessly abandoned their followers to the mercy of the torturers while they acquired villas in the south of France.

Torture or incarceration under socialism retained some faint appearance of rationality. You knew roughly why someone had been airbrushed, tried, imprisoned or caused to vanish. The systematic exercise of injustice was conducted with reference to norms of civilization, fraudulent though these might be. In Buenos Aires I began to understand that it was possible to envisage a world in which nothing was fully comprehensible except the sudden, arbitrary exercise of violence. I learnt, too, that it wasn't entirely fanciful to speak of fascism as a virus of sorts or a disease. In Argentina the fascist idea had begun with the Peróns, and with their fancy-dress imitations of Mussolini. It was given significance in vast and repetitious parades in which the love of Juan and Evita for the *descamisados* was commemorated, attaining a bizarre apotheosis in Evita's long, public death, in which participation was formally required, with punishments for those who declined to do so. Now fascism appeared to have infected an entire society, to the degree that one might wonder whether it would ever be possible for Argentina to return to something like normality. The people I was interviewing were worried about being associated with a foreign reporter, but some of them did speak to me. I remember a woman who told me, sobbing, that she knew no family in which someone had not disappeared. 'I know no one who has been spared,' she repeated. 'No one in Buenos Aires. It affects all of us.'

Walking about the streets after meeting the woman, I was picked up by a black car containing three men in suits. I had my passport and I showed it to them. They asked me a few, mainly perfunctory questions. The men in the car sat silently, impassive in the dusk. They were dressed in old shiny suits. There was a smell of American cigarettes and one of them was chewing gum noisily, without stopping. From time to time a short-wave radio crackled. They drove me around and let me out far from the city centre, on a piece of wasteland. When I left the car, I felt that I had been holding my breath for the past half hour and I wanted to go somewhere, anywhere, far away. I remember sitting on the pavement, vomiting until I was utterly exhausted.

Friends told me that I had been stupid, and that I was lucky to escape with my life. However, I suppose I should feel grateful to those men because they gave me a lifelong interest. I now wanted to know about the moment at which whatever it was that caused a society to close up, destroying itself, usually irreversibly, became fully operative. In the short term, returning from Argentina, I found that I didn't believe in very much. (This, I discovered, was a syndrome – other people plunged into situations similar to the Argentine darkness were affected in the same way, and it took them longer to recover the more intense or more hazardous the exposure had been.) Over the years, among other interests, I began to read and think about fascism. I wondered whether it would ever be possible to say why people were attracted to hatred. I wanted to know whether it was indeed possible to speak of a fascist or authoritarian personality. And I suppose I also wondered whether what we called fascism might return in a different guise.

I now knew that, given the chance, cruelty bred more cruelty. I had developed a practical sense of fascism, framed around the question of what, if anything, might be done to impede its return. Meanwhile it was those who had chosen fascism as an alternative, and who had bequeathed us their reasons for doing so, who now spoke to me. They were the Hamlets, not the Iagos, of international fascism. They would tell me more about why it remained attractive. I could also see their descendants at work and play in Paris. A forgotten aspect of the 1970s is the fear of fascism that existed at the time. Around the playgrounds of the West were highly remunerated freelancers like Carlos. But European states were also menaced by domestic terrorists from the Extreme Left such as the Italian Red Brigades, who kidnapped Aldo Moro or the German RAF, popularly known as the Baader Meinhof gang. An unhealthy ambivalence existed towards such figures. The question discussed in those days was not merely whether these terrorists were 'fascists' – much ink was spilt on this matter in a style of which Orwell would rightly have disapproved – but whether, through excessively brutal responses to them, so-called liberal states like Italy of the Federal Republic of Germany had not also revealed themselves in their true authoritarian-fascist colours. Of course, the purpose of the terrorists was to show up what they regarded as the brutal 'fascist' mechanisms behind the sham Potemkin Village front of democracy – but there were many outside their ranks who found these arguments attractive.

In 1968 Pier Paolo Pasolini annoyed his admirers by criticizing rioting students:

When yesterday in the Valle Giulia you came to blows
With the cops,
I sympathized with the cops!
Because the cops are the sons of the poor.[2]

What Pasolini called 'sacred hooliganism' was in reality an impatience with the boredom levels implied by bourgeois politics. This was still a freely available attitude in the 1970s. It appeared that hostility to democracy had never wholly been extinguished in Europe. Most students from what would become known as the generation of 1968 declared themselves to be left-wing. But a minority, particularly in France, retained more ambiguous allegiances. Fashion encouraged such lengthy flirtations.

My friend Patrick loved to talk about ideology in the way that others went on about rock groups or, in our time, Internet sites. Too refined, messed-up in an over-educated way, dropping names over cup after cup of black coffee, he would never be mistaken for a 'son of the poor'. He had been a Maoist in 1968, during the Paris uprisings, but by the time we met he appeared to belong to an extreme-right group called Nouvel Ordre, though he implied that this was only temporary. Exactly whom or what he was busy infiltrating and on whose behalf was never self-evident. At that time he was always travelling at short notice to odd places in the Middle East. He appeared to know something about making bombs. Patrick was tallish, with stringy, faux-Aryan dyed fair hair and a half-distracted manner, and he was usually dressed in black. I felt he liked to look like the Prince of Darkness. He was always en route – going from one potential assignment to another. For Patrick the sociopathic present evoked rich possibilities of intrigue. *Les réseaux* – networks – were the staple of his monologues. Everyone was connected to everyone else, right as well as left. I realized rapidly that I had no means of knowing whether much of what he was saying was true or not. It was possible that he worked for the DST – the French Secret Service – and what he described as his family's military background appeared to render this likely. This might explain his half-earnest cultivation of an English reporter. But it was just as possible that Patrick had no serious connections to the red and black underground, and that he merely liked hanging out in cafes.

I knew a bit about what was now called Vichy, and its brother phenomenon of collaborationism; but it was Patrick who first filled me in. Presciently, he was convinced that the imaginative power of communism was waning, and that we would all shortly realize that the true importance of Europe – its dirty half-secret, if you like – was its history of blackness. Patrick was very intelligent in the best French way, nuanced but flaky. At that moment, books and films about the collaborationist past were just beginning to appear in large quantities, and he was scathing about them. 'Don't bother,' he would say. 'They are ridiculous. Bertolucci is Hollywood, Malle is worse.' Instead I must know about the French official class who were all around me. People went along with things in France; they were expensively encouraged to do so by the conformist education system. But I must also encounter the true believers. To do so I must disabuse myself of the very English notion that cynicism or despair precluded belief. The example of France during the 1940s overturned this notion. I must understand that although these people had made the wrong choices, they had been right to make them. They were believers. In another of our sessions he talked about boredom, and how any society, even the most sophisticated one, required the cultivation of signs, symbols and collective rituals. In this respect fascism, he implied, had an edge over its rival, socialism. The buckles, marching songs, uniforms were of superior quality – just look at their continuing appeal to collectors. He was sure that the European roots of fascism went deep. No one should imagine that it had simply gone away. 'Look around you,' he said. 'Just look around you.' The last time I saw him he was off on another trip and I asked him finally whether he thought of himself as a fascist. All he did was shrug. 'You can be a fascist without fascism,' he said.

Now I heard that Patrick was married to someone with a hyphenated first name and safely lodged in one of the stuffiest French state companies. There were rumours of his involvement in one of the large-scale scandals of the late years of French socialism. As I found my way around the contemporary scene I recalled his views about the fascinations of fascism. Not that we lived in a Europe that resembled the one of the 1930s, far from it – but it did indeed seem as if something central to the idea or practice of fascism just wouldn't go away.

I packed many history books on these voyages, carting them from one hotel room to another and reading late at night; and I was surprised to find how many of the best books about fascism were written by English or Americans. Like most Anglo-Saxons, I found fascism fascinating because (with the exception of Buenos Aires) it was so far from my own impeccably calm historical experience. But I was also wised up enough to know early on that the word fascism, in the sense conventionally given to it, posed many problems. George Orwell, among others, doubted that it had much meaning. It had been used about farmers, tobacconists, Chiang Kai-Shek, homosexuality, astrology, women, and even dogs, he noted:

> Yet underneath all this mess there does lie a kind of buried meaning ... even the people who recklessly fling the word 'fascist' in every direction attach at any rate an emotional significance to it. By 'fascism' they mean, roughly speaking, something cruel, unscrupulous, arrogant, obscurantist, anti-liberal and anti-working class. Except for the relatively small number of fascist sympathizers, almost any English person would accept 'bully' as a synonym for 'fascist'. That is about as near to a definition as this much-abused word has come.[3]

Good for a scary evening in 1944, when the V1s were passing over London, this wasn't quite enough for the present. It didn't explain why so many people had taken the bullies seriously and had been prepared to die for them. And it didn't explain the fascination exercised by the movement or its aesthetic properties – the black boots, the silly buckles and funny hats, the endless wasteful performances laid on in the name of solidarity organized around common hatred. By the time he wrote *1984*, just before his death, Orwell appeared to have tired of fascism, regarding it as a mid-century dead end no longer capable of capturing the imagination. A totalitarianism the more shocking because it derived from the humanist pretensions of socialism now triumphed. By comparison with the horrors of Ingsoc, the vanished world of the mid-century dictators seemed small beer. Orwell chided the anti-fascists. They were looking backwards and they were also committing serious linguistic abuse. He came to believe that anti-fascism merely disguised the awful things going on in the so-called socialist world, perpetrated in the name of freedom and justice.

'If nationalism is the excessive distortion of patriotism,' the historian Eugen Weber wrote, 'fascism is a similar distortion of nationalism: militaristic, aggressive, totalitarian in its exclusion of alternatives.'[4] He might have added that it was also irrational, and thus (for its practitioners at least) had the advantage that it couldn't be argued with. As doctrine, fascism was concerned with the fetishistic aspects of the world: it succeeded best where, out of injured pride or anger, totems could be conjured up. Only the maddest of its fellow-travellers, such as the socialite Unity Mitford, paid much attention to the idea that the movement might reach across cherished frontiers, uniting its believers in the common ground of embattled nationalist differences. However, the melody of fascism was a different matter. Leave aside such mundane differences of uniforms and the music remained. And it was composed in equal parts of pessimism and redemption. Fascism relied on the attractive and simple presumption according to which immorality, exercised on behalf of shared prejudice or hatred, was legitimate. Simply, it told people the world was so unutterably awful that any means of shared self-redemption would be allowed. It meant that groups of people could, and did, do what they felt like to make themselves feel better.

After the Leader – a figure considered essential to fascism, and of whom I was to encounter a copious supply of candidates – another fascist type was the Doomed Hero. Flops were tolerated if they crashed their planes or wrote bad poetry. Converts to fascism became its staunchest believers, but they could also nudge along as ballast in the movement – all they had to do was seem elegant or merely cynical. Now that the principal aspect of fascism had disappeared, which was its total control of the modern state, it was possible to see that the movement had to a large degree been composed of people who didn't really believe in anything at all. There were plenty of those around in Europe, and they constituted the decorative class of fascism. To use communist terminology, they were the fellow-travellers of the movement. Their existence established beyond doubt the fact that, given some sort of choice, a great many people disliked the implications of democracy and wouldn't plump for what they saw as the arbitrary destructiveness of capitalism.

The publication in 1992 of the memoirs of Drieu la Rochelle revived the memory of this type. Drieu was a half-successful 1930s novelist (his best book, *Le feu follet*, about a suicide, was later adapted by Louis Malle) who lived at the edges of the Paris beau monde, seducing the wives of industrialists and toying with the end of democracy between the good meals still to be had during the Occupation. He was too lazy, and also too stuck in his weariness, to think of joining de Gaulle. In 1940 he was approached by the German invaders and asked to become the head of the *Nouvelle Revue Française*, France's best-known literary review. He was to be a figurehead of the new European culture imposed on France by its occupiers. By all accounts Drieu did a perfectly good job, even advancing the prospects of those he knew to be opponents of the regime, but whom he nonetheless judged to be good writers or merely *braves types*. However, his diaries show him to have been at odds with the morosely dutiful *personnage* he daily presented to his German friends. In between worrying about his haemorrhoids or his sexual performance and reading Indian mysticism – serenity eluded him, as one might have expected – he entered a spiral of depression. When it was clear that Germany had lost the war he resolved to kill himself, and he did so with his usual sense of style, hiding out in a country estate at the end of 1944 while his enemies tracked him down.

By now the Occupation and its horrors had become the stuff of kitsch fiction. This was not why Drieu interested me. Instead I was concerned with the degree to which, as a type, he resembled so many people whom it was my privilege to know, professionally and personally. I was becoming familiar with the notion of cynicism as a belief system. It seemed that Patrick had been right: you could simply believe in nothing at all, turning the absence of belief into a creed of sorts. However, this required the presence of increasing quantities of hatred, and Drieu, like many of the people I was meeting, was what contemporary psychologists would call an addictive personality. Hatred, rather than food or sex, was his principal addiction. Drieu's fruitcake high style was miles away from the semi-literate outpourings to be found on the Internet, but the emotions (and the posturing) weren't so different:

> I wish to die as a Roman . . .
>
> I loved England, the greatest success of nordic [sic] civilization. But I abandoned her because she was rendered rotten by too much success.
>
> I hate Jews. I always knew that I hated them. When I married Colette Jéramec [his first wife] I knew what I was doing and what an idiocy I was committing. I never could fuck her because of that.
>
> The Germans are assholes, too. Complete assholes, arrogant, clumsy. But they are also passionate, like myself. They are all I ever wanted to be. I only wish to die with them.[5]

The sense of never quite belonging was often to be found among fascists, and this was why the impoverished Drieu resented his moneyed wife. But anti-Semitism was also what held his world – what there was of it anyhow – together. It explained the social or cultural decline that appeared to threaten him personally. Among those I met who professed to believe that it was the Arabs or Islam that now posed a greater threat to Europe, I was interested to find that a distrust of Jews nonetheless prevailed. It had become a primary hatred, legitimating the elevation of lesser aversions. As long as there was hatred in Europe, I knew that the long shadow of anti-Semitism would be there, too.

In 1997, a friend in Paris gave me a copy of what proved to be the most distasteful book I had ever encountered. This was not *Mein Kampf*, which was by comparison boring and evasive; nor was it the odious *La France Juive* by Edouard Drumont, published at the time of the Dreyfus affair; nor indeed the notoriously faked Protocols of the Elders of Zion, still available in the 1990s on Moscow bookstalls. Louis-Ferdinand Céline's *Bagatelles pour un massacre* was first published in 1937, selling very well, and it was reprinted in the war, when paper was scarce. After the war Céline never mentioned the book. Although his works were tastefully assembled in the Pléiade collection, a certificate of literary pre-eminence, Céline's estate never allowed *Bagatelles* to be reprinted.[6]

At the time Céline's outburst appeared its author was known as a novelist whose best work, *Journey to the End of the Night*, had appeared to presage a new democratic form in which the anonymous and hopeless were given expression against the existing rules of the game which specified that only the bourgeois were worthy of fictional attention. Céline became what was probably the first instance of anti-celebrity – a man who thrived from the hatred he incurred. Like his hero Bardamu, he appeared to his many admirers to be the forgotten man of 1930s Europe. He had been in the trenches during the Great War and he had wandered around the worst corners of the French Empire, in West Africa. Also, he had been to Chicago and Los Angeles where, like most French people, he found much to dislike. The Communist Party acclaimed *Journey to the End of the Night*; it was thought to be capable of telling the comrades what a life lacking a consciousness of the future might consist of. Céline was a dog lover and a vegetarian, and was married to a woman who taught progressive dance. He made his living as a doctor, usually in the most impoverished areas of Paris. But few were prepared for the revelation that he was also an impassioned anti-Semite.

Céline's paranoid, atrocious ideas (many, many times he suggested in print or to friends that Jews should be exterminated, and he wasn't joking) existed in mysterious counterpoint with his literary genius. Even as he comprehensively denied humanity to one group of people he could evoke the utmost feelings of sympathy for his hopeless *paumés* – the lost ordinary Frenchmen of his time. In that respect, considered merely as a literary problem, Céline was far more intractable than genteel anti-Semites like T. S. Eliot. However, I became interested in his work for entirely different reasons. Nowadays Céline was a cult writer of the Far Right and many of his ideas closely resembled those of the National Front polemicists. Céline's racism, for instance, which was of the deepest, blackest kind, was based on his conception of culture. He believed that civilization, if it meant anything at all, should be founded on the difference between groups or individuals. Céline was sufficiently well educated to understand that the race theories implied by German anti-Semitism were nonsense – indeed he found the seriousness of Germans ridiculous. But culture was important to him, and he believed that a culture could die as easily as any other organism. Looking around him, Céline announced that France was mortally threatened. The last vestiges of Frenchness would be extinguished in the next war. The 'bagatelles' of which he wrote were a form of consolation offered before the imminent prospect of Armageddon, and they consisted of telling fellow

Frenchmen that it remained the obligation of every French-man to hate Jews. For Jews were the founder members of the international class of capitalists. They were middlemen (like many anti-Semites, Céline believed that Jews didn't make anything except money) of popular culture. Jews were those on behalf of whom the next war would be fought. Jewishness found expression in the English language, which had been annexed and destroyed in much the same way as French shortly would be. Above all Jewishness could be identified in the mass, homogenized multiculturalism of America, which would sooner or later destroy France. Jews and blacks were the enemies. Around the Front, and within French extreme right-wing circles, these views were widespread. They formed the basis of most of the pamphlets put out by GRECE, an influential organization purporting to defend European values. Each time I heard a Front speaker allude fatuously to their bêtes noires, Steven Spielberg and Michael Jackson, I thought of Céline.

His half-grammatical rants still have the power to shock. Like his successors, Céline was skilled at evoking liberal rights even while he destroyed them. He demanded the right to freedom of expression in order to spread poison. So-called free speech, he suggested, meant that the world was infected by 'Jew fascism'. He was claiming as his due the reciprocal right to be heard:

> This is what I think of as the intermediary activity of Yids: editors, agents, publicists ... under the influence of films, Jewish scenarios, cultural hoodlums, rotten people ... it's an order, hidden or overt, that what remains of French artistic production, already so feeble, so little important, is in the process of dying and must die ... The Jews have to have everything, that's what it all comes down to ...

> What all of us hate about Jews is their arrogance, their demands to have everything, the dervish-rhythms of their endless martyrology, their hideous tom-tom beat . . .[7]

In 1943 Céline encountered the German writer Ernst Jünger at a tea party of the German Institute. Jünger's job was to look after French writers who were suitable objects of German sponsorship, giving them handouts. He was a decorated war veteran, a fastidious conservative, and a very serious man who believed in German–French fellowship. But Jünger was taken aback when Céline asked him why the German army didn't just get on with it and kill every Jew. 'I did learn something from listening to him speak for over two hours,' Jünger wrote in his diary that day. 'He expressed the monstrous power of nihilism. People like him hear only one melody. They are like machines which go forwards until they are broken in pieces.'[8]

Should racism be overtly expressed or not? At that time, as in ours, good taste (or the lack of it) was considered to be an important feature of civilization. One might conclude that what Jünger really objected to was a lack of circumspection. For his admirers, however, Céline possessed the redeeming quality of authenticity. In 1944 he followed the ageing survivors of the collaborationist Vichy government to Sigmarigen, a castle in Middle Germany, where the Germans kept them in a state of half-imprisonment, allowing Pétain and the motley collection of civil servants and retired generals who still surrounded him on short walks through the winter countryside. After the briefest sojourn in Denmark after the war, where he avoided imprisonment, Céline returned to France. He never apologized for his views; indeed, he continued to hold them, entertaining visitors to his small house with the notion that the Holocaust had never existed ('*ces magiques chambers à gaz'*) even while he insisted, apparently with great seriousness, that one of the greatest outrages of the time was the Nobel committee's refusal to consider him seriously.

After the collapse of 1945, fascism was placed under interdiction. It was possible to invite ex-communists to colloquies at the height of the Cold War and they might even be found jobs if they recanted publicly. But true fascists (as opposed to the many abettors and place-servers, who were reclaimed, often with excessive haste) remained beyond polite consideration. The fear of fascism remained, and it didn't go away. There were sightings of Nazis throughout the world, particularly in Argentina and Paraguay. Parallel to the journalistic quests for these survivors, however, lay a lesser-known enterprise. This consisted of trying to ascertain whether fascism was capable of spreading beyond its European nexus, and thus might be considered as a phenomenon of universal significance. Led by Max Horkheimer and T. W. Adorno, two German émigrés from the Frankfurt School, a team of sociologists interviewed hundreds of people in the Los Angeles area in 1950. They, too, were looking for fascists – but they went to the suburbs of Southern California. 'What tissues in the life of our modern society remain cancerous?'[9] they asked. 'And what within the individual organism responds to certain stimuli in our culture with attitudes and acts of aggression?' Respondents were ranked according to various complementary scales, to give an idea of the degrees of anti-Jewish prejudice, ethnocentrism and 'antidemocratic' feelings:

1–2. The Jews must be considered a bad influence on Christian culture and civilization.
1–5. One trouble with Jewish businessmen is that they stick

together and connive, so that a gentile doesn't have a fair
chance in competition.

1–8 Jewish power and control in money matters is far out of
proportion to the number of Jews in the total population.[10]

Adorno and his colleagues discovered that there was indeed
such a thing as an 'authoritarian personality'. It was to be
found usually (though not exclusively) among males who
were not specially well educated, and it went with patriarchal
attitudes to the matter of family authority. 'Conservative
embattled . . .' was the authoritarian motto, and its adherents
could be found in many different places, in particular at the
edge of disadvantage. Those who felt threatened in their jobs,
or who were worried about a world changing too rapidly for
them, were particularly affected. The armed forces appeared
to provide a testing ground for such types.

These were attitudes that I found in contemporary
Europe. But I was interested to discover that, unlike the
contemporary European sociologists I encountered, these
Southern Californian pioneers were not pessimistic in their
conclusions. They appeared to believe in a benign form of
social conditioning. If it was possible to think of an authoritarian type, created by circumstances, one might also conclude that people became tolerant or liberal-minded for
reasons that could be fathomed. Adorno and his investigators
examined the tolerant and democratic in their sample. They
were better educated, more frequently female. Their view of
life was more positive. Bigotry, the investigators concluded,
might be vanquished through education and the beneficent
influence of popular culture. Peer pressure would assist in the
struggle. In due course they could envisage a world where
there would be more democrats and fewer fascists.

But in Europe the situation was somewhat different. Here,

in countries like Germany and Italy, substantial portions of the population had gone along with acts of cruelty, accepting the removal of democratic rights from minorities. Briefly, the occupying US forces ran de-indoctrination classes, but these were abandoned when the outbreak of the Cold War required the cultivation of anti-communism. At a deeper level, unsusceptible to the analyses of social science, the fascist past posed an enormous problem. It was not so much a question of what should be done with the ex-fascists – many of them occupied the same places they had done in the previous regime – but of what lessons, if any, could be drawn from the entire experience.

Marcello Clerici, the hero of Alberto Moravia's 1951 novel *The Conformist*, was molested as a child by a chauffeur, and he shot and killed the man. Horrified at what he had done, but eager to conceal the facts, he was in permanent flight. What seemed to him to be an escape took him deeper and deeper into the spirit of conformity – into a loveless marriage and meaningless spying work deep within the fascist bureaucracy:

> He remembered that formerly he possessed a rich interior life, tumultuous and barely understood. Now everything about him was over-defined, as if he had been extinguished: a few simple ideas, a few over-rigid beliefs had replaced his generous and confused sense of self . . . The most conspicuous change in his life during the past seventeen years was the utter disappearance of a vitality caused by so much unexpected and perhaps abnormal instinct. All that had been replaced by something grey and mediocre: a sense of normality.[11]

Stripped of its mid-century bourgeois props, Clerici's abused past might not seem so unusual to us these days; but his solution was the one taken by many Europeans. Look, Moravia was saying, the danger never came from badges and uniforms, it came from the rest of us, who permitted all this to exist. And we should not think that the system that permitted fascism to flourish was dead. But Moravia also meant Europeans to understand that post-war Europe was not so distanced after all from its forbidden past. The same sort of people flourished within identical, conformist bureaucracies. Moravia, who was a communist, could only be aware that he himself was still under surveillance, perhaps even watched over by the same people who had guarded him during the fascist era, and that they would retire in comfort, sunning themselves in small villas by the Adriatic in the company of their grandchildren.

Destroyed in Europe, post-war fascism continued to exist in diminished form. Its real face was thought to be hidden, its true nature preserved in anonymous networks; and a comeback was awaited each time a bomb went off or a synagogue was defaced. The truth was somewhat more banal. Fascists subsisted meagrely on the fringes of Europe, somewhere between outrage and anonymity. If they kept quiet, middle-ranking fascists were allowed their place in state or private bureaucracies. The scandal of their presence implied, correctly, that governments placed stability above justice; Europe and its American allies were less concerned with a reviving black threat than they were attentive to the need to combat communism. But the fascist parties were outlawed, and this meant that it was not easy for those who had been fascist politicians to rehabilitate themselves. Nobody was interested in a revival of their old and catastrophic ideas, and nobody believed protestations to the effect that they had changed. The ex-fascists resolved this problem by adopting a code. They began to wear suits rather than uniforms and they now claimed to eschew violence. From time to time (when no one but their reduced core of supporters was listening, or when they forgot themselves in the flood of oratory) they sounded like their old selves.

Oswald Mosley had created a militaristic, anti-Semitic movement in 1930s Britain, dressing his followers in black shirts and staging large-scale rallies in emulation of Hitler and Mussolini. He was imprisoned during the war and went into exile afterwards, living in France and Ireland. But Mosley wished to rehabilitate himself, and he therefore stood for parliament in post-war Britain. He tried to depict himself as a peace-loving sage, but he was not entirely successful. Here he is campaigning in London in 1959, described by his son:

> There was dad on top of a van again and bellowing; so much older now with his grey hair and grey suit . . . I had expected that he at least would be putting over the aspect of his case that was reasonable; but . . . there he was roaring on about such things as black men being able to live on tins of cat food, and teenage girls being kept in attics. And there were all the clean-faced young men around his van guarding him; and somewhere, I suppose, the fingers of the devotees of the dark god tearing at him.[12]

Fascists were caught somewhere between the desire for clean faces and the presence of the dark god. They might, certainly, have abandoned much of the traditional clobber, but it was also periodically necessary for them to deliver something of the real thing. Mosley was an early, primitive instance of the desire to hide, all the while displaying oneself.

In 1933 the teenage Patrick Leigh Fermor was hitchhiking through Europe when he came across the Westphalian town of Goch:

The town was hung with National Socialist flags and the window of an outfitter's shop held a display of Party equipment: swastika arm-bands, daggers for the Hitler Youth, blouses for Hitler Maidens and brown shirts for grown-up SA men; swastika buttonholes were arranged in a pattern which read Heil Hitler . . . in some of the photographs Goebbels sat at his desk and Goering appeared in SA uniform; in a white uniform; in voluminous leather shorts; nursing a lion cub; in tails and white tie and in a fur collar and plumed hunting hat, aiming a sporting gun. But those of Hitler as a bare-headed Brownshirt, or in a belted mackintosh or a double-breasted uniform and a peaked cap or patting the head of a flaxen-haired and gap-toothed little girl offering him a bunch of daisies, outnumbered the others . . .[13]

You had to look somewhat harder in order to find the fascists of our day. However, it appeared that they hadn't changed too much. The same gimcrack objects were to be purchased in similar circumstances of unreassuring banality. The same pretensions to represent the reality of the *volk* were to be found.

In a rainswept tent near Antwerp, I attended the family festival of the Flemish separatist Vlaams Blok. Many of the *blokkers* had spent their student days breaking immigrant heads, but they now insisted that they had placed such rash acts behind them. Impeccably democratic in organization, their movement would pursue its aims – these included the eviction of foreigners and the creation of a Flemish state proof against immigration – within the context of the European Union. Replete with beer and oysters and lulled by the strains of Flemish bluegrass, these militants were the image of good bourgeois. They insisted that they were not racist – all they wanted was their own culture. Why should it be so difficult to be Flemish? I remembered what the novelist Albert

Cohen had said – that there were many occasions when good folk came together for the purpose of hating other people. I began to think that shared hatred, rather than the chic of uniforms, constituted the real legacy of fascism. Little about the pursuit of ethnic identity could seem excessive in places where such activities had always been acceptable.

But were these people really fascists? I walked past stalls selling stickers and beer mats decorated with the black lion of Flanders, and the slogan *Belgie Baarst!* (Die Belgium!). I bought a slim pamphlet entitled *Qu'est-ce que le fascisme?*(What is Fascism?):

> Fascism is not a doctrine. It is a time-honoured will, obscure and very ancient – and it is written into our soul. If it is different for each nation, that is because each nation possesses its way of saving itself. Such knowledge can be found only at the heart of things. So the fascist idea can't be grafted on, or transplanted. You cannot spray it on to any plant. But those who are fascists truly feel it before they believe in it – they experience the idea more deeply than others . . .[14]

This was written in 1962, and it seemed ridiculous then. Its author, Maurice Bardèche, was the brother-in-law of the famous collaborationist Robert Brasillach, also a writer, who was executed despite the protests of his peers in 1945. In Europe these days, the contemporary spirit of correctness meant that no one admitting he was a fascist was likely to be taken very seriously by electors. True, much of old-style fascism had consisted of lies, but it had been nonetheless easy to understand what the dictators had in mind. These days more subtle evasions were required.

I learned that the new mob wore sports clothes instead of uniforms. They had adopted the language, if not the attitudes, of democracy. On the whole, allowing for periodical gaffes, they eschewed overt racism. They defended themselves against charges of bigotry with the assertion that it was the project of 'multiculturalism' – the word was never defined – and not the existence of individual Arabs, Turks or Africans in Europe, which caused all the trouble. The Vlaams Blok were at pains not to offend the rich community of Orthodox Jews who did the diamond-cutting in Antwerp, providing much of the town's wealth. A previous generation of the party's leaders were Nazi sympathizers or collaborationists; but the present lot insisted that they were not anti-Semites. All Europeans would be welcome in the new Flemish state – it would even be possible, if he so wished, for an Englishman to become Flemish, and to feel proud of his new identity. Everyone, indeed, but the real foreigners would be welcome. The party's ideologist seemed quite surprised when I suggested that some foreigners might not want to leave Blokland. 'I don't know what we'd do in that situation,' he said.

Looking for fascism, I became used to searching for the European future in the past. What I could not have anticipated, however, were the changes simultaneously wrought to memory itself, and the half-obliteration of whatever it was that had once been serious. In 1998 the German magazine *Focus* ran an interview with an Austrian bus conductor called Adolf Hittler. Despite many urgings the man had refused to change his name, and it appeared that he had lost jobs, and his wife, too, as a consequence of his obduracy. 'They call in the middle of the night,' he said. 'They say, "We've got one in the gas chamber for you,"' he complained. Kitsch in its origins, the primary 1930s attraction of fascism was by now lost to us, buried beneath obsolescent uniforms and fake moustaches. But I also had to remember that fascism was still taken seriously. It was easy to give or take offence, and there were many places where irony was interdicted. Usage was of more than etymological significance, involving the life and death of reputations.

Fifteen years after he had first drawn attention to the similarities between fascism and communism, the German historian Ernst Nolte could still complain of the attacks to which he had been subjected. In Germany, he suggested, even discussing Hitler and Stalin together placed one on a level with the other 'revisionists' for whom the camps weren't so important.[15] In 1982 the Israeli historian Zeev Sternhell was fined a symbolic one franc by a French court for having referred to the sociologist Bertrand de Jouvenel as a fascist. 'What I have learnt,' Sternhell said, 'is that on the terrain of ideas everything is permitted, but one does not have the right to touch persons. One can speak of fascism, but not of fascists.'[16]

Of course, I could joke about what I was doing; indeed, I found that I had to do so. 'Take me to the fascists,' I'd say. In *Seinfeld* I noticed that a character referred to a waiter as a 'soup Nazi'. The F word subsisted somewhere between the mildest description of negative chic and ultimate outrage. It was used to titillate, or to offend, or both. Over fifty years ago, Simone de Beauvoir described a fashionable Left Bank cellar for the illumination of her Chicago boyfriend, Nelson Algren:

Most of the people were either existentialist (including myself) or communist or fascist. There was a very strange, crazy and hateful man who should have been shot after the Liberation and who danced with a drunk, hateful girl; they had some other ex-collaborationist and pro-fascist boys with them. In the end of the evening, the fascist ones made some unpleasant reflection about Jews; and a communist boy asked what was the matter with Jews? So some existentialists came and said to the communists they must make a kind of union for just a while and fight the fascists with their fists. But the communists would not, and they began to argue harshly with the existentialists.[17]

As for contemporary Europe, in Berlin the Far Right gathered to drink German standard beer at a dive called the Café Germania, on the walls of which were hung images from Teutonic mythology. Had it been legal to hang an image of Adolf in the midst he would have been present. 'PARIS FACHO: ILS SONT PARTOUT' was the title of a special issue of a listings magazine. It recounted the various bookshops, clothes shops, caves, cafes, boot manufacturers and purveyors of black or brown shirts in the capital. In Predappio, where Mussolini was born, rival emporia vied with each other to supply bottles of wine, black pom-pom hats, busts, shirts, boots, disco versions of *Giovinezza*, keyrings and watches. Nowadays Mussolini looked like an Italian member of the Addams family, and it wasn't possible to say how many of these apparently fulsome tributes to the Duce were made or sold in a spirit of irony. Perhaps no one really knew any more.

At the same time, the F word had not wholly lost its meaning, and it was also perhaps appropriate for the *Observer* leader writer, contemplating the derangement or sordid cynicism which had led members of the Real IRA to place a huge charge in Omagh High Street, to call the bombers not just 'pure evil', but also 'fascists'. I could find nothing wrong with this usage. 'All you fascists bound to lose,' sang Billy Bragg, borrowing the 1930s lyrics of Woody Guthrie; and I hoped he was right. However, I also realized that my relationship with those who called themselves anti-fascists might be problematic. A few years ago I was responsible for a film in which three neo-Nazis went to Auschwitz, where they met a Holocaust survivor, arguing in situ that, appearances to the contrary, the place in which she had been incarcerated as a teenager had no genocidal function what-soever. I wasn't surprised when there were complaints about the film, but I was taken aback by the sacks of mail which followed a discussion programme in which members of the BNP (along with neo-fascists flown in from Continental Europe) took part.

The anti-fascists still believed that such people should not be granted the privilege of media attention. The irrational, as well as horrifying, aspects of fascism were cited as grounds for continued bannings. No spirit of charity was extended to those who might believe that it made little or no sense permanently to exclude people with distasteful or ridiculous ideas from the scope of rational or civilized debate. Arguments to the effect that it might be good to know one's enemies received no takers among such folk. They suggested that in this instance free speech might be seen as a betrayal of the most basic human values. The argument, familiar from the 1930s, to the effect that freedom was capable of under-mining itself still held sway. I discovered that such ideas were far more prevalent in Europe than I could have imagined. Indeed they had grown in importance over the past decade, and they now amounted to a new orthodoxy, in some respects rivalling in importance the threat to democracy against which they were directed.

Anti-fascism, like fascism itself, came from the age of the Popular Front and the dictatorships, and it spoke in what had become an outdated idiom. Expressed simply, the idea was that democracy or capitalism – the two were more or less interchangeable – bred fascism. 'Fascism', wrote the authors of *Fascism for Whom?* published in 1938, 'is the product of democratic decay'.[18] Many first-generation anti-fascist militants were communists and they placed little trust in the institutions of liberal democracy – or indeed the prospect of civilized debate as a means of containing hatreds. They believed that fascists should be banned, or at least censored, before they could do any harm. To suggest anything less was for a long time to give evidence of weakness in the face of a common enemy.

These ideas found systematic expression in post-war Europe. After so many atrocities, the attitude of Europeans to the phenomenon of hatred was one of chastened horror. They recalled the race polemics of the 1930s, identifying them with press corruption; and they didn't want to hear them again. They didn't want to allow freedoms to those who abused them or didn't believe in them. For the moment, which turned out to be a very long one, there would be no equivalent culture of First Amendment libertarianism in the new Europe – and there was no one ready to defend the fascists.

However, it wasn't enough to ban parties with racist ideas, driving them underground. Instead, many concluded that the phenomenon of racism must be attacked. 'Anti-Semitism', wrote Jean-Paul Sartre in 1955, 'is not within the category of thought which must be protected by the right to free opinion.'[19] He meant that there were many things which people should not be encouraged to think, let alone say; and that these opinions should be countered by legal means or, if these ultimately proved insufficient, by the establishment of a propagandist civic culture of antiracism. During the 1970s, most European countries amended their laws in order to make it easier to punish obnoxiously racist views. Where there was a choice between correctness and the claims of free speech, it was agreed that the former should prevail. Lawsuits were brought by governments and private parties against race-haters. Those who claimed that the Holocaust had never happened – they were a small sect in the 1970s, but they became more numerous during the 1980s, partly as a conse-quence of so much publicity – became the target of many judicial proceedings.

As a consequence the distinction between hate graffiti and half-rational argument, never very easy to make, became increasingly blurred. It was enough to demonstrate that ideas, in addition to being false, were also dangerous. In 1980 the American linguist and left-winger Noam Chomsky was chas-tised for asserting that Robert Faurisson, a French literary professor, should be allowed to publish his views about the Holocaust, no matter how absurd or distasteful these were; and that he should not have been sacked from his position at Lyon University. No one in France accepted or even appar-ently understood Chomsky's point – that free speech only began to mean something when the most unpleasant ideas were protected. Instead, Chomsky was assailed for daring, as an American, to venture on what must be considered to be French turf. The point was that only French people truly understood the enormity of Faurisson's behaviour, and that only they were capable of judging him.

Were Europeans really interested in freedom of speech? Would they rather not use the power of the state to suppress whatever it was that they still found embarrassing about the dark past? I encountered these attitudes in many unexpected places. Sitting behind a cluttered desk in his Paris apartment, Claude Lanzmann, the maker of *Shoah*, became angry when I suggested that the time had perhaps come, given the easy access to the Internet, to abandon some of the more conspic-uous attempts to police unpleasant views. 'You are talking of crimes, not opinions,' he said, echoing his mentor Sartre. 'You must not dignify such views by the name of speech.'

When I persisted, citing the First Amendment, he told me that as a BBC reporter I should know better than to apply bad American inventions to serious things. Not wholly politely, he showed me the door.

It took me a while to realize that my own attitudes elicited hostility, and even when I did, I wasn't sure how to react. Should I be talking to these people? To those for whom the answer was no, any distress I might incur on my assignment merely served to teach me a lesson in the futility of my ways. Although I liked to think that I was immune to the notion that I might, secretly, share at least some of the views of those I was seeing, I dealt with such criticisms only with great difficulty. On one of the occasions when I interviewed the leader of the French National Front, I took with me a book entitled *Le procès de Jean-Marie Le Pen* (*The Trial of Jean-Marie Le Pen*), and I wasn't surprised when he brushed it aside. (Though he later sued the author, winning the case with a modest award of damages.) The book was a novel – or a 'real fiction', as one critic had called it. It recounted the perverse efforts of a young Jewish defence lawyer to defend an FN thug who had murdered an Algerian. The lawyer's strategy was to allow the defendant all the rope he wished. He wished to shift blame from his client to the man whom he considered to be the real author of his sentiments, and thus guilty of murder: Jean-Marie Le Pen. Of course, this effort was doomed to failure. It wasn't possible to 'try' Le Pen for a crime he hadn't committed. All one could do was accuse him, ineffectually, of being responsible for the circumstances in which hatred thrived. As I had discovered, far from hurting Le Pen or his followers, accusations of this nature merely reinforced their sense of embattled solidarity.

We could take part in demonstrations against Le Pen, compile or merely watch news bulletins, insult militants or be insulted by them – in the end, perhaps nothing made that much difference. But the author, Mathieu Lindon, while acknowledging these problems, called for what he appeared to believe were radical solutions. He and his hero demanded a 'permanent trial' of Le Pen. Racism would only be defeated if the full legal and propagandist resources of the state were directed towards its eradication. In effect he was calling for the kind of ideological limits once placed on free speech in the countries of socialist Europe:

> There is no need to go to court in order to try Le Pen, for the trial occurs everywhere he is, at any moment when he is speaking. He is his own trial, his own condemnation and ours. We try to shove him into a corner of our consciousness not to have to hear him speak, but he is everywhere, he's looking for outrage and we give him just what he wants. If he must be fought by judicial means, let's try him for incitement to murder, for racial hatred . . .[20]

Should one ban entire categories of speech, as Sartre had wished? Did it make sense to outlaw parties or movements? Whatever we in Europe resolved to do about the enemies in our midst appeared to me as important as the fact that they existed at all. But it was relevant, too, that we lived in a world where the market was more or less unstoppable. It had become capable of translating any idea into the stuff of merchandise. Grand figures such as Claude Lanzmann and his heirs were not capable of imposing moral or ideological uniformity. Perhaps they never had been – but the forces of cultural pluralism, distressing though these might often seem, were far stronger than thirty years ago. The small kiosk where the young Hitler is said to have acquired race-hate texts was global now, accessible at the press of a button.

As recently as 1997 a German court gave a suspended

one-year jail sentence to the European manager of the Internet company Compuserve. His crime was to have transmitted to Germany racist sites (and pornography) which had originated in the United States – and it didn't appear to matter that the flow of information was beyond his control. In Europe the opposition to these aspects of the freeing up of information was deep-seated. Many of the people I spoke to believed that the fascist threat of the 1990s was on a par with the crisis of European democracy of the 1970s, when the German and Italian states appeared to be menaced by terrorists. The current ascent of racism was more threatening because its means of propagation were cultural. For such stern critics, the libertarian position, apparently based on insouciance, was reprehensible.

I didn't like censorship, but I could understand the ferocity of such arguments. At the same time I could see that their validity was being daily undermined – and not just by the new technology. For we were distanced from the mid-century horrors, even as we were more capable of being entertained by their memory. 'Are you going to see the man called Hitler?' my daughter once asked me. The professor with whom I went looking for Nazis always wore black. 'It does help,' he said apologetically. 'They may not think you are one of them, but it's a form of camouflage.' Without quite realizing it, I began to do the same thing.

Not long ago I had watched a remarkable compilation of the feel-good music and images of Hitler's Germany, shot in colour. The young film-maker wished to show that the spirit of MTV had existed in Goebbels' day and that, bizarre though this might seem, efforts had been made to represent Adolf Hitler, *lederhosen*, hounds and silly hat, as a sex object. His film was roundly criticized for its frivolity, particularly by the mostly middle-aged Germans present. I couldn't agree with such censure. In 1998 the Polish photographer Piotr Uklanski assembled a roomful of photographs of Hollywood Nazis. Here they were dressed in deepest black, Telly Savalas, Curt Jurgens, Dirk Bogarde, Peter O'Toole, James Mason, some eighty of them glaring balefully at the camera through fake monocles or black patches. The purpose of the exhibition, self-evidently, was to document what had become our Nazi problem; but I wasn't surprised when Uklanski, too, was attacked for glamorizing his subject.

At the heart of the argument about what should or should not be permitted was the press, or its rapidly growing electronic or digital siblings, television and the Internet. Neutrality was the traditional norm of news reporting. However, I realized early on that journalistic neutrality posed its own special set of problems with respect to the Far Right. What did a reporter do in such circumstances – try to understand the fascists or denounce them? Exactly how was it possible to show them as they were, without courting accusations of complicity?

A liberal from what I had now learnt to call the 'Anglo-Saxon tradition' of qualified freedoms, possessing no simple answer to these problems, I went back to the warnings of Hugh Greene, brother of the novelist. As a correspondent for the *Daily Telegraph* in Berlin during the 1930s, Greene had comprehensive, first-hand experience of the Nazis. Years later, in 1965, when he was head of the BBC, he tried to incorporate such knowledge within a prescriptive framework of journalism:

There are some respects in which [journalism] is not neutral, unbiased or impartial. That is where there are clashes for and against the basic moral values – truthfulness, justice, freedom, compassion, tolerance. Nor do I believe that we should be

impartial about certain things like racialism, or extreme forms
of political belief. Being too good 'democrats' in these matters
could open the way to the destruction of democracy itself . . .[21]

Hailed at the time for their wisdom, these lines now seemed
profoundly threatening as well as prescient. For Greene could
not have anticipated the competitiveness of news – or indeed
the degree to which information had become another form
of currency. Nor could he have wholly understood the way
in which journalists, simply by reporting events or interviewing people, might allow themselves to be used by those whom
they hated or despised. In that respect, life had become more
difficult for a journalist since his day. However, Greene's
message was more slippery, as I now realized. He, too,
appeared to think that in the good cause of democracy,
censorship might be required. At the very least he was calling
for reporters to observe the proprieties. Unusually for someone who had once been a reporter, he believed in reticence.

'Everything is what it is,' Isaiah Berlin had written. 'Liberty is liberty, not equality or fairness or justice or culture, or
human happiness or a quiet conscience.'[22] I tended to believe
that those who wished to defend freedom of speech must
address the matter of what they, too, would ultimately find
intolerable. As I went round Germany I listened to many
coherent arguments from the mouths of liberal censors. Perhaps, I reflected, it was possible to be 'too good a "democrat"' – though I somehow doubted it. However, it was easy
for a journalist to connive in the manufacture of hatreds, of
that I could be certain. Some days I felt that my own support
of freedoms was based in a sustainable view of the world,
and that there could be no real danger to democracy in
Europe, at least from the depleted specimens of fascism
before my eyes. Other days, when things were less good, I

told myself that the fears were grounded in historical wisdom, and that there was no reason anyone should not expect a return of horrors in Europe. I resolved to struggle with these matters, just as I would struggle with the fascists. Meanwhile, I reflected, it was no doubt good to live in doubt. This is what I told myself each time I set out on the black road.

# FÜHRERS OF NOTHING

'All those years, I was a Führer of nothing.'
Ewald Althans

I noticed Kai Diesner's white knuckles when he stood between the two policemen. Unsuccessfully, nervously, he tried to anticipate their movements, shifting when they did from side to side. I imagined that this was his way of appearing to be in charge of a situation which he was far from being able to dominate. While they were dressed in the usual police pseudo-functional new German muds-and-greens, he wore the anti-dandy, British-originated new Nazi uniform: a Fred Perry polo shirt, Lee jeans, Doc Marten boots. Small, pasty, his pale cheeks scraped rough and his skull shaved, Diesner rose and sat punctiliously, nodding whenever the judge addressed him either directly or through his lawyer. He never looked at the public gallery where I sat with the rest of the press. Where the testimony concerned his own murderous actions, especially when these were recounted in horrible detail, he became abstracted or observed details of the outsize, bland tapestry depicting ships blown about by German-looking mythological figures as they approached the crenellated medieval port of Lübeck.

Diesner had killed one man and maimed another. He was the first Nazi whom it had been my privilege to observe freely, at more or less close quarters. From his prison cell he wrote poems in which he presented himself as a warrior engaged in conflict with the state. He quoted from runes, observing the sacred memory on his birthday of AH or 18, as he referred to the Führer, using the code coyly adopted to circumvent censorship. Amid what he conceived of as the contemporary lack of belief, he spoke ardently of pagan stoicism. I recalled what the urbane prosecutor, tilting his chair back under Humphrey Bogart posters, had told me. Diesner was a new type, in the sense that he had some sort of worldview more ample than the simple and systematized recirculation of hatred. He appeared to believe in all this paltry Nordic business. It enabled him to conclude that foreigners had the cosmological status of devils. And there was nothing under-privileged about Diesner's background. His mother had worked in one of the GDR hard-currency stores for foreigners – which made her, relatively speaking, well off. Unlike many of his own generation, who were summarily rendered unemployed, he had served a long (and apparently successful) apprenticeship at Siemens. Although his girlfriends said he was violent and fanatical, it didn't appear that he had ever attacked them. I asked the prosecutor if he knew why Diesner had done these things and he laughed, pulling at the sleeves of his natty Boss jacket. 'If he knows, he won't say,' he replied. 'I don't know whether he does know.' Perhaps it was part of the warrior idea to explain that no explanation should be necessary, the prosecutor continued. Why should he ever need to justify something that (to him at least) made complete sense? So Diesner had declined to address the press, contenting himself with the Adolf Hitler birthday letters. He wasn't apparently a wheel of any sorts in the local neo-Nazi world. If he had belonged to a cell, the police hadn't found one. It did seem that he had incubated the idea of being Führer in relative solitude. Then one day he went out and committed barbarous acts. But why did he do these things?

In the past days I'd encountered police chiefs and social workers and prosecutors. These people – they were well-educated, like most Germans they spoke deliberately, and they were the sort of people whom we had learnt to define as caring – shared the conviction that what they were doing was the right thing. The polite prosecutor had gone into the Nazi business shortly after leaving law school, and he had spent the last fifteen years interrogating or trying them. Now he smiled at me through small, lozenge-shaped steel glasses. I could see him as a journalist or an executive of an innovative consultancy, and I liked him. 'I do still feel good every time one of them goes to prison,' he explained. 'So, yes, you could say that I have no doubts about my job – none whatsoever.' The social workers and policemen I had so far met on the Nazi trail sounded like judges, and I wasn't surprised to find a prosecutor who sounded like a journalist. But I was bothered by the question, suppressed amid the overwhelming statistical flow, of how dangerous Nazis were. All right, they were horrible and sometimes, just as they did in Britain, gangs of louts went out, got drunk and killed foreigners. But this, as I had begun to realize, wasn't quite what people meant when they talked about a Nazi threat. Obviously Diesner was dangerous – he had, it would seem, killed someone. And yet I found it hard to accept that in some places Nazis systematically operated 'no foreigners' areas, standing guard to exclude intruders. I had no problems entering and parking anywhere I wished, though it could be said that I wasn't the kind of foreigner whom Nazis would necessarily wish to exclude. I wondered whether the threat wasn't exaggerated, granting legitimacy to a not so small complex of vigilant officialdom. Were there really so many members of the extreme right wing? Did they represent a threat or a nuisance value? Did their hate-filled presence on prime time do more than periodically cause foreigners not to buy German cars?

Although the other functionaries whom I had encountered responded coolly to this line of questioning, the prosecutor took it seriously. He insisted that, yes, Diesner was in his own limited way a new type, and I must understand this. Outside politics, he was almost anonymous – and one must imagine Diesners springing up anywhere, reconstituting the old hierarchy of Nazism as a series of anarchist-style cells where every man could be a Führer. It was this combination of reclusiveness and fanaticism that interested him. 'I don't think it's enough to say that he might fifty years ago have been a guard in a camp,' he said. 'And I don't think it's enough to judge these people solely by reference to the past that we know about. One really does want to know why someone like him does these things. And that's difficult – perhaps it is a vain hope after all. They don't always change their views in prison, no matter how hard we try. They stay the same.' But this was the new Germany and I realized that he was teasing me, smiling. 'All this will be a problem for you if you're looking for Nazis,' he said.

On 6 November 1995, Diesner, irritated by the vocal and disruptive presence of *autonome* – the left-wing anarchist gangs who dressed up in leather and sported cockatoo hair-dos – during a neo-Nazi demonstration, decided to do something about it. He took his pit bull, Willy, and his pump-action gun, and he went to the local bookshop, which was the centre of the leftist scene in Lübeck, where he shot the owner, badly wounding him. Then he drove off in his small red car with the pit bull, stopping each night in fields or in the parking areas of autobahns. He didn't attack anyone else – it appeared from his testimony, though he was reticent on this point, that he had no idea what to do with himself now that he had committed a crime. But Diesner had switched licence plates from one car to another and he was driving illegally. It would seem that this began to worry him. On Sunday morning, when a policeman knocked on the window of the car, he panicked, pushing the door open, firing once in the policeman's face and, when the man staggered backwards, firing again. Mortally wounded, the policeman fell to the ground. Taking the pit bull and his gun, Diesner escaped to the fields.

Lübeck, an old Baltic city, was where Thomas Mann chose to depict the rise and fall of the old Protestant bourgeoisie of pre-modern Germany, and in his courteous pedantry our silver-haired judge appeared to have stepped from an updated made-for-TV *Buddenbrooks*. The back of the courtroom was lined with hefty ring folders, containing evidence, which he consulted from time to time. He smiled at the small army of social workers, assistants and stand-in jurors. (This wasn't a jury trial in the English sense; they were present to ensure due procedure was adhered to, and they flipped industriously through the indexed volumes, checking testimony against already recorded evidence, looking earnestly over the defendant towards us.)

Sobbing, pausing to wipe his tears, the police witness told how he had crossed the autobahn in search of help for the dying man. He hadn't been able to save his friend. By the time the helicopters arrived Diesner had got to the nearby wood and it had taken the best part of a morning, and a hundred policemen, to surround the fugitive and the pit bull

– they had finally surrendered only when it was clear that the situation was hopeless. We went back and forth over the small number of facts available in relation to this simple, futile crime. The judge ran his court with a scrupulousness verging on piety. Diesner's lawyer suggested that his client had been threatened by the policeman, but it was clear that he himself didn't believe this. We hung around the courtroom during the breaks, sitting in the sunshine on the English-looking lawn before the courthouse. Severe young women from the Berlin press were taking copious notes. When I asked one of them if Diesner was exceptional, she blinked. 'He is not typical,' she explained. 'Perhaps special in his courage. But that is not so unusual among the *rechtsextremismus* – the Far Right.'

Sentenced to life in prison, Diesner was, as even someone as unreflective as himself must understand, finished. As a Celtic warrior and combatant for Adolf we would see no more of him, and he would be middle-aged and spent by the time he emerged to confront the complications of the Germany which he despised. But I had met him early in my search for Nazis, and he became a spirit level of sorts. Each time I seemed about to be overcome by the kitsch of the subject – the rococo censorship, the hideousness of their uniforms or the hatefulness of their views – I thought of Diesner. He was serious, at the very least, and I could legitimately consider him to be a talisman. He told me something of what I was looking for. I did try to see him in prison, but I wasn't surprised when he declined. Meanwhile I considered what, in the circumstances of our time, could be said to define a real Nazi. What did these clothes and scarified heads express? Was it pure hatred? Or the blindest rage? Or were these merely the fantasies of the journalists, social workers, or judges (I included myself here) who, as they had

Diesner, surrounded these Nazis, forming a dense protective cordon around them?

But there was another aspect of my sighting of Diesner that bothered me, and that was what might be termed the problem of scale or perspective. It was as if I had seen him down the institutional equivalent of a long lens. I had merely sighted him, after all; and it transpired that I knew less about him, or what he stood for, now that I had seen him. From my conversations with German friends it appeared that this was how they, too, experienced those said to be the enemies of German civilization. Everyone believed they knew what these Nazis stood for, but no one was personally acquainted with them. The question of their relationship to contemporary Germany was a problematic one. How German, after all, were these Nazis? Their parties were under permanent surveillance, and their trophies – Third Reich flags, swastika badges, brown shirts, even such relatively antiquated symbols as the Kaiser Wilhelm battle flag and the Celtic cross – were declared illegal. To survive, and circumnavigate these bannings, Nazis were obliged to encode their real message of hatred within a complex set of essentially harmless social formulae – either that or they screamed unintelligibly. They were allowed to parade occasionally, so long as they behaved themselves. Just as significantly, however, nobody in Germany that I had met believed that they would ever cease to exist. Doomed to serve as a reminder of the past, therefore, the Nazis were the object of perpetual vigilance. They had become the means whereby Germans reminded themselves of their own democratic good faith. They were what remained of the abhorred, unregenerate old Germany – and thus, like buildings, books from the period, black and white newsreels, or endlessly recorded and replayed memories of terminal infamy, worthy of conservation.

I thought of the tight atmosphere in Germany when I next went to Denmark. Here it was possible to park outside a seaside villa in Greve, a nondescript small town forty kilometres from Copenhagen. You rang the doorbell and a stout young man clad like a lumberjack opened the door. This was Jonni Hansen, leader of the Danish National Socialist Party and the local Führer. Hansen worked part-time in a kindergarten, but this didn't bother anyone; and he was allowed to operate a local radio station in the evening, from which he broadcast military marches and Holocaust denial news. (Bizarrely, I learnt that he received a subsidy of £3,000 from the Danish Ministry of Culture to operate this 'independent' radio station.) The Danish Nazis periodically fought with the Far Left, but they also stood in elections, polling 0.5 per cent of the vote. Their principal importance was as an irritant or test of social democratic tolerance. The German authorities, who were trying to stop the flow of racist CDs shipped in pig trucks from Copenhagen to Kiel, sometimes lodged protests. Meanwhile Jonni affably entertained visiting journalists with his rich display of hatreds.

'Racism. Yes Please!' a sticker said. For me, Jonni's principal interest lay as a prototype. If Nazis were countenanced elsewhere in Europe they might resemble him and his friends. If they did they would be pedantically law-abiding, insisting to the point of tedium that they should not be discriminated against on the grounds that they held hateful views, which they would of course express with the utmost sobriety, thus evading the charge that they were actually disseminating hatreds. They would also (I enjoyed this irony) claim funds from the EU in order to campaign against democratic Europe. But I was to be astonished again and again when I accompanied Jonni and his friends on their visits to suburban streets. They were indeed Nazis, and it was as if I had arrived in a small town at some point in the 1930s, miraculously preserved. For Jonni's diminutive *volk* – about a dozen of them, young, womenless men, hanging out in the house, failing to clean up the dog turds when they weren't photocopying racist pamphlets – were better than the most artfully constructed heritage site. Everything Adolf Hitler had done was fine, they assured me – and he was not to blame for the bad things attached to his name. A swastika barbecue stood in the back yard, but its presence was not to be interpreted in a spirit of postmodernism. It meant exactly what it would have meant had Denmark remained a suburbanized portion of the German Reich. Pork would indiscreetly have been enjoyed in the Danish portion of the Reich by Danes and Germans alike – no doubt the barbecue would have been of the quality expected in Denmark. Meanwhile Jonni less than tastefully explained that he was against race mixing because of his belief in the superiority of the White Race. There should be no Jews in Denmark, he suggested, even if their antecedents had been Danish citizens for centuries. Jonni disapproved of my own views, which he considered to be frivolous. The greatest threat to us all, Danes or no, he insisted, was multiculturalism. And I wasn't being serious about the White Race. 'I don't approve of your person,' he repeated. 'Or of your views. I get this shit from the media every day.' Stubbornly the Führer of Greve went through the Nazi catechism. Not a single Jew had died in what we mistakenly called the Holocaust. Some day, he and his followers would come to power, but legally, as Hitler had done. Meanwhile he intended to practise what he described as honest racism – and the idea struck me as being specially Danish. When a car tooted at us as we stood together by the roadside, Hansen insisted that this meant that a supporter had greeted him. He raised his middle finger to show what happened when he encountered an opponent.

Given his circumstances in quiet and prosperous Denmark, Hansen was absurd; but the decision to tolerate him was serious enough. Notoriously, in relation to pornography as well as the Far Right, the Danish Constitution was the freest in Europe. It distinguished between the expression of ideas, which was legal, and the encouragement of hatred, which was not. (A year later, he was arrested and charged for driving his car in a way that might have injured the left-wingers who had demonstrated outside and attacked his HQ.) This meant that Jonni would be guaranteed freedom to speak and stand for office no matter how much he and his likes appeared to threaten democracy. Even as a young civil servant in the Ministry of Justice earnestly explained this to me, I began to doubt it. It seemed to me that Jonni and his friends were tolerated because they were harmless. They were a form of easily purchased luxury in a society both relaxed enough to have afforded a sense of humour and sufficiently earnest to have guaranteed freedom of speech. These conditions pertained in the expansive air of Danish Europe, but not, it was clear, in the new Germany where Jonni would some time ago have found himself doing the contemporary equivalent of sewing mailbags.

A few months later I flew to the old East Germany. In Munich, where I stopped on the way, the glass atrium of the hotel contained three brand-new BMW convertibles filled with the overpowering scent of new leather upholstery. I was on my way to a May Day demonstration which had been alternately banned and declared legal in a succession of complicated and contradictory judgements in state and federal courts. Outside Leipzig the autobahns were filled with six thousand police taken from all over Germany. One after another, brand-new VW vans moved in convoy loaded up with riot gear. I was filmed many times by police cameramen, stopped and frisked. It was an unseasonably warm day, and the centre of Leipzig resembled a large military encampment in which security had been entrusted to the sort of professional zealots employed by millennial cults. The park to which I was directed was green and sticky, and I climbed a grassy mound. Here I seated myself amid scrubby, acrid-smelling bushes in the shade of the tomb-like monument marking the spot on which, in October 1813, Napoleon's Imperial army was finally destroyed by the soldiers of the Prussian state. From this vantage point, afforded a magnificent perspective that would have been envied by nineteenth-century war correspondents, I saw trucks equipped with water cannon lumber through narrow streets lined with suburban gardens. Suddenly, there was a noise of stone on metal and they began to squirt water at the *autonomen*. For two hours, before our eyes, the police methodically doused these small groups of irate leftists. A journalist from the *Berliner Tagesblatt* lent me her field glasses so that I could pick out the rock throwers. I followed one blue-haired *antifa* as he was pursued through the streets by a cannon until the water appeared to run out, and what had been first a spray became a fitful drip and then a sad trickle. He turned towards the lumbering image of authority, screaming abuse.

Soon afterwards, music began to play on a small adjacent parade ground. Column by column, young men marched from their buses into the park. Like Diesner, they had shaved their heads; and they, too, were dressed in jeans and Fred Perry shirts. I skirted these groups, trying to talk to them, but I was rebuffed. A photographer by my side saw his camera removed, opened up and smashed to the ground. I tried to separate faces or physiques from the gathering crowd, but I could register only types. Some of these young men were horribly bloated, others were skinny. Amid the odd trench coat or forage cap, I could pick out Goebbels and Goering lookalikes, dressed in spiffier leather or wearing the armbands that marked them out (for the police, too, I reflected) as leaders. These Nazis looked as if they had rummaged through a giant thrift shop – in their disguises they bore some parody resemblance to the ragged armies of the 1960s counterculture. But unlike those who became known as the children of Marx and Coca-Cola, they were not well-disposed to the accompanying press, to whom they had little or nothing to say. When the music swelled and military marches were played they froze away from us. This was their moment, and they were not going to miss the opportunity of retreating further and further into the approved posture of hatred. I tried several times to speak to them before I realized that they, too, were prisoners – of the cordon of police surrounding them, to be sure, but also of the press, pestering them like myself. They were at the centre of a large *ausstellung* – a ponderously contrived exhibition of hatred. Like Diesner, and whether they liked it or not, they were also on trial.

Ostensibly, these were followers of the NPD, a nationalist party founded in the 1960s, which had recently enjoyed a revival among young people in particular, scoring well in East German local elections. But the NPD was a flag of convenience for these young adherents of the Extreme Right. Instead of Nazis they now called themselves national (or nationalist) socialists, by which they affected to mean, not wholly convincingly, that they were merely socialists who also believed in the integrity of German culture. As the speeches about the evils of capitalism or the selling-out of Germany progressed, policemen and dogs ventured into the crowd, confiscating the Kaiser Wilhelm battle flags that sprouted amid the anodyne black, red and white NPD banners. This seemed to me like *übereifer* – an instance of excessive zeal. My Anglo-Saxon reflexes inclined me against so conspicuous an instance of crowd control, and I was astonished by the level of judicial or administrative doublethink implied by the notion of first permitting a demonstration, then seeming to cancel it; and, lastly, hindering those who wished to attend it from making their way to the deer park within which they would laboriously be cordoned off from anyone who might wish to hear whatever it was that they wished to say. But I found that I was rapidly set right by the journalists around me. This was the largest gathering of neo-Nazis in twenty years, an Associated Press man told me; and he was shocked to be German. 'Never would I have thought this possible,' he kept saying. He would have to tell his young children about the awfulness of what he had seen. A bearded correspondent from a Berlin left-wing agency was meanwhile exercised by the earlier spraying of leftists. For him the morning's events testified to the fact that, given the opportunity, the German police always dressed to the right. He didn't agree with my observations about the excessive police presence or the number of VWs. 'Once a fascist, always a fascist,' he muttered, as he set me right.

Between the park and the ranks of coaches ready to receive the returning Nazis stood ranks of policewomen in their twenties wearing white helmets and black breastplates, with designer nightsticks made of the kind of solid plastic to be found in Porsche accessories. I walked back through an utterly empty city. The photographer whose film was wrecked was on the evening news; so were the banners, shaven heads and chants. But this appeared to be a well-known story, and nothing was thought to be worthy of

explanation. Once again, I found myself a reluctant participant in a ritual of exorcism. Look, these people are here, the
smartly dressed newscaster was saying. They are awful and
we must pay attention – sackcloth and ashes are still de
rigueur. But they are not so awful as to merit any real
disruption of our lives; indeed (and one must grasp this
paradox to be a real German, this was what the pictures now
told me) they make sense of who we have become, and what
we henceforth wish to be. Flicking between a porn channel
and the Nazis, I realized that Germany – so central to our
perceptions of Europe, so big and sometimes so friendly
seeming – was also a very difficult place.

In London, I tried to read the numerous press cuttings
and books which described how, after all these years, the
Nazis constituted a threat to civilization. It was hard, unforgiving work; but one could trace, year by year, the national
obsession. From the beginning a revival of Nazism was what
the occupying forces, Americans in particular, expected and
chiefly feared; and they earnestly scrutinized the rubble for
early warning signs of revived danger. It seemed that they
had been right to do so. Polls done in the American Occupied
Zone in 1947 revealed that between 47 and 55 per cent of
Germans believed that National Socialism, contrary to all
available evidence, was a good idea badly carried out.
Between 55 and 65 per cent of Germans still thought that
'some races (were) more fit to rule than others'.[1] Other
samplings revealed a surliness towards the occupiers coupled
with a sense of nostalgia for banished national grandeur.
From the beginning, the authorities of the new Germany, too,
dreaded any recrudescence of Nazism. It was to forestall such
an occurrence that German constitutional lawyers formulated
the notion of democracy existing in a legitimate state of self-
defence. The new Basic Law of 1950 made it possible for the

Constitutional Court in Karlsruhe to ban political parties. A handful of neo-Nazi parties had sprung up, scoring more than decently in elections. In 1952, following a request from Adenauer's government, the new court banned the most prominent of them, the Sozialistische Reichspartei. Dissolved, the party could neither hold meetings nor raise money. No longer eligible for the various subsidies available to political parties, it ceased to exist. Happily, no further action needed to be taken against the other parties.

Half-banned, fringe Nazi groups riposted by going half-underground. The earliest neo-Nazis were disgruntled veterans who hated the Soviet and American or British occupiers indiscriminately. They believed that the Third Reich, given better luck, would have succeeded in its insane war aims; and they insisted, pedantically, in small journals or at veterans' meetings, that too much fuss had been made about the Holocaust. Pride in being German wasn't a crime, nor, as it turned out, had Hitler's hostility to Marxism proved unfounded. Cranky, vocal, these survivors from the banished past became the irreducible hard core of the Far Right. In bad times – when the *Wirtschaftswunder* showed signs of sputtering – they were joined by a more amorphous group: those who were left behind or thought they might be, the malcontented, the poorly educated, all those who had reason to despise the empty surfaces of post-war Germany. There were gratuitous, horrifying acts of violence, against Germans as well as Turkish immigrants and, later, asylum-seekers. But it was nonetheless possible for the authorities to control the neo-Nazis. Germans who believed in democracy could tell themselves that the legal curbs placed on extremist activities were effective. They could say to the world that, thanks to the stout and unrelenting efforts made on their behalf, German democracy was able to defend itself.

And yet the situation was more complicated to the east, in the German Democratic Republic. Here the anti-fascist antecedents of the communist regime gave the new state a prior claim on the collective conscience, but this was rapidly abused. Commemorations of Nazism were regularly organized at such camps as Sachsenhausen, conveniently situated near Berlin, at the end of the S bahn; and the party turned out *en masse*, in suits and carrying banners. It became routine for speakers to attack the Federal Republic (which was fair enough) pointing the finger at many ex-Nazis occupying prominent positions in the West. But the rewriting of history, prevalent in all Eastern bloc socialist states, was soon directed towards the Nazi past. The Germanness of Hitler was eliminated in Marxist-Leninist theoretical writings, where his connections with capitalism were instead deemed of paramount importance. Historians interpreted the Weimar period as a succession of 'fascisms' of which *Hitlerfascismus* was the logical outcome.[2] This meant that the Federal Republic could be easily classified as an unregenerate 'fascist' state, by comparison with the 'democratic' East. Between the 1950s and the fall of the East German regime in 1989 nothing was permitted that might have destroyed this lie.

In 1983, I was astounded to accompany a schoolteacher and his twelve-year-old charges to the Berlin Historical Museum. All the exhibits glowingly described the anti-fascist character of the GDR – because there were no capitalists in socialist Germany, it seemed as if there had also been no Nazis. Meanwhile the pieties of anti-fascism proved one of the few distractions available to the beaten populace under socialism. The GDR ostensibly guaranteed freedom of expression, but it banned 'works which present war as inevitable and foster hatred for other peoples'.[3] Anti-fascism was therefore used to justify the creation of an educational dictatorship of awesome strictness, and a schooling system proof against the most rudimentary forms of enquiry. Censorship in the GDR was taken as seriously as indoctrination. In their determination to link the capitalist West to the Nazi past, the Stasi – the GDR secret police – even organized their own networks of neo-Nazis, sponsoring bombings and hold-ups. It was as a consequence of their efforts, it now appeared, that the Köln synagogue was plastered with swastikas in 1959, causing a wave of global outrage and much self-searching at home.

Were Germans right in thus using the law to interdict fascism? In 1948, George Orwell, struggling with the second draft of *1984* in a sanatorium, wrote to a friend complaining about the demands to outlaw Sir Oswald Mosley's fascist party. He observed that the fascists were now not important in Britain:

> The central thing one has to come to terms with is the argument, always advanced by those advocating repressive legislation, that 'you cannot allow democracy to be used to overthrow democracy – you cannot allow freedom to those who merely use it in order to destroy freedom.' . . . If you carry this to its conclusion there can be no case for allowing any political or intellectual freedom whatever. Evidently therefore it is a matter of distinguishing between a real & a merely theoretical threat to democracy, & no one should be persecuted for expressing his opinions, however antisocial, and no political organization suppressed, unless it can be shown that there is a substantial threat to the stability of the state . . .[4]

The new German Nazis were not a threat to democracy, that was clear. But Orwell was not living in a country in which genocidal terror had reached unprecedented proportions. And censorship did not destroy democracy in Germany – whatever was said to this effect in the GDR, the Federal

Republic did not become a fascist regime. The restrictions on free speech seemed benign, or not quite as malign as Orwell might have feared. This was at least how things seemed to most Germans during the years of the Cold War.

'We really are quite a tolerant people,' a friend explained to me. 'Nobody cares now if you take your clothes off in the Munich Englische Garten. Nazism is the only bad thing left to us.' In the angst-ridden soap of German popular consciousness, having a Nazi for a son was the worst that could happen – it far exceeded in importance any other domestic atrocity. Germans were therefore upset at the beginning of the 1990s, after the Wall was destroyed and Germany reunified, when there was what appeared to be a serious return of neo-Nazism. In 1992 neo-Nazis attacked a refugee centre in Rostock. This was how an American journalist (following the German press) described the after-effect:

> Alarm bells started to ring in foreign embassies and boardrooms, as photos of neo-Nazi youth hurling Molotov cocktails at immigrant hostels flashed around the world. Suddenly people were asking questions that until then had seemed unthinkable: Could it happen again? Had the German demons returned? 'This is how something began that ended at Auschwitz,' said Manfred Stolpe, premier of the German state of Brandenburg. 'These riots are the worst thing that has happened in Germany since 1945.'[5]

At some moments of the early 1990s, it seemed briefly as if an entire generation of young Germans in the East had 'gone Nazi'. The apocalyptic language was everywhere – 'HATE IN ROSTOCK' was how NDR titled its evening news, in lurid pink lettering. 'ROSTOCK IS EVERYWHERE' said *Stern* magazine, anticipating the imminent collapse of the rule of law throughout Germany.

In Rostock I visited the centre in the presence of an NDR camera crew interviewing the social workers for the fifth anniversary of this outrage – short of copy, they ended by interviewing me about why I was there. It had been terrible to be besieged inside the building for two days, and the Rostock police had been less than competent. However, things had quietened down. No plaque had been installed on the building, but the Rostock chief of police, fresh from the West and bearing a startling resemblance to Harrison Ford, was adamant that these things would never happen again. At the local school, teachers had developed a pairing system to ensure that newcomers from different cultures wouldn't be overwhelmed by the spectacle of so many blue-eyed, pig-tailed classmates. The principal concern in Rostock lay not with such lofty questions as whether and why the Nazis would return, but how to stop them setting foot within the city limits.

But this was not the entire story, and those who had assiduously sounded the alarm had been right to do so. Something bizarre had occurred in Germany, and it had to do with the wholly new country, brought so abruptly into being by the pulling down of the Wall, and the pathetic, anticlimactic end of the old GDR. Germans were faced with a bankrupt, derelict piece of real estate about which the truth hadn't been told for many years. They also inherited a serious policing problem – no one could rely on the hopeless hacks and ex-border guards from the GDR, and they proved unable to counter the neo-Nazis. But the Wall coming down had created chaos of a different, deeper nature. What was Germany after all? What relation did the post-war arrangements bear to the real, historic Germany? Briefly, it became possible to think of Germany from scratch, as if it were rubble again, except that Europe had changed, and Germany was no longer ringed with hostile occupying powers. It was into that space that the neo-Nazis marched, wearing the borrowed English gear and shouting old-for-new slogans. They failed – of course they were never going to succeed; they, as well as everyone else, knew that – but in their failure they reminded Germans of what might have been. And they seemed momentarily, to the German Left as well as the Far Right, to provide a means of rededication to the totems of the recent past.

Nonetheless, even with the benefit of hindsight, it wasn't easy to explain the phenomenon of neo-Nazism in the early 1990s. Was the movement as serious as people had imagined? Part of the problem I encountered was that many participants had recanted, criss-crossing Germany dressed in black leather to denounce their former selves. Their glamour made them attractive, but it ensured, too, that they were never taken entirely seriously, and they followed groups like the Black Panthers into the limbo reserved for those to whom excess media attention had proved as damaging as the police. Now they were important for the media primarily as retrospection or as fetishes.

When I met Ingo Hasselbach he was sitting at a film festival with his Palestinian fiancée, surrounded by a small crowd of admirers. Professionally amiable, by now skilled in self-presentation, Hasselbach was, as he described himself in his memoirs, 'an Aryan poster boy'.[6] Photos of him had appeared in the *New Yorker*, and he was the star of two documentary films. Hasselbach's memoirs, ghosted by an American journalist, described in detail the awfulness of growing up in the GDR. His journalist/propagandist father, from whom his mother was separated, was in charge of youth indoctrination, and this seemed to have begun his disenchantment with the orthodoxies of anti-fascism. Ingo's schooldays in the elite academies of Marxism-Leninism completed the job – and as a teenager he became a professional breaker of left-wing heads. He ascended to the position, largely imaginary, of Gauleiter of Berlin. At one time, between media appearances and well-publicized battles, he even had the time to found his own party.

However, his memoirs were too eager to please to be wholly convincing, and the violence, by the standards of those coming from British hooligans or SAS veterans, was oddly muted. Ingo told of derring-do amid the squats and broken *antifa* heads in the breathless but oddly removed style with which boys' books (the ones read avidly by young imperialist Germans) once recounted the adventures of young Britishers at the furthest frontiers of Empire. Fighting took place, it seemed, but no one was maimed or killed. It appeared that Hasselbach had become skilled at the extraction of money from foreign television crews. He was the man everyone called when they needed a Nazi. Exactly why Nazism had attracted him, or what at any moment he thought he was doing in the cause of right-wing revolution, was already hidden behind the over-artful portrait of deviance happily returned to normality that he now presented to a receptive public. Like his father, after a mild detour, Hasselbach had become an anti-Nazi propagandist.

More interesting to me was the bizarre career of Ewald Althans. Playing Goebbels to Ingo's Röhm, he had specialized in agitprop rather than head-breaking. Another documentary film *Beruf: neo-Nazi* (*Profession: neo-Nazi*) had been made with his collusion. Meeting Althans some years ago, I was struck by his intelligence, all the while wondering whether it would ever be possible to fathom what was genuine fanaticism and what was inspired self-publicity. During the early 1990s Althans ran a small PR business in Munich, distributing pamphlets. He appeared on a number of platforms, often in the company of the British historian David Irving. Althans' parents were so-correct teachers from a small town in West Germany, and it seemed that they were upset by their son's vocal anti-Semitism – they felt disgraced by what he had become. Clean-cut, dressed in natty suits and denims, with cropped hair and the right Aryan eye-and-skin colouring, Althans was the model of modern neo-Nazism. He was also a homosexual, and he announced the imminent triumph of Nazism as a 'lifestyle religion'. He blithely told journalists that multiculturalism was a negation of the democratic ideal. 'Why should I have to live next to a group of spear-chucking negroes?' he asked. But Althans appeared also to be a Holocaust denier, and the most bizarre sequence of the film showed him in Auschwitz, shouting at a group of Jewish visitors that the gas chambers they had just seen were fakes. As its makers must have anticipated, *Beruf: neo-Nazi* was banned in Germany. In 1993, Althans was arrested. He was tried twice – at the second trial in Berlin, for what he had said in the film, which had conveniently been exhibited in a cinema for one night, thus allowing charges to be brought. At this trial, witnesses testified that he had been a police spy during his career as a propagandist, and that his contact book had provided the police with the means whereby most of the neo-Nazis were tailed or later arrested. Having served his prison term, Althans was now in hiding outside Germany. I was frustrated by my inability to locate him.

By now I was tired of hearing what over-educated German specialists had to say about the Nazis – what I needed to know, it seemed, was what they, the Nazis, might tell me, directly or not, about Germans. Or about the Germany, appalling as it might be, that they wanted. Or indeed about themselves. I still couldn't really believe that it was possible to have been born after 1945 and still want to be a Nazi. But I was lucky, passing through Paris, to meet the man I'll call Gerhard. He reminded me of my old acquaintance Patrick, grown somewhat tubbier. Half-German, half-French, brought up in the Rhineland during the Allied occupation, he belonged to the class of people I had been familiar with during the Cold War – those equipped with bugging devices and familiar with the jargon (if not the location) of message drops. Conspiratorial, paranoid, an expert in martial arts, Gerhard was also contradictory in his attitudes. He professed, nervously, an admiration for the vanishing social discipline in the various more or less distasteful regimes it had been his lot to oversee or infiltrate for the past thirty-odd years. But, like many Europeans, Gerhard had recently switched targets, and instead of pursuing communists he kept tabs on the Far Right.

Gerhard dressed in various shades of black or grey, making long cell-phone calls in a variety of codes. The old faux-matiness with which he addressed the comrades had shifted reference, becoming his proper form of greeting for the fascists. He pooh-poohed my excessively relaxed Anglo-Saxon ideas. The extremists did communicate with each other, across boundaries or over the Internet. True, Europe wasn't immediately going to be overrun by a black peril; but these people were nastiness incarnate. They could be a danger if they were ever allowed to be. It was Gerhard who began to tell me about the complex mechanics of surveillance applied to the Far Right. For him the critical aspect of this surveillance was its painstaking legality. Built on new foundations, post-war Germany had been forced to evolve a system of snooping that was wholly transparent. It was even possible for him to suggest that, just as the world had learnt from the Germans how to make cars or win at football, so, too, we might learn from them about the theory and practice of low-level, user-friendly espionage. When I said that I found it hard to believe that espionage could be conducted in so civilized a fashion, he offered to show me how it worked.

We met on a sunny day in a red-brick campus near a stretch of autobahn, on the outskirts of Köln, between an engineering plant and a management retraining centre. Here we were lightly frisked, given nutritious cakes and fruit juice, and marched down long corridors. We endured briefings and, in between them, short waits. There were graphs and organigrams to digest rapidly. In the corridors notices hung informing employees of their rights and reciprocal obligations to discretion. Large, happy paintings reinforced the notion of progressive, painlessly ingested educational practices. In a room full of computers, racist publications were meticulously displayed on large tables, graded according to nastiness.

I listened to facts and figures from a youngish researcher wearing jeans and hippie shoes. Although the number of right-wing extremists had fallen slightly in the past year, from 46,100 to 45,300, it seemed the number of 'violence-prone extremists' (neo-Nazis and skinheads) had risen somewhat.[7] Politely, the researcher tried to make sense of these distinctions for me. The inaptly named Verfassungschützbehörde – the word meant Office for the Protection of the Constitution – classified 'extreme-right' activists according to the degree to which they were dangerous. It was estimated that there were at least 2,500 very dangerous extremists and another 7,500 violent skinheads. Around them could be discerned their followers and, beyond those, members of the Far Right parties who should be seen as sympathizers. Circling these, merging with them, were the twenty-odd per cent of the German population for whom extremism was, if not attractive, at least tolerable. A high proportion of these were to be found in the *Länder* of East Germany, or among the undereducated and backward. These figures remained pretty constant, it seemed, though the frequency of violent acts appeared to be affected by outside factors – unemployment, for instance.

But I needed to understand more about this. What I knew about the data regarding violent extremist acts was that it was very difficult to make comparisons between countries because of the different ways in which violence was reported or the incomplete state of police statistics. Britain and Germany seemed to boast the highest levels of racial violence.[8] However, the German definition of a racist act, or a violent racist act, covered just about everything; and in Britain reports were collated on the basis of what victims, and not merely policemen, had to say. (Other countries collected data differently – France for instance, logically if bizarrely, failed to separate attacks on naturalized black or North African French from those on white French, on the grounds that the former were not 'foreigners'.) It was therefore difficult to conclude that one European country was 'more racist' or 'more violently racist' than another. What one could say, however, was that racist incidents, violent or not, had increased enormously in Germany after reunification, by five times in two years, and that most of the increase was accounted for by the reclaimed Eastern *Länder*.[9] In the past four years an epidemic of violence had occurred, and the figures demonstrated that it hadn't yet run its course.

It also seemed possible that the discussion or coverage of violent acts encouraged them. But my mentor dismissed any notion that the press, even in part, was responsible for the Nazis, or that this need be the case. 'It depends how you decide to describe them,' he said. 'There are good and bad ways of showing that the problem exists.' The bad ways, he told me, were much in evidence shortly after reunification in endless scare stories. The idea that Germany was in flames had indeed encouraged the pouring of kerosene. I asked him whether Mrs Thatcher had been right in her famous assertion to the effect that terrorism survived by means of the oxygen of publicity. 'In some respects,' he said, smiling cautiously.

I wanted to ask how it was decided that a person was an extremist. But my interlocutor was describing a system in operation, with an extensive and tested record to defend. The German state, he explained, had been created in the light of American or British models. From its beginnings it had appeared to be threatened from two sources: by the communists in power in the old GDR or their proxies intent on subversion; and by the Far Right. Although the emergency was over, the German constitution nonetheless recognized the danger inherent in extremism. Nothing yet had occurred to cause the relevant clauses to be abolished. Rapidly, he went through the defining features of the Far Right. They might believe in the idea that the German people had a unique destiny, based on blood origins. They might think that an elitist political party, organized around a Führer, was the best way to accomplish this. They were perhaps covert or hidden anti-Semites. They probably rejected the idea that a society was composed of many different belief systems and ethnic groups. They liked obedience and blind trust, revelling in military values. Perhaps they practised revisionism, implying that the crimes of the Third Reich were not as horrifying as the record indicated. In general they were pessimistic about democracy, or the prospects of humankind. They had a tendency to admire terroristic acts, and they were opposed to the idea of Europe.

I asked whether any one of these traits was enough to define a right-winger – or whether it was necessary to adhere to two or more of these misguided beliefs. But my teacher misunderstood these observations. He imagined that I was suggesting that his work was arbitrary. Not so, he said. The Verfassungschütz proceeded methodically. Its agents weren't allowed to carry guns – all the 13,000 operatives did was accumulate data. The important thing was to be dispassionate under any circumstances. Certain parties were banned anyhow; and one had to determine by meticulous scrutiny who and where the real right-wingers were. An initial period of study established the likelihood of suspects to conform to these criteria. After that the matter was placed before a committee composed of the German great and good – policemen, politicians, civil servants – so that a proper determination could be made. And only after that could the bugging begin. Once begun, it was done in earnest – most calls of the Far Right made from *handys* (mobile phones) were intercepted. I asked him how many agents I could expect to find in the average neo-Nazi meeting. 'Out of ten?' he asked. 'Let's say at least two. At every meeting at least two.'

Downscaled from Big Brotherdom, constitutionally sanctioned and performed between glasses of the best fruit juice, this was a Little-Brother-and-a-half, a utopian project of democratic surveillance. Next I was taken through more corridors to a large office. Here I found myself in the presence of the head of the Verfassungschütz, Dr Peter Frisch. The office was large and airy, furnished with outsize black plastic sofas. It resembled those occupied by important Soviet bloc officials twenty years ago, only it was more luxurious. Its occupant got to his feet, blinking through thick glasses. Sombre and deliberate in his responses, Dr Frisch spoke in the very long sentences of the German administrative class. If I had been required to single out someone definitively representative of the mourning that characterized the post-war German generation, it would have been him. He told me that as a young man he had studied the history of National

Socialism. After that, he had sworn to dedicate his life to ensuring that it would never happen again. Liberty, it seemed to him, could only survive if it was circumscribed by law – otherwise its enemies would possess freedoms which they could then use to overthrow the state. Painstakingly, he began to tell me that this was what Hitler had been able to do. Those in positions of responsibility in the ill-fated Weimar Republic were in a position to stop Hitler, but they had failed to do so. There had been a slogan among liberals in universities: 'We are so liberal that we even grant the freedom to destroy liberty.' In 1928 Goebbels wrote in *Angriff*, the SS newspaper: 'We have come to the Reichstag in order to destroy it. If democracy is stupid enough to reward us for doing this, this is the problem of democracy.' So perhaps, Dr Frisch implied, you could be too liberal – every German should know this. And perhaps this was a lesson for our times. 'Men are weak,' he kept saying. 'And we must be strong.' At any rate, he concluded, Germany should take no risks. It must be seen to be ever-vigilant, by friends and enemies alike. When I asked him how long it might be before the restrictions were lifted or relaxed, he made an attempt at a smile. 'Not in my lifetime,' he said. 'Perhaps in a hundred years.'

Near Bonn, where we started our guided tour, the Nazis were to be found in woods, amid German families with dogs and picnic ware. They had hung a plastic bag from a tree, in which they placed empty beer cans. Soberly, they sat in a ring while a septuagenarian Führer addressed them. This was Friedhelm Busse, who had been jailed for attempted bank robbery during the 1970s, and who was now regarded as the grandfather of the neo-Nazis. Busse wore a T-shirt over his gut, and he suffered from many years of poor dental work. His speech was long-winded, filled with denunciations. Not entirely convincingly he treated the Federal Republic as if it were an occupying power, sponsored by international capitalism. But he and his very young followers became more animated when he talked about the police. It seemed that they had wished to rent a hall, but that this had not been possible. Not out of any complex conceptual fusion of greenness and *heimat*, but because it was the only option open to them, they were sitting amid trees. Busse told me that his aim was not to rehabilitate Hitler, but to find him a legitimate place in the German pantheon. I began to tell him that this appeared to me to be more or less the same thing. However, at this moment, on cue, the police arrived, and the Nazis began to scatter. A policeman interrogated the fugitives carrying bottles of beer and deckchairs. 'Did anyone speak here?' he asked. 'Did Busse speak? I'll know about it from my informers if you don't tell the truth.' One young woman became agitated. 'We didn't even sing,' she told the policeman.

As long ago as the 1960s the Left had been regaled with the idea of 'repressive tolerance' – the paranoid-Marxist idea, mooted by émigré Germans like Herbert Marcuse and their hippie-activist followers, that there were things which so-called liberal states could afford to allow because they sustained the fiction of freedoms without touching what were considered to be the real underpinnings of state power. Sceptical about this formulation, I had abandoned it after becoming acquainted with real repression. But now it seemed more relevant – at least in parody form. 'You pretend to hold real meetings, and we'll pretend to suppress them' was how the police addressed the existence of Nazis. Not needing to be repressive, they nonetheless performed a ritual of exclusion on our behalf. For them, Nazi-hunting had become a giant board game, electronically configured at enormous expense, across which cars, journalists and police spies moved.

Still, I told myself, we were finding the Nazis. In Marzahn, a horrible *plattbau* suburb of East Berlin which stretched for miles in each direction, a teenage gang hung out next to the supermarket. They were interesting, Gerhard explained, because they weren't yet Nazis. They had no jobs and they were drinking beer. They were poised somewhere between a horrifying acceptance of the disaster which had struck their lives and a desire, half-formulated, to avoid it. They hated social workers and capitalism. And they talked about how foreigners had been given everything that they had never been entitled to. I could have been in Leicester or Bradford, Le Havre or Marseilles. There was nothing 'racist' or 'fascist' about these lost children, and nothing shocking or hard to explain about their views. But they came accompanied by a woman with a small dog, who sat in the sun next to them making notes. She wasn't a police spy, according to Gerhard. Instead she was the recruiting officer of the local cell of the NPD, and she would soon harden these kids, turning them in the space of a year from disaffected adolescents to militants. But I had no means of gauging the accuracy of Gerhard's observations.

In Rosenberg, a model village of Baden-Würtemberg, we encountered a punk hatred band called the Wolfsrudel (the Werewolves) who performed toned-down racist songs in execrable Euro-English, and whose impeccable monotone was said to be up and coming in the half-respectable skin scene. They made a show of saying that they and their lyrics were censored (I learned that they did indeed submit their songs to the authorities) but they refused to tell me what it was they would have liked to say, on the reasonable grounds that this would get them into trouble. Bored of their music, I walked by the side of small gardens planted with geraniums and hollyhocks. The mayor of Rosenberg was a young Christian Democrat in his thirties who spoke perfect, unaccented English. He explained that there was no unemployment in the area and no foreigners. He didn't know why the hatred was attractive, but it was he who had made the hall available to the Werewolves. Sometimes, he suggested to me mildly, it was better to look after sick or deviant members of a family. That way one knew what was going on.

I had expected something wilder, but I was interested to see that these kids had acknowledged only the remotest parentage of AH, as they, too, were forced to call him. Often it was the memory of other Nazis, like Rudolf Hess or Otto Strasser, which animated them. I found myself in the midst of a rescored, colorized Warner Brothers plot, a new-old *On the Waterfront*. Among the social workers and spies were sententious Karl Maldens a-plenty and even the odd Marlon Brando. As for the kids, most of them too old for their parts, they were still unhappily alienated, to use the oddly appropriate 1950s word. Like their fictional predecessors, they didn't want to have anything to do with the surrounding world which so ardently sought to care for them and render them, by its own lights, normal. But I recalled the current theory, according to which the neo-Nazis were more dangerous than they had been ten years before – because they had effectively merged with the youth culture of the disaffected East. These 'post-Nazis' organized *Kameradenschaften* – gangs or looser associations outside politics but nonetheless capable of spreading the word. The triangular patches, different-coloured laces, or numbers on Fred Perry T-shirts served to identify them. They wore equipment made by the British sporting goods firm Lonsdale because it was the only way the letters NSDA (they stood for the Nazi NSDAP) could be shown in Germany. Meanwhile they policed bits of the *plattbau* cities, placing them beyond the reach of the cops and putting foreigners at hazard.

In Thuringia, around the small town of Saalfeld, I had the opportunity of putting these theories to the test. Here there had been a riot a few months previously. Nazis had come from all over Germany, and several left-wing *autonomen* were hurt. The head of police, who had been imported from Bavaria and regarded his posting as a relatively upright member of the old British colonial police might have done, was apologetic. We drove through the *plattbau* and were rebuffed by a group of teenagers sitting with a pit bull outside the local cafe. Then, with the help of the local Verfassung-schütz, we contacted the local social workers. I sat down in a small, well-equipped office with a man who had shoulder-length hair and beard, giving him the air of an oleograph Christ. By now it was getting late, and his hair was backlit by the fading light. He and his assistants were indeed pessimistic, but the view they offered was slightly different. To them it appeared that the Nazis were unreachable. They might seem to hold dialogues, but their real purpose was to evade authority. The mindset they acquired outlasted adolescence. If they acquired jobs, or families, they would still remain tied to extremism. An entire generation in the East, having been let down by communism, had no belief in capitalism. At the same time the social workers didn't entirely share the view that these kids were dangerous. Being Nazis, or whatever they called themselves, kept them off the streets and gave them things to do. In Saalfeld there were no Turks to kick anyhow.

Mirko, the leader of the *Kameradenschaft*, lived with his family down a small road, opposite what appeared to be an ivy-covered late-Gothic folly which was falling to pieces. His mother was handsome in a rumpled-looking way, wearing a polyester jumpsuit; and she sat with us among the domestic bric-a-brac and family photos, holding the pit bull while we talked. Mirko was small, neatly dressed in dyed fatigues, and already, at the age of eighteen, quite the politician. I was interested that his parents had been communists, and that he and his brother were both attracted to the Far Right. His mother told me that this had nothing to do with Hitler. Everything had collapsed around them and it was necessary to do something. What Mirko did for them kept the kids from breaking things. She added that she was proud of him – and that anyhow there were far too many foreigners in Germany. She, too, thought that so much censorship was absurd, and that Mirko and his friends ought to be able to say what they wished. Everybody likes the kids around here, she repeated. No one finds anything wrong with what they are doing. 'Do you find anything wrong?' she asked me.

Next day was Father's Day, and the roadsides were filled with middle-aged men carrying shoulder-height wooden sticks on which they had placed a variety of different forms of headgear. They waved at the car, staggering on and off the road, and I noticed that they were extremely drunk. We drove higher and higher into the hills while Gerhard explained to me the relation between romanticism and the German national idea. He was convinced that kids like Mirko existed in dreams of their own, at a pre-terrorist, pre-revolutionary stage. They might become dangerous later, he asserted, though at present they were merely a dissident sub-culture. But it was their conspicuous, willed banality that interested me. It seemed that they had learned to evade the requirements of social workers and politics by the simple expedient of copying them. Bourgeois society had its own rules, *nicht war*? Well, if that was the case, they would adopt their own. But theirs would be authentic, in the sense that they would more accurately reflect the *real* Germany than those of the bastardized society around them. Otherwise they would just play the game.

I kept my eye on the small white Peugeot carrying Mirko, his friend André and their two punkish, hair-sculpted, black-lipsticked girlfriends. Now we were high up and the fields were filled with black-and-white cows. If anyone wished to create a retro Germany, I reflected, Thuringia was the place. Neglected for forty-odd years, it was the real *völkisch* thing elsewhere stamped out by liberal capitalism. If they were sensible, no Turks would come here. We stopped in a village and walked together, and then we went through a terrace filled with geraniums and old men with sticks, up a wooden staircase and into a large wood-panelled room hung with antlers. Here there was a balcony, overlooking woods, cows, small houses, a railway line and a blue, washed sky with smallish, dainty clouds.

They had wanted this mise en scène – to show off their uniforms, and because it was theirs, their Germany above all. Once again, what they said that afternoon wasn't new, but it was nonetheless remarkable. It was what their grandparents, quizzed by a visitor, would have no doubt said in the 1930s, and it could have come from the many thousands of testimonies assembled by historians in an attempt to demonstrate why it was that the German people adhered to or acquiesced in National Socialism. They had read books, hurriedly and selectively, like most adolescents, and they were careful not to break the law. It was as easy to tiptoe around interdiction as it had been to modify the Bundeswehr uniforms they wore. They weren't democrats and they had racist views. I listened to the usual fantasies linking Hitler with genuine socialism.

The two girls conceded that the Reich had been wrong to consign women to the kitchen and hearth – though they did say that they would only consider having children with German men. None of them could decide whether English people should be considered to be Aryans. But they were more concerned, for the moment at least, to be drinking apple juice. Later, as they explained, the time for drunkenness would come – and later, too, I imagined, the social workers would try to find out what we had said to them. But it wouldn't matter anyhow, because Gerhard, busy whispering to them separately, would already have given his own report. These teenagers were intelligent enough to know all this. They knew exactly how far they should go. What they must do was to evoke anxiety among the army of half well-wishers surrounding them. What they must not incur was the stigma of definitive transgression.

It was late when we left the village, and I was by now tired. But I felt elated, as if I had discovered something. You see, I wanted to tell Gerhard, these are just kids. The whole apparatus of surveillance is ridiculous. Nothing is wrong here. Germany is an entirely normal place. But there was something the *Kameraden* wanted to show us, and I was in for a surprise. In a disused garage of a *plattbau*, they unpacked from the boot of a Trabbi a large selection of the CDs which the German police were so anxious to confiscate. Next they showed us a large, brightly coloured board game. Modelled on Monopoly, but making use of traditional Gothic script, the game was called Pogrom. It required participants to rid Germany of Jews, by acquiring cities and putting up 'German' houses. You passed Adolf Hitler instead of Go, and you could land on the *Gaswerk*. I noticed that it was possible to collect concentration camps, though bizarrely Auschwitz cost the same 4,000 marks – I didn't understand at what date the currency was fixed, but I imagined it was accurately calculated in terms of 1930s spending power – as the lesser establishments of Dachau and Majdanek. SA or SS cards gave rewards or penalties to the players. Neatly, in emulation of the originals, the German houses were gabled. The representation of Jews on the board was worthy of illustrations from *Der Stürmer*.

Having wanted them to be harmless, I now felt let down by these little Nazis. In what I knew was a very English way, I kept saying that the game was obscene. It existed not to divert, but to stir hatred – though I wasn't sure that this was entirely the case. That was what Gerhard thought, of course, but he was also happy to tell me that many of them (those shipped from the US, or downloaded on the Internet) were much worse. And in the US the game would be perfectly legal. 'You can't say these kids are harmless,' he said to me. And the game, or things like it, made relevant or necessary all the tedious aspects of surveillance in which he, in the course of his career, had become implicated. 'You need the state to fight against fascists,' he said. Of course, I didn't want to accept this perspective. I suppose I had recalled the poem of Cavafy about the barbarians endlessly hanging around the gates of the city, breeding fear, who one day plunged everyone into confusion by failing to show up. Whatever would Germany do without its barbarians? But now, inconveniently, I had to admit that some barbarians – a small tribe, poorly equipped, only a shadow of their antecedents – remained. It was certainly worth taking them seriously.

Not long afterwards, in London, I was surprised to receive a phone call from Ewald Althans' lawyer. His client, it transpired, was living in exile in Antwerp, where he was improbably running a travel agency specializing in gay tourism. But he was prepared to meet me, as long as it wasn't near his new home. So I stood one cold morning in front of the Cathedral of Cologne, and waited for him beside a flower shop under the blackened spires. Prison had aged Althans, giving him a sombre, harried expression; but his eyes stared at me in the same way. We went to a nearby *bierstubl*. Althans explained that the shaved head wasn't part of the neo-Nazi kit, but that he had contracted a skin disease in prison. He had abandoned the uniform along with the ideas. Everything about the Nazi past had been consigned to the past of the other person he had been before he came out. I asked him the same question again and again. Everything? Was he really not the same person? He began to tell me about the boredom of growing up in a small town, and about how attractive it had been to discover something that everybody found reprehensible. He had been a bright adolescent and then his scholarship was removed. That was why he stayed a Nazi. And he did believe in the whole thing. He was an anti-Semite, and he reviled multiculturalism as much as he hated the blandness of contemporary Germany. Also, he discovered that he was a homosexual. The problem for him was that he made his money out of 'the scene' and it was therefore difficult for him to quit. Only very slowly, after he had been to Canada, did he realize that it all meant nothing. And now he had a new life and a new relationship. He didn't really want to come back to Germany.

I was disarmed by Althans' army-base American accent. Althans was a skilled fantasist; but I did feel that this new account of his life was more or less reliable. It certainly made better sense than the myth of national revolution implied by his past provocations. Althans was also less harsh than he had been. Imprisoned first in the Landsberg prison where Hitler was kept, and then in Berlin where he was placed in solitary confinement, Althans learnt French, reading Jean Genet and Michel Foucault. However, he was still bitter about the way he had been treated, suggesting that he had been entrapped by the film-maker whose work had been used in his trial. He resented the judge's summing-up, in which he had been described as being as dangerous as Goebbels. Although he did seem to have abandoned the cause, the hostility towards 'normal' Germany hadn't left him. Hour after hour as we sat, he came back to this theme. All his Nazi career proved to him now was that in Germany you couldn't disagree. If you did, they would come and get you quickly. And a substantial set of rewards existed for those whose job it was to punish or confine. That was the real function of the system that Germans mistakenly referred to as democracy. 'For ten years I was never out of the media,' he said. 'And I was nothing – *nothing*, you realize. I was the Führer of nothing. It didn't matter what I did or said; nothing made any difference. But they created me, they allowed me to exist; and then, when it was convenient, they destroyed me. It's as simple as that.'

I told him about the Nazis I had met and their beliefs. 'Kids,' he said. 'Well, you know, we did have something. We had some sort of ideology. We did believe in something, though it may have been wrong.' I asked him whether there was anything at all he had kept from what must have been ten wasted years of his life. 'Oh, something about the discipline,' he said. 'Some sense that whatever I did I would never belong.' I left him standing in front of the *bierstubl*. It was raining, and the grey sky was turning black. On the way back to catch a bus, I noticed how in so affluent a Germany almost every item of clothing on sale was black, no matter how expensive, and how many of them were made of leather.

As punishment or bondage, the past was still here, and I could suddenly experience the weight against which all Germans, and not just the Nazis, interminably struggled. I couldn't see how we Europeans would be rid of it for a long time.

# LIES IN OUR TIME

'People only remember the history that is convenient to them.'
Adolf Hitler

It was a raw early winter morning the day I went to David Irving's apartment, and the historian was struggling with an overloaded travel schedule and low-level domestic crises. With his old-fashioned pinstriped suit, bushy eyebrows and brusque, erratic manner, he looked definitively out of place in contemporary London. Some sort of vestige of military or naval bearing, carefully cultivated, gave him the air of having stepped from the sort of British film in which the Empire still was within spitting distance and ratings saluted punctually. But I also noticed that this chosen role of Irving's, as contrived as Steed's in the old television series *The Avengers*, and as dated by now, hadn't included the prerogative of contentment. Spurts of energy lit up a flushed, sombre countenance, and I thought of Milton's angels hopelessly stranded by their burning lake. Irving's left eye twitched continuously, adding a quotient of pain to his blasted demeanour.

Friends responded with words of caution when I told them I was going to see Irving. I should be careful of him, they said. He changed his mind, altering his own texts. He was always suing people. The habit of taking what he wanted out of documents, or historical situations, was extended to people. I should certainly never expect to be told anything approximating to the truth. Irving, for his part, denied these allegations, representing himself as a serious historian wronged by those who found his views to be unpalatable. He claimed that he alone understood the truth about Nazism. 'I never have dared see him,' one of them, a historian, said. 'I know too much about how Nazism can turn your head inside out.' I had told Irving that I wished to talk about a subject that was beginning to preoccupy me – the views of the small sect who believed, or at least affected to, that the Holocaust never happened, and the bans imposed on them. Because he was lonely, or envisaged with pleasure the arrival of another easily entrapped liberal journalist, the prospect of talking about this subject appealed to him. 'Everybody thinks I'm a denier, but I'm not,' he boomed over the phone. 'I'm also not a Holocaust historian. I've never written a book about it. I don't think I could do now.'

As it turned out, however, Irving didn't linger at the gas chambers. Instead, he talked about his own 'war' – against governments, rival scholars, anti-race campaigners, churlish booksellers and immigration officials, against anyone, indeed, who seemed disposed to question the unique position he occupied, that of lonely volcano of the Right and defender of the lost honour of the Third Reich. The story of Irving – I noticed that he was inclined to use the third person about himself – raised in the most acute form the question of exactly what, and in what circumstances, should be permitted in the guise of freedom of speech. 'I am persecuted,' Irving said. 'Really I am. Well, I can walk around London, that's true. But I am a martyr to my views. I have been made to suffer for what I believe. I tell those who don't believe me: "Look into it, look at David Irving's War."' Irving made no secret of his views, far from it; and he had never done so. Over the years, however, his line of defence had altered. He now claimed the right to be heard, I noticed, not primarily because his views were necessarily true or worthwhile. They were his, and to him that was enough. He was not going to let go of them, and he certainly wasn't going to be muted or suppressed. He didn't address the dilemma of whether there were some views that should be suppressed because they were hateful or dangerous. Only one question was posed by his existence: should David Irving be allowed?

Irving's Danish companion Bente, who was much younger than him, blonde and attractive, came in with their four-year-old daughter Jessica. I'd heard that she didn't agree with Irving's views, but on this occasion she smiled tolerantly. We sat and waited while he arranged a trip to Florida, where he owned a small house. Irving handed me a stack of copies of his own *Action Report*, printed on yellow paper. The edition recounted the withdrawal of Irving's biography of Goebbels by the New York publishing house St Martin's Press in 1996; and it told a stirring, exemplary tale of triumph against the odds. Criticized, argued over, Irving suddenly found himself at the centre of a storm of controversy in Manhattan. Many came to the defence of his book, but no one wished to publish it. Irving concluded, probably correctly, that no large international publisher would henceforth touch his work, and that he must fend for himself. He had pneumonia at the time, but he distributed copies of the book, which he had had printed himself, by driving a small van around Britain. The newsletter explained how he even stayed to argue with bookshop staff who told him they would never stock a book he had written or published.

I saw the four of us seated in what to any outsider would appear the circumstances of sated bourgeois comfort. Then I reminded myself how intensely Irving was hated – few people in Britain elicited such unqualified, embittered feelings of resentment or unalloyed loathing. Irving didn't enjoy the sort of security that might have come with a successful career. Like the dark protagonists whose exploits were chronicled in his books, his life was devoted to combat, albeit in the muffled circumstances of late-century suburban England. *A Radical's Diary*, Irving's clarion call to supporters, was written in the inflammatory, injured tone I associated with Lord Beaverbrook's dying-Empire-and-bourgeoisie newspapers of the 1950s. It was filled with rants about 'The Mob' of 'jostling, threatening lunatic left-wing screechers and thugs . . . blacks, Jews, homosexuals and underworld characters' who attacked him at signings. Bailiffs tried to serve summons for offences committed in Germany or France. The previous year his eldest daughter had a car accident in which her legs were crushed so badly that one of them had to be amputated. 'The fight continues!' Irving exclaimed.

However, I also noticed that his newsletter was filled with darker, less tractable preoccupations: alleged disputes over Anne Frank's estate; squabbles over anti-Semitic remarks in local American schoolboards; students arrested in New England dormitories for daubing swastikas on their dormitory walls; professors who didn't accept that Jews had been gassed in the camps, and whom the authorities wished to retire early rather than sack. Irving's news items came from Germany, France, Japan and, above all, the United States. One news item gleefully described the contents of a faked letter ostensibly signed by the Chief Rabbi of Britain and appealing for contributors to Steven Spielberg's Shoah Visual History Foundation, based in Los Angeles. 'How many other apparent "victims" are actually out there and alive and well, if we could only find them,' the faker had written.

A clock ticked in the big, anonymous Mayfair apartment. There were framed copies of 1930s Nazi newspapers on the walls and large filing cabinets. Rather than a historian's lair, the study resembled a small research centre or an expensive dental practice. The big desk was empty, aside from a laptop and a photograph of a stack of dollar bills next to a copy of the previous Wednesday week's *Daily Telegraph*. Noticing my interest in the photograph, Irving interrupted his phone call. 'Supporters,' he exclaimed. 'They send me money. There are decent people around.' I wondered at his use of this so English word, with its echoes of Orwell. It seemed that decency was in short supply in Irving's world. Certainly, in his view, it was not displayed by the group of people whom he referred to in his newsletter as 'the traditional enemies' of freedom of speech, meaning, as it turned out, Jews or liberals. 'Nothing could be clearer than the division between Jewish and non-Jewish reviewers of my work,' Irving remarked. 'They wait until buckets of glop have been poured over my reputation, then salve their own liberal consciences,' was how he described the behaviour of the liberal reporters who had first written articles critical of the publishers of his book, and later, when they had got round to reading it, acknowledged its qualities.

Irving explained to me that he had become interested in Nazism because he wished to find out how the British Empire was destroyed. 'Think of my generation. Everyone was saying all these people were stupid or evil,' he said. 'Then I began to meet all the people who had known Hitler. And they weren't at all stupid. They also told me he was brilliant. So I got to know them, and they gave me their letters or documents. And they also began to explain that world to me.' He wrote his first book, one of the first accounts of the bombing of Dresden to render the full scale of Allied atrocity, when he was twenty-five. Although he had never taught at university, and learnt German on a building site, he was acknowledged to be an authority on the subject of Nazism and praised as a popular historian. *Hitler's War*, his two-volume history of World War Two, told from the vantage point of the Führer, was widely praised for its understanding of military skills as well as its empathy with monomania. But from the beginning, Irving was regarded with misgivings by many of his peers. He was not (this was a persistent gripe, though it would surely not have seemed important had it not been for Irving's notoriety) a *trained* historian, and his appetite for publicity went with the cultivation of increasingly extreme views. Determinedly, in part because the activity of provocation appealed to him, Irving skirted the boundary between more or less respectable 'revisionism' (the practice of overturning received historical ideas) and outright apology. From the beginning of his career he appeared to be determined to attempt to open the question of whether Hitler was guilty or not – if only by posing the question of whether the Allies weren't as guilty as he was.

At the time of the publication of *Hitler's War*, Irving offered $1,000 (a somewhat larger sum in the 1970s) to anyone who could show him a document that directly associated Hitler with the Holocaust. No one responded to this challenge, repeated on TV shows, and Irving was emboldened. While not denying that many Jews had been murdered, he began to refer to the Holocaust as a 'myth'. Meanwhile his speaking tours in Britain were disrupted by students – and he began to address audiences drawn from the Extreme Right in Germany, Austria and the United States. With near fatal consequences for his career, Irving began to think of himself, like the man whom he apparently admired, as a sage or even a leader as well as a skilled researcher and polemicist. He founded *Focal Point*, his own publishing company, dabbling with extreme right-wing politics in Britain. In 1989 he encouraged and published the Leuchter report, a supposedly scientific study of the Auschwitz gas chambers conducted by Fred Leuchter, a maverick figure who constructed or examined killing apparatus in American prisons. Leuchter's company, it later transpired, worked according to a scale of fees – $30,000 for a lethal injection system, $80,000 for a gallows and $200,000 for a gas chamber. For states without the proper facilities Leuchter had devised an 'execution trailer' complete with a lethal-injection machine, a steel holding cell, and a viewing room for officials.[1]

And yet it was Irving who went to Auschwitz with Leuchter, in search of soil and brick samples, accompanied by the notorious Holocaust denier Robert Faurisson; and Irving who advocated that he be used as a witness in the Canadian trial of Ernest Zündel, another Holocaust denier. Irving lent what remained of his good name and his polemical skills to their cause. Praising Leuchter's 'integrity' and 'scrupulous methods', Irving accused the state of Israel of swindling West Germany by demanding over ninety billion marks in reparations. Fined in Germany, he now called on the court to 'fight a battle for the German people and put an end to the blood lie of the Holocaust'. All over Europe he explained to audiences of cranks and fanatics that the gas chambers at Auschwitz were fakes. 'I am a non-believer,' he told a Danish television interviewer in 1991. He now appeared to believe that what he called the entire deception of Auschwitz – Irving's language became steadily more extreme – could be laid at the door of the British Psychological Warfare Executive. It was they who had first spread the rumour in 1942, according to which the Germans were using gas chambers to kill millions of Jews and social undesirables. After the war the Allies completed the job – I believed this was what he meant – turning what had been an ordinary work camp into an early variety of the theme park, dedicated to atrocity. Irving's campaign drove him deeper into messianism and away from history.

In Britain, Irving was suddenly less popular. Questions were asked in Parliament about prosecuting him, and there was an outcry when the *Sunday Times* proposed to use him as a translator of Goebbels' diaries. (This was ironic, as Irving pointed out, in view of the fact that it was he who had exposed the fake Hitler diaries, published by the same paper some years previously.) Irving, the American historian Deborah Lipstadt wrote, 'is one of the most dangerous spokespersons for Holocaust denial'.[2] She meant that his credentials as a historian were real, and that these gave weight to what she perceived as his distortions. But Irving was also adept at defending himself, and he was prepared to sue those who attacked him. Year by year the list of his enemies grew as his 'war' turned into a caricature of Hitler's. Suddenly, Irving became the object of hostility on the part of a coalition of near global character. He was banned from entering Germany, and deported from Canada. Other countries like Australia, South Africa, Austria, Italy closed their frontiers or their archives to him. It seemed as if Irving's many enemies were determined to show that it was possible to silence him.

'You'll end by hating me,' Irving said lugubriously, stretching his arms and yawning in an affectation of ennui. 'Everyone does.' The line wasn't convincing; and I felt it had been used many times before. Like many of those whose company I had begun to keep, Irving used outrage like a carefully administered drug, adding to the dosage until some sort of state of liberal intolerance was finally reached. Perhaps he really did want to know how much of himself would be accepted. But I realized that it was also more complicated. There were many things that Irving couldn't control – too many, it was clear, for his own satisfaction. He tried so hard to be buttoned up, and he failed, spilling out more than he anticipated. Many things, most of all the prospect of boredom or neglect (for him, they were almost the same thing) appeared to cause such lapses. Seated across the table from him, I wondered about his relationship to the brutal, unsightly caricature of himself that he had become. But most of all I wondered about his anti-Semitism.

This was the winter of 1997 and we were sitting in a distant, unheated corner of the kind of London Italian restaurant that might have been fashionable in the 1970s, long before the arrival of arrugula. Irving complained about the amount of time it took to eat a steak. Surely, he suggested, there was a more efficient way of absorbing energy. Food should come cubed for easy consumption, and be of uniform taste. He began to talk about discipline – without the spirit of regularity he would have achieved nothing in life. 'I don't sleep much,' he said. I asked him whether he was an anti-Semite, and he turned melodramatically from the cubes remaining on his plate. 'I'm not an anti-Semite,' he said. 'I have resisted it. I have had good reasons to become an anti-Semite, but I feel no hostility towards Jews.'

I suggested that he had made what many would regard as a number of anti-Semitic remarks. 'About the Holocaust?' he asked. 'It's peripheral, a minor matter. Jewish history is boring. The Jews go on about it because it's the only thing that happened to them in 3,000 years.' Then he said, 'You have to be crude. No one listens if you aren't.' Later, he contrasted what he saw as the offence given by Jews with his own transgressions against correctness. 'What I've done is nothing compared to what they do every day,' he said. 'And they will be paid back in kind. What happened after Weimar – the last time they were allowed to acquire so much power – is nothing compared to the reckoning that awaits them.'

Irving didn't like the word 'denier' – it appeared to him to imply that those who said the Holocaust hadn't occurred were motivated by other than purely factual considerations, possessing the motivation of fanatics. He thought either that there hadn't been any gas chambers, or that fewer people had been killed by gassing than was imagined. 'Oh, you can find real deniers,' he said. 'Some of them I wouldn't put behind my left shoulder. These people are the purest anti-Semites. I believe the Holocaust is a myth. Wars are full of acts of what I call "innocentcide" – entire populations or armies are killed by bombs, and Hitler's war was no different from the war on the Allied side. I believe that 95 per cent of the people who died in the camps, perished of hunger – there probably weren't many functioning gas chambers. Look at the real history of the camps, and you'd have to say about your granny: "She died on her legs, she wasn't murdered." And people don't want to know that their relatives died covered with lice.'

This wasn't exactly what Irving had been saying a few years ago. At that time he had stated categorically that the gas chambers were fakes. I asked Irving whether his struggle against what he described as official lies had been worthwhile. No large-scale revival of Nazism had so far taken place. His views were still considered to be marginal and cranky, and he had surely wasted many years of his life in his campaign. 'No,' he said. 'There comes a point where you have to say no. Too many lies. I couldn't bear to hear their version the whole time. And anyhow, revisionism has had some effect. Holocaust museums are springing up everywhere, like McDonald's. We now know that the gas chamber at Auschwitz is a fake. People have ceased to claim that human beings were made into soap. In 1948 it was said that four million people were killed at Auschwitz, and now the figure is acknowledged to be closer to one million. So these are all real developments. I have achieved something, you know.'

The question of whether Irving did or didn't believe in what he was saying had appeared important to me, but the more I listened the less I was able to make this distinction. Hold such views, I told myself, and you must be identified with them, you could never escape them. It didn't matter whether you really believed in them or not. But now it was as if the room had become dark and I was transported out of the plastic flowers and Formica of the restaurant to a dim plain peopled with shrouded, indistinguishable shapes. Whatever sympathy I might periodically feel for Irving's literary travails, I felt a steel wall suddenly erected between us. And I didn't know how to react to these assertions. If I appeared to be provoked I would seem petulant – and I knew that I would be playing Irving's game. If I didn't I would merely seem feeble.

It also was hard to talk to Irving because he shifted position ceaselessly while retaining his dogmatism, like a flag fixed on a heaving deck. He was able to present himself as a victim while retaining the demeanour of a hanging judge. The trenchant, violent aspects of his conversation – they came spaced out between routine mouthfuls of unappreciated, stuffed-down food, as they had been in his office between telephone calls – were thus awesome as well as ridiculous. 'I do regret what I said. Oh yes, endlessly,' he said. 'And I regret where I said it. It's the determination not to be suffocated, you see. I've made colossal errors. I've chosen the worst friends. I've been hostage to my own stupidity. I'd appear with anyone – the grand wizard of this or that, any old skinhead capable of tying up his Doc Martens. But I wanted to speak out, you see.'

As we talked, I began to think of Irving's conversational style in the light of his models from nature. To the real Nazis, pretty much anything was allowed in the way of brazenness or cynicism. They, too, regarded in a positive light the claims of comprehensive untruth, attaching to lack of belief or scruples a kind of perverse glamour. One might say that for them lying – and admitting they had done so – was the equivalent of the Masonic oaths which they abhorred. (I had found some perverse regard for this attitude in Irving's own books – it came across, particularly in his study of Goebbels, as a kind of heartless jauntiness by means of which indifference could be first disguised and then repackaged. 'Yes, they're awful – but don't worry about it,' he was saying. 'Don't worry too much, because everyone is awful.') But Irving now sounded different to me, both more modern and ultimately less convincing. I didn't quite believe in his bravado or his pathos. Listening to him, I thought of Hollywood Nazis and the more recent phenomenon of the male renewal movement, which propelled grown men into the woods in search of lost supremacy.

Irving began to talk about what he feared most about the direction his life had taken. Had I heard of H. W. Wickes? He had sued a Canadian insurance company after he was injured at work, only to be countersued, thus losing his livelihood, his remaining funds and ultimately, it would seem, his sanity. For thirty years Wickes stood outside the offices of the insurance company wearing a placard. He wrote to Hitler, Himmler, Stalin – and he also wrote to Irving when the latter had just published his first book. Irving had discovered Wickes's letter to Hitler in the archives. 'I saw him once,' Irving explained. 'But I did nothing for him – although he sent me a Christmas card every year until he died.' He paused, arranging the cutlery on his plate, frowning. 'I suppose his story shows that you mustn't let yourself become obsessed,' he said. As we stood together in the wintry street, he returned to the subject of Wickes. 'I do fear obsessions,' he said, nodding stiffly towards me.

As Irving had promised, a packet of papers arrived shortly after our meeting. He had obtained these under the Freedom of Information Act shortly after he was banned from Canada. It appeared that Irving had tried to enter Canada via Niagara Falls, but he was stopped by a diligent customs officer, and taken to the local police station. The following dialogue of the deaf ensued:

Q. But why did you travel so far out of the way before entering?
A. I had a four-day speaking engagement in Pittsburg [sic]. From there I went straight up.
Q. What was the purpose of your trip to Canada?
A. I was to give a series of talks on free speech.

In 1992, Irving was convicted of slander in Germany. His offence, allegedly, was to have told a meeting of the Jugend-bildungswerk, a neo-Nazi group: 'By now we know – and I'm sure I don't need to point this out – that there never were any gas chambers in Auschwitz.' Translated, the court judgement was reproduced in full:

> Anyone who denies the murder of Jews during the 'Third
> Reich' – and the accused has deliberately done so, as he
> himself confirmed in the course of the main hearing – slanders
> each and every Jew (cf. BGHZ 75.160 for further documen-
> tation). The persecution of the Jews solely on grounds of their
> ethnic origin, as it was practised under the National Socialist
> reign, is a historical and legal fact. It culminated in the killing
> of millions of Jewish men, women and children in extermina-
> tion camps, one of which was Auschwitz-Birkenau, in which
> at least 1 million Jews were murdered by means of gas
> (Zyklon B) . . . Denial of these facts also constitutes slandering
> the murdered Jews.

Setting the fine of 10,000 marks the judge took into account,
by way of mitigation, the fact that Irving admitted his
offence, making no secret of his views. However, Irving was
using 'revisionist' ideas to sell his work, and this – it was a
characteristically German reaction, reflecting the high view in
which historians were still held in the Federal Republic – had
shocked the judge. At the meeting where he had uttered these
offensive words, the judge noted disapprovingly, Irving had
been surrounded 'by stacks of some 200 books', selling
revisionism as one might dog food or deodorants.

Nonetheless the most interesting item in Irving's package
was a fifty-odd page document supplied to the Canadian
authorities by the Board of Deputies of British Jews and, one
must imagine, used as background material when the case
against Irving was being considered. This was a detailed
account of Irving's background, private life and career, and
it had been annotated, often in a spirit of approval, by Irving
himself. I learnt that his mother's name was Beryl Irene, that
his father, having served in the Battle of Jutland, had written
books about the British navy; and that the young Irving,
acknowledged to be a brilliant linguist and mathematician,

had also displayed an interest in Germany unusual for an Englishman. An early scandal – it involved printing racist cartoons and soliciting money from organizations such as Sir Oswald Mosley's fascist paper *Action* – led to his dismissal from the post of editor of the London University student magazine. It was shortly after this that Irving, in an interview with the *Daily Mail*, described himself as a 'mild fascist', a description which he later claimed to regret. 'I had a fine time,' is how he described his visit to Berchtesgaden, Hitler's mountain retreat. 'It is a shrine for me.' Page after page followed in which Irving was observed eating horrible food and speaking at right-wing dining clubs, or sighted on obscure, ill-lit platforms garlanded with fading Union Jacks. But I noticed that there were interesting gaps in the account, too. Although the anonymous author (like many other investigators) believed that Irving had received funds from right-wing organizations, no evidence of the gifts was available. The question of whether Iving was rich (as his enemies maintained) or poor (as he so frequently declared) was thus left open.

Was Irving an anti-Semite? If he was, how did he acquire these views? In this respect the author was at what seemed to be extraordinary pains to appear even-handed. Irving, to be sure, hinted at Jewish conspiracies; but he was 'too clever an opponent' to admit to being anti-Semitic. The most that one might deduce from the friends he kept was that he was prey to 'anti-Jewish sentiment'. The author of the document from the Board of Deputies of British Jews conceded that Irving had often done valuable work, unearthing fresh material through his own unrivalled contacts with the survivors among the Nazi brass, their wives, secretaries and heirs. When it came to analysing Irving's attitude to Adolf Hitler, a spirit of judiciousness similarly was on display:

6.1 By limiting Hitler's culpability for the horrors of the Holocaust, he could remove Hitler's image as evil incarnate. By further alleging that Hitler was actively opposed to the Holocaust, Irving made him appear as a positive figure . . .

6.2 Hitler's ignorance of the Holocaust leads very neatly into Irving's attempts to portray him as a mere human . . . The theory is a simple one – if Hitler is just another human, then how can he be the devil? In conjunction with this, he attempts to portray Hitler as a wartime leader whose activities were no different from those of other leaders.

Irving, the document concluded, might perhaps be called a Hitler apologist – though the author lacked the space, or perhaps indeed the stomach, to explain exactly what that meant. But he was neither an anti-Semite nor a Nazi, and it seemed that these were important distinctions. I noticed that Irving had registered approval at this point in the manuscript with a minute affirmative tick accompanied by a neat and decisive yes.

At one time, I had read everything I could lay my hands on about the Holocaust – memoirs, histories, polemics. I had been to Auschwitz on many occasions, but the idea that bits of it might be faked was news to me. Who would have added to the sum of so much atrocity? Why would they have bothered to do it? I recalled a painting by the American artist R. B. Kitaj. It showed a prosperous, cultivated train passenger, a Jewish businessman or publisher, passing a landscape in which a concentration camp appeared to have been built. Kitaj was perhaps implying that we all, whether we liked it or not, were atrocity tourists. But now we had to deal with something much worse. We had to envisage the possibility of the existence of a group of people who either thought the Holocaust hadn't happened or (which was just as bad) were of the opinion that it didn't matter much, one way or the other.

For weeks after seeing Irving, I began to have many bad dreams. Holocaust denial took me to a place which was familiar in its awfulness and yet suddenly shrouded. I didn't believe that any of the hypotheses posed by deniers were remotely plausible, but their existence forced me to ask certain questions. I wondered what the world would look like if they were right. I also wondered how it was possible to believe such things. Would those views be around in another hundred years? The existence of Holocaust denial made me wonder why, after the labours of so many historians, it was still difficult to say for certain what had happened at Auschwitz. Perhaps the historians were partly to blame, but we too – jaded, habituated to the daily passing off of lies as truth – were no doubt complicit. In this sense, it seemed to me, something of the guilt implied by the existence of Auschwitz would always remain, lodged near the heart of what we no longer had the nerve to call civilization. It was this idea – that perhaps we would never be able to settle the matter of Auschwitz – that gave me pause.

I began to search for denial on the Internet. The sites were easily reached through servers bearing the images of Hitler and Rudolf Hess, or pieces of sartorial advice regarding Celtic crosses and the like. You could purchase racist CDs from PO Box numbers which, I imagined, were located in Nebraska, and you could order White Power T-shirts, too. It seemed sad that so astonishing an instrument of rationality should be used for trash. They were part of the immeasurable, oceanic wreckage implied by the cherished contemporary notion of an Age of Information. Many books chastising or rebutting deniers had been written, but with some exceptions they didn't seem adequate to their subject. They couldn't explain why it was that anyone would hold these views. I was baffled by this problem until I found Muriel

Spark's 1970s novel *The Abbess of Crewe*, a replaying of the Watergate scandal in the exotic circumstances of a nunnery, in which the hard work of bugging is done by novices whose efforts are organized by a cadre of nuns. When representatives of the mass media arrived at the gates with embarrassing questions, the Abbess, a woman of style as well as wisdom, was dismissive. 'They'll make some sort of garble,' she says. 'Garble is what we need, Sisters. We are leaving the sphere of history and are about to enter that of mythology. Mythology is nothing more than history garbled; likewise history is mythology garbled and is nothing more in all the history of man.'[3]

Nowadays it seemed that 'garble' lay all about us. Did it matter that so many people appeared to think, despite the evidence, that Princess Diana was murdered? Or that NASA had staged the moon landing in some back lot at Houston? Or that the lead singer of Nirvana, Kurt Cobain, rather than taking an overdose of heroin and shooting himself, had been murdered by his wife Courtney Love? Under the jumbled signs of postmodernism it was fashionable to suggest that lies didn't matter much, or that they were at least 'interesting', and should thus, like good gossip, be retold. Garbling was the stuff of daily journalism, and the means by which entertainment bled away the last vestiges of truth or austerity from our lives. However, it was still agreed that no act in history had resembled the Holocaust in its awfulness, and it followed that lies, or even half-truths told in relation to the event, would seem uniquely painful. From this perspective alone Holocaust denial must be important.

But I learnt, too, that the sense of disconnection from horror wasn't new, and it had been experienced by many survivors. Lying on his wooden bunk in Auschwitz, the young Primo Levi dreamed the same dream each night.[4] Far away in Italy his sister and a friend of hers were sitting at a table, and he was trying to recapture for them the sensations of internment. He told them about the bunk neighbour, who was so heavy that he couldn't be moved; about ceaseless hunger, beatings at the hands of guards, lice control. He could even begin to explain the disappearance of sick or old prisoners, taken away on arrival or removed later when they could no longer work. At first the sensation of being able to explain what was happening was intensely pleasurable. But something went badly wrong. Dreaming, Levi could see those whom he loved, as if they were next to him; but he also understood that they didn't hear him. Panicking, he experienced intense, crushing grief 'like certain barely remembered pains of one's early infancy' just before waking. And yet the dream had an after effect, too. Retelling it to a friend Levi was astonished to discover that he, too, and almost everyone else in the camp had experienced the dream, in more or less identical circumstances, over and over again.

Levi's earliest work, *If This is a Man*, offered little in the way of false consolation. However, it did seem to insist – in its very existence, implying the survival of its author against all odds, for which the calm, level prose gave thanks – that some reckoning with the truth could take place. But Levi's last book *The Drowned and the Saved*, completed shortly before his suicide in 1987, was less optimistic about the prospects of truth:

Some mechanisms are known which falsify memory under particular conditions: traumas, not only cerebral ones; interference by other 'competitive' memories; abnormal conditions of consciousness; repressions; blockages. Nevertheless, even under normal conditions a slow degradation is at work, an obfuscation of outlines, a so to speak, physiological oblivion, which few memories resist. It is certain that practice (in this case, frequent re-evocation) keeps memories fresh and alive in the same manner in which a muscle that is often used remains efficient; but it is also true that a memory evoked too often, and expressed in the form of a story, tends to become fixed in a stereotype . . .[5]

Levi knew that the past could be killed by censorship or that it might in time be destroyed. He didn't mention, though he must have been aware of it, the possibility that its death might prematurely be induced by clever, unscrupulous anaesthetists. I wondered how Levi must have reacted to the news that what he had experienced – irreparably, with so much pain returning each year – hadn't happened at all. How would he have responded to the presence of site after Internet site proclaiming the Holocaust to be a lie?

Holocaust denial contained almost as many varieties of dogma as it did believers. Its importance lay well beyond its narrow field of dispute, primarily because, like child's putty, it was indestructible, returning history to its distorted shape no matter how many complicated corrections were performed in the name of truth. The idea of 'historical revision' came from a group of left-wing American historians, working in the inter-war isolationist period, who examined the record of German atrocities during World War One, concluding that many of them were fakes devised by clerks in Allied Chancelleries. History, it was thus suggested, had been used to get young men to kill each other. The implication was that no 'official' version should be believed without extensive re-examination.[6]

The first significant revisionist was Harry Elmer Barnes, who taught at Smith College, and he appealed to the widespread sense that history, far from rewarding Americans for their sacrifices, had cheated them by leaving them adrift in an imperfect world. Rather than conclude that this was how things often happened, he believed that the public had been duped. His case was strengthened by the fact that the British had cannily utilized 'black' (i.e. fake) propaganda in their struggle against Germany. The efforts of Barnes and his colleagues meant that the Allies were reluctant to make use of German atrocities during the next war, although these were known to have taken place. But these revisionists also provided ostensibly principled grounds for disbelieving the atrocities after the war. No matter how much evidence was made public, it could always be said that this was faked or exaggerated. A historical precedent existed for running down Germany, after all. To begin with, the revisionists merely asserted that some, if not all, of the evidence at Nuremberg, was likely to be untrue. But the movement became more extreme as the years went by, and by the 1970s, when Irving came on the scene, revisionism was inseparable from the more radical idea that the Holocaust had never happened.

Revisionism sounded respectable, even vaguely scientific, and it became the preferred, genteel style in which deniers liked to be addressed. Revisionists or deniers were located throughout the world, in Japan, America, Sweden, France and Switzerland. In Los Angeles, protected by the First Amendment, the Institute of Historical Review held conferences and published pamphlets. Revisionists represented a cross-section of the late twentieth-century professional bourgeoisie – though few were historians, others claimed some expertise in chemistry and many ran their own printing or publishing businesses. Cranky and stubborn, the deniers might perhaps have been left to well-deserved obscurity.

However, a number of them existed on the fringes of various right-wing groups. Revision, or denial, was attractive to right-wing politicians, concerned to exploit the possibilities implicit in the 'revision' of ideas about the Holocaust without overtly adhering to them. Did such people really believe that the Holocaust never happened? Well, yes and no, or maybe.

Denial was a certain way of provoking familiar liberal enemies, particularly if they were Jewish. It secured easy publicity; and it also caused anguish among journalists, who were uncertain how to deal with it. Now it became possible to suggest that Hitler wasn't so bad after all. And the Holocaust itself? Well, that could now be depicted as a modern myth, an invention of Jewish victim culture and officially sanctioned opportunism. Thus reduced in scale, its bodies long ago disposed of, the Holocaust became nothing more than a means of retrospectively establishing the legitimacy of war. It had become a myth and a tool – its real function, and never mind whether it had actually happened or not, was to extract reparations from the German state, or merely to perpetuate the idea that Israel, because of the circumstances of its creation, was owed unique consideration.

Grotesquely expressed, wounding to those whose relatives had disappeared in the camps, these ideas nonetheless appeared to gain ground by ceaseless repetition and exposure. There was nothing new about the arguments, and indeed there couldn't be, since they were based not on research but repeated assertions. It was easy to conclude that denial wasn't real, or indeed deeply held, or that it was just another growth on the plant of anti-Semitism. Those who now alleged, stoutly and without shame, that no Jews had died in the camps were in many instances those who might have wished them all dead in the first place. What made it all worse was the popularity of denial in the Arab world – and the contributions made by rich Gulf states to legal fighting funds where deniers were prosecuted. It was easy to regard the phenomenon of denial as a giant fake perpetrated on the scale of the notorious Protocols of the Elders of Zion, and with similar malign intent.

In the United States, the existence of the First Amendment protecting freedom of speech ensured that Holocaust denial entered the growing realm of popular culture, periodically becoming the stuff of daytime TV debates. 'Stay tuned,' the presenter Montel Williams told his audience as he prepared them for a group of camp survivors, assembled to counter the deniers seated on the other side of the studio. 'After the break we'll find out whether the Holocaust is myth or truth.'[7] For the historian Deborah Liptstadt the dilemma was whether to appear on these shows, thus contributing to what she rightly considered to be the systematized demeaning of atrocity, or whether to leave the field to the deniers. With some misgivings, she chose the latter – but she was also criticized, not entirely justly I felt, for this decision.

Elsewhere Holocaust denial also provided an intriguing test with respect to the effectiveness of liberal censorship. Deniers rejected the various laws designed to uphold the notion that millions of people had died in the camps. They were prepared to fight the 'thought police' (much of their polemical vocabulary, not convincingly, was taken from George Orwell) in court. Some of them had lost their jobs as well as a substantial amount of money in pursuit of what they claimed to be the truth. With some justice they were able to point to the institutionalized hypocrisy whereby they were singled out for harassment while their communist enemies, many of whom had been apologists for Stalinist atrocities, could publish pretty much what they liked.

In Germany, the Constitution outlawed Holocaust denial.

The earliest deniers were ex-SS men, or veterans' associations. During the 1950s and 1960s, German judges, supported by public opinion, dished out fines or jail sentences with exemplary swiftness. The German way of handling right-wing dissent appeared to be successful, and in due course it was adopted by other European countries, including Belgium, Austria and Switzerland. Any reluctance to evoke the law, and thus the power of the state, in relation to the matter of memory or historical accuracy, was rapidly extinguished. In France Holocaust denial was for a long time either ignored or considered within the context of laws making racially discriminatory speech illegal. But in 1990 the Assembly passed fresh legislation. What became known as the Fabius-Gayssot law was named after its two most prominent sponsors, an ex-Minister of François Mitterrand's, heir to a thriving antiques business, and a communist deputy who was later placed in charge of France's railways.

The new law made it an offence to 'contest the existence of one or many crimes against humanity as they are defined by the statute of the international military tribunal of London of 8 August 1945'. Although the wording was ambiguous, raising the possibility that other 'crimes against humanity' committed at different times and against other ethnic groups might also be covered, this ensured that it would be used in relation to the Holocaust. Offenders could be punished according to a sliding scale ranging from a month to a year's imprisonment, or from 2,000 to 30,000 francs.[8] Like their predecessors, the censors of the ancien régime, French judges were lenient and understanding in their interpretation of the law. Although more than fifty successful prosecutions had taken place by 1998, only one offender, the editor of Révision, a small-circulation magazine, had served a full year's sentence.

While I talked to Europe's new censors, I also reread John Stuart Mill. I was at once overcome by a feeling of wonder for the days when it could be assumed that intellectual debate, left to itself, would provide the right conclusions. Mill lived before such atrocities as the Somme or Auschwitz. He did believe that humans were essentially good and rational. Perhaps communities did require to protect themselves against those who wished to 'produce evil',[9] but it seemed to him that such cases would be rare indeed. Meanwhile Mill was able to welcome controversy. He enjoyed the prospect of stupidity being routed by wisdom. He could speak passionately of how humanity was robbed everywhere that debate was stifled – of the 'opportunity of exchanging error for truth'. And he could even suggest that truth, as a consequence of its collision with falsehood, emerged clearer and livelier.

Far from invariably encouraging the spread of wisdom, as nineteenth-century opponents of censorship like John Stuart Mill had hoped, freedom of speech had led in many instances to the propagation of monstrous hatreds. If we understood anything, we Europeans now knew that governments lied – they muzzled their opponents while claiming a monopoly of truth

Perhaps the weight of the past century meant that Europeans were no longer terribly interested in politics. They had suffered from many varieties of extremism in the past, and they would enjoy the privilege of freedoms so long as these didn't come burdened with any excessive obligations. They would certainly be reluctant to go to the stake for the likes of Holocaust deniers. Meanwhile, people were tried and sentenced. A significant apparatus of state censorship was in place. This was perhaps why many European liberals, making

111

the best of a bad job, tended to focus on the bad faith of deniers. Either they were unhinged, or they were frivolously turning the Holocaust into a fashionable taboo. The activity of denial was in itself anti-Semitic. No dialogue, the historian Pierre Vidal-Naquet suggested, was possible between an astrophysicist and a 'researcher' who believed that the moon was made of cheese[10] – though he was uneasy about the prosecution of deniers. Vidal-Naquet's mother died in Auschwitz. Although his speciality was ancient history, he had spent many years attacking the varieties of denial. But he was now unhappy with the way things had worked out. 'The law is bad,' he told me, when I went to see him in Paris. 'Could we have a better law like this? I don't know.'

In 1979, after a brief exchange of views, France's establishment paper *Le Monde* closed its columns to the deniers, with the worthy if somewhat premature observation that controversy about the Holocaust need not, and shouldn't, continue. When the American linguist and political activist Noam Chomsky came to the defence of the French denier Robert Faurisson he was attacked for his pains. It was suggested that he didn't know anything about the man whom he was defending, hadn't read his book, and that he should anyhow have kept silent on a matter that was, properly speaking, French. 'Why does he expend so much energy and so much tenderness on the publishers and defenders of neo-Nazis . . . and so much anger on those who fight them?'[11] asked Pierre Vidal-Naquet. No one seemed specially interested when Chomsky echoed Voltaire, to the effect that the most shocking ideas were those that demanded to be vigorously defended.[12]

After a long period in which he wouldn't speak to French journalists, in 1998 Noam Chomsky gave an interview to *Le Monde*. His views had hardened in the intervening years:

Q. Don't you believe that in the interest of liberty and democracy it might sometimes be necessary to limit the right to freedom of expression . . . ?

A. This is the position of Goebbels, of Zhdanov and of Khomeini, and I don't agree. Freedom of expression is essential to mankind. It's an inalienable right.[13]

For Chomsky, however, freedom of speech wasn't an absolute. It was possible, he intimated, to imagine a situation in which he and the interviewer tried to rob a bank together. If Chomsky were to say 'Shoot!' in that context, no protection should of course be afforded. But freedoms had increased over the years in America, and this was, Chomsky intimated, a good thing. I polled Parisians to find out what they thought. This was the year of Clinton and Monica, and such opinions were often dismissed. They were symptoms of American callowness or lack of savoir faire. I found non- or anti-Voltairean views all over Paris. 'We don't require to know what these people think,' Laurent Joffroy, the young Parisian editor of the left-wing *Nouvel Observateur* told me at a dinner well attended by the liberal and well-heeled. 'First, because we already know what they have to say. Second, because it's all lies.'

The problem was that censorship, once installed, had acquired its supporters. By the 1990s, the struggle against 'race hate' had become the dominant European correctness, and minority groups struggled to secure legal protection from those deemed to be their potential or actual aggressors. Jewish groups were drawn into the barrage of claims and counter-claims implied by this development. It was they, sometimes acting in conjunction with the state, sometimes alone, who brought cases against the deniers. Censorship thus meant that honour could be upheld. A less happy result was that those who were convicted were free to appropriate the status of those whom they were judged to have dishonoured, declaring themselves to be victims of 'Jewish lobbies'.

Britain had so far resisted such legislation, but there were those who felt that it was nonetheless needed. In December 1997, I attended a meeting at Chatham House in Grosvenor Square organized by the Institute of Jewish Policy Research. The atmosphere was measured, though it was clear that the subject touched the deepest sources of anguish among British Jews. Speakers were divided over whether Holocaust denial was inherently propagandist or not. According to David Cesarani, who supervised London's Wiener library, wrote biographies and taught the history of the Holocaust, the fact that denial had existed for so long was important. It was by now a fully blown conspiracy theory and, like one of the odd plants beloved of 1950s science-fiction writers, it grew independently of whatever attempts were made to snuff it out. Far Right parties, if they were to succeed throughout Europe, needed to avoid being restricted to their traditional constituencies – and to do so, they must 'sanitize' the Third Reich. The example of Germany and France showed that freedom of speech wasn't affected by such limited curbs – rather than serious historians, retired dentists or amateur chemists were the primary target of laws. 'Should we mind that David Irving's itinerary is rather limited?' Cesarani asked. 'At least he can go to more places than Slobodan Milošević.'

Counting the speakers and listening to the applause, I concluded that the audience was divided evenly. Holocaust survivors calling for legal action were more than politely clapped; but so, too, were those who had come to Britain in search of liberty (or whose parents had done), and felt it should be retained. 'What is the point of free speech if it's stopped when it's offensive?' an ex-refugee asked. The grand historian Max Beloff, now in his eighties, pointed out that twentieth-century history was a battlefield in which rival versions, many of them absurd, had been disputed. For forty-odd years, representatives of the Soviet Union had insisted, against the claims of evidence known to scholars, that the Gulag didn't exist. It would have been gratifying to have imprisoned a number of French intellectuals, including Jean-Paul Sartre, who shared such views. (Sartre didn't in fact share these views, as I knew – worse still, perhaps, he believed that right-thinking people should keep quiet about the Gulag, lest the proletarians become demotivated. '*Il ne faut pas déprimer Billancourt*,' he declared famously.) But would it have been such a good thing? The Labour politician Mike Gapes referred with enthusiasm to the steps taken by governments to prohibit Holocaust denial. It was possible to discipline and therefore inhibit racism by legal means. As in other things, Britain should accept the European way of doing things. However, I noticed that the lawyers who spoke were less certain. Experience had taught Geoffrey Bindman the virtues of caution. He advocated a more modest project, consisting of extending the scope of British libel laws, so that it was acknowledged that a group of people, defined by their ethnic origins, could be libelled as easily as an individual. 'I've practised law so long that I'm entitled to feel cynical about its possibilities,' Bindman observed.

I remembered these words a month later when I stood in a large marble hall outside Courtroom 16 of the *Palais de Justice* in Paris. One hundred years previously, almost to the day, Émile Zola, hat in hand, appeared in the same building to defend the publication of *J'accuse*, his famous letter to President Félix Faure.[14] In defending Alfred Dreyfus, Zola went against the public opinion of his day, providing a template for the modern, secular intellectual, whose role henceforth was to stand for freedom of expression as well as justice. However, Zola's stand was unpopular, and he was right to fear for his life. A correspondent from the anti-Dreyfusard *France-Soir* noted with satisfaction how ugly crowds had to be kept away from the dapper author. '*À bas Zola! À bas les Juifs!*' they cried each day. When Zola was sentenced to a year in prison for his defence of the truth, the courtroom got to its feet and applauded.

On this somewhat more muted occasion, journalists from Qatar TV and Tokyo jostled with skinny teenagers in yarmulkas, black-robed lawyers holding files and women wearing headscarves. Alongside white-haired worker priests and *ancien résistants* were young Parisian *fachos* dressed in black, with elegantly half-shaven heads. I shook hands with the dapper Maître Vergès, notorious for defending Klaus Barbie and, more recently, Carlos the Jackal; and I noticed that his hair was clumsily dyed. His current client, Roger Garaudy, was tall and stooped, with white hair, dressed impeccably in an English blazer. Happy to be the centre of attention, the octogenarian sociologist smiled at those around him, dispensing *embrassades* to those who had come to testify in his defence.

Garaudy's fifty-third book was on trial, a slim volume entitled *The Founding Myths of Israeli Politics*. It was available on the Internet, and had already been published in ten countries. The French edition had been printed at his own expense, in a samizdat edition. There was nothing specially original, or indeed coherent, about the book. Garaudy, too, insisted that the camps hadn't contained gas chambers and that, viewed as metaphor or not, the Holocaust thus never happened. What made the book important, in French eyes, was Garaudy's celebrity. He had been a member of the Resistance and, until he left the party in 1970 (rather late as his critics suggested), a leading communist intellectual. Garaudy converted to Christianity, but he surprised everyone by changing his beliefs again, espousing Islam and becoming a critic of the state of Israel. Unlike most French people, he took Islam seriously enough to write books interpreting the Koran. Although viewed as something of a joke in sophisticated Paris circles, Garaudy had proved an adept literary operator, securing the endorsement of the renowned grey-bearded Abbé Pierre, defender of the poor and homeless. By linking himself with an ex-atheist turned Muslim, the abbé appeared to revive a traditional strain of French-Catholic anti-Semitism, and this ensured that the 'affaire Garaudy' received much attention among French intellectuals. 'Holocaust: Victory for the Revisionists' is how the weekly Événement du Jeudi described the collaboration of priest and scholar.

But I had come to meet the prominent denier Robert Faurisson, who was attending the trial as an observer. Small, with grey hair and the kind of gold-rimmed glasses that in France are a reliable sign of pedagogical vocation, carrying a beret and a topcoat, the professor sat near to the front of the courtroom, scribbling in a notepad. When I approached him during a break, he was shaking hands with two young admirers. Faurisson's mother was from England, and he spoke a fluent if accented English stuffed with literary archaisms. 'Garaudy must be delighted by this lot,' he said. 'What a galère!' We sat through a lengthy interrogation of the printer of Garaudy's book, a stout man with a twitch and the rhetorical manner of a Cordelier street militant from the French Revolution. Pierre Guillaume, I had learnt, was a sectarian Trotskyist. He and his associates had begun to interest themselves in Holocaust denial during the 1970s, out of a generalized hostility towards imperial powers – the victors of World War Two – coupled with a sympathy to the Palestinian cause. It was he who had published Faurisson's first text. Now Guillaume complained about the straits in which he and his family had been placed by the law. He was only fulfilling a service to humanity by printing such texts. 'Absurd,' Faurisson whispered loudly.

The courtroom strategy of Vergès and his young assistant was by now evident; it consisted of making Zolaesque speeches designed to discredit the law. They even spoke of taking the case to the European court of Human Rights in Strasbourg. Faurisson found all this somewhat ridiculous. 'They know nothing,' he repeated, over and over again. 'If they took the trouble to find out more, they might seem less ridiculous.' I said that it seemed as if Maître Vergès, given his relative state of ignorance, wasn't doing a bad job. Perhaps the idea of the law, or the way it was drafted, was ridiculous. But Faurisson would have none of this. 'Mr Fraser,' he said, grabbing my sleeve, making a hissing noise like a small snake. 'When you know more you will understand that for a thing to exist, it doesn't matter whether it is absurd or not.'

During breaks a crowd of well-wishers gathered around the professor. It turned out that the circle of denial was a small one – the printer Pierre Guillaume was defended by Eric Delcroix, who had stood as a candidate for the National Front, and who represented the professor as well as being his son-in-law. Among cultists, the Fabius-Gayssot law was known as the *lex Faurissonia*. We sat through the interrogation of Roger Garaudy. 'An old fool,' Faurisson remarked as the sociologist asked to be allowed to sit down. By now I was attuned to the ritual absurdity of the proceedings. Garaudy had prudently resorted to euphemism in his book, and yet he did unequivocally assert that there was no proof that anyone had been killed in a gas chamber. This was enough to convict him. However, legal nicety or social protocol insisted that the judge, seeking the appearance of fairness, should also conduct his own investigation. Garaudy was therefore asked to re-rehearse his entire intellectual development. The judge wanted to know why certain passages were different in the original edition (the one privately circulated in France and later used for translation). Did this mean that the author – laudably, one must suppose, from the judge's unctuous tone – had wished to comply with French law? Or did it mean that Garaudy had prudently watered down his views for publication in the hope of receiving a smaller fine? The judge, a handsome sixtysomething with a roguish eye, sounded as if he was marshalling the conversation at a chic Paris dinner party composed of the polite and half-informed. Garaudy for his part insisted that he was a philo-Semite, and that he despised not only Hitler, but his successors, the neo-Nazis, and their allies in the National Front. His concern was solely with historical accuracy. Again, Faurisson hissed in my ear. 'Playing to the gallery,' he said. 'None of them is serious.'

Next day I went to the small, old-fashioned *Librairie du Savoir*, tucked away in a small Left Bank street and run by a Romanian husband and wife. Downstairs, half-hidden among the collection of ex-samizdat texts and monographs about the Romanian Royal family was *Verité historique ou verité politique?* (*Historical or Political Truth?*). This was an account, mostly in his own words, of Faurisson's discoveries and his martyrdom at the hands of the French state and the Zionist lobby. As I read it on the Eurostar I was first perplexed and then, despite what in my vanity I considered to be deep reserves of journalistic unshockability, horrified. Once again I was falling – and further and more quickly than when I met Irving.

Robert Faurisson grew up in the remote and sleepy French

countryside during the less than idyllic circumstances of World War Two. He gave a brightly coloured account of his childhood that might have come from a Louis Malle movie:

> My name is Robert Faurisson, I'm half-British. During the war I was a child, I was nicknamed *l'Angliche* and on my desk I didn't carve the word 'Liberty' like [the poet] Eluard asked us to do. Instead I inscribed the words 'Death to Laval' and I wrote as soon as I could, for I was courageous, 'Hitler is a shit . . .' When I listened to the BBC, which I did incessantly, I heard '4,000 tons of bombs on Hamburg,' and I said: 'That's great, but why not 8,000?' When women, old men, children were roasted in phosphorus, I found all of that quite all right. Oradour, with 625 dead, made me feel indignant; Dresden where there were probably 135,000 dead . . . that was fine.[15]

Faurisson also recounted that as a child he saw a collaborator being walked through the village streets at bayonet point. 'Why don't they get on with it and kill him?' he asked his elder brother. I wasn't sure whether to believe in this account of Faurisson's early pro-Allied zeal. It sounded too neat – though small boys might well have encouraged the summary execution of collaborators in 1945. Still, Faurisson apparently began to revise these simple notions of guilt and punishment after the trials and mass killings that followed the war. By the 1950s, he explained, he took the side of a colleague who was suspected of belonging to the terrorist French Algerian OAS.

> That's how real British people react. I know that this is sometimes difficult to understand. And I hate it when people spit on a corpse. I always ask myself why people spit on corpses.[16]

Faurisson made a living from the obscure and uncontroversial field of literary analysis. It was while he was teaching at a provincial girls' school at Vichy that he published an analysis of Rimbaud's famous poem *Voyelles*.

> A noir, E blanc, U vert, O bleu: voyelles
> Je dirai quelque jour vos naissances latentes[17]
> A is black, E white, U green, O blue: Oh you vowels,
> One day I'll describe exactly how you were born

Where other scholars had linked the meaning of Rimbaud's verses either to the subconscious or, if they believed literature arose from more literature, from the history of the symbolist movement, for Faurisson the letters A and U were inverted figures of female genitalia, while the letter E, tilted upright, spelt out a woman's breasts. In the 1950s views such as these were neither widespread nor popular. Out of a sense of *pudeur*, or fear for the consequences, Faurisson didn't sign the article. Ten years later, when it came to the Holocaust, he was to prove less circumspect.

I called Faurisson, and I began to ask him about his work. Perhaps, too, like his critics – the historian Pierre Vidal-Naquet had called Faurisson an 'Eichmann of paper'[18] – I hoped to discover that his views were inauthentic, in the sense that they were politically motivated. Some of his interest in me, as with Irving, arose from the prospect of securing another convert; but the BBC also appeared to evoke tender memories. Those who had known him for a long time, like Vidal-Naquet, insisted that he had always harboured 'revisionist' views, but Faurisson denied this. It seemed that his obsession with the camps came about slowly, as a consequence of the tourist visits he made in middle age to Auschwitz, Majdanek and Dachau. He took samples in these places, in the style of a Victorian entomologist, or grubbed about the museums. The Institute of Jewish Documentation in Paris also helped him with this apparently innocent research. However, as one would expect from any French intellectual, theory played a part in his conversion. Faurisson was influenced by the work of Paul Rassinier, first published in early 1950s. Rassinier was the kind of last-ditch believer of a type to be found in the Gulag, maintaining that it was all a mistake and that Stalin could never have wished to send him there. He was a French socialist and pacifist who joined the Resistance, was caught, tortured and sent to Ravens-brück. When he returned to France, however, far from acknowledging the hell he had experienced, Rassinier concluded that he and the other deportees had exaggerated or invented their sufferings. The Germans had merely wanted to create penal colonies, and they had left administration of the camps to those in their charge. The victims, therefore, bore responsibility for their own suffering. So, of course, did the Allies – this was an absurd assertion with which I was already familiar – whose bombing raids had made it impossible for the Germans to feed the inmates.

In 1974, at a time when his ideas were already well known, Faurisson was appointed to a professorship at Lyon University. He began to submit articles to the press. Many newspapers refused to publish Faurisson's 'findings',[19] but he persisted. In the end Le Monde gave him space – not, as the editors explained, because his views were in themselves considered worthy of comment, but because a renowned survivor of the Vichy regime, the ex-commissioner for Jewish Affairs Darquier de Pellepoix, had just pronounced on the subject. This meant that Faurisson's contribution could be considered as a 'right to reply', thus absolving the newspaper of charges of having initiated the debate. Accordingly, Faurisson listed his 'findings' succinctly. No proof existed of the gas chambers. There were no convincing eyewitness accounts, and the ruined sites at Auschwitz gave no signs of having been used for the purpose of killing people. The scale of gassings apparently required at Auschwitz rendered them improbable. If it was difficult for Americans to kill one prisoner, how many more problems would the daily killing of thousands have created? The surviving gas chambers shown to tourists were post-war fakes. But Faurisson was also careful to distinguish himself from anti-Semites or Vichy apologists. Unlike them he was a disinterested observer and, more important, a humanist. 'The non-existence of gas chambers is good news for poor humanity,' he concluded; and, more rashly, 'Hitler never suggested that anyone should be killed because of his race or religion.' But the activists who came to disrupt Faurisson's classes were not convinced. The slogan 'Faurisson is killing the dead' was painted on walls, and the Jewish Union of Students called for his suspension. Finally, the university authorities cancelled his course on Marcel Proust, explaining that it was impossible to guarantee the professor's safety. After a long and unpleasant wrangle, Faurisson was forced to leave the university.

Sometimes, reading Faurisson's texts on the Internet, I wondered whether it wasn't literary studies, rather than denial, that should be abolished. With little taste for, or indeed comprehension of, the messiness of things, the professor treated the camps as if they were a literary construct. Documents were scrutinized for the slightest inconsistency – and they were rejected instantly if they failed to measure up to his own entirely perverse standards. Anything coming from a Jew was thought to be unreliable. The accounts of ex-Nazis extracted at the Nuremberg Trials or later were treated like the staged confessions of the communist show trials of Stalin-ism – as items of propaganda. The insistence that 'proof' of gassing must be found, but that all the people capable of establishing it must not be taken seriously – members of the *Sonderkommando* who had cleaned up, SS supervisors, the odd survivor or escapee – was worse than perverse. Faurisson couldn't, or wouldn't, understand that the Nazis might have wished to kill the Jews quietly and without fuss. He didn't even wish to confront the possibility that documents might have been written in code in order to hide what was going on.

'Special action', for instance, was the term often used for gassing. The diary of the Auschwitz doctor Johann Paul Kremer was filled with barely coded references to the horror of these events. But Faurisson remarked blandly that no German would have had the need to conceal anything in Auschwitz, and that the entries must therefore refer to something else. Kremer wrote:

> Today I was present at a special action at the women's camp; the ultimate in horror. The military doctor was right to say that we find ourselves at the *anus mundi*. At night, around 8 p.m., I attended another special action carried out on people from Holland. Because of the special rations dished out on these occasions – one fifth of a litre of alcohol, five cigarettes, one hundred grammes of sausage and bread – the men fall over each other to attend such occasions . . .[20]

The phrase '*anus mundi*', according to Faurisson, didn't refer to any ultimate horror. Instead, it described the diarrhoea of those suffering from typhus. The people from Holland hadn't been gassed, they had died of typhus. Like the good textual critic he had once been, Faurisson endlessly examined the discrepancies – they were mostly insignificant – between the various post-war transcriptions of the diary in Polish, French and English. This allowed him to reject the entire diary. A similar approach led him to conclude, wrongly, that Anne Frank's diary was also a fake.

Meanwhile the professor took the word *Vergasung* to mean that the gas of Auschwitz had been used not to kill but to delouse. Auschwitz, Faurisson affected to believe, was a penal camp and not a place of extermination. He even suggested that the Germans had been right to ship children to Auschwitz – because it was a way of training them for life.[21] Whatever was inconvenient, he elected not to see; and whatever appeared to support his theory – there was not much that did – he pursued with wearying pedantry. Sometimes, in their apparently hapless cultivation of delusion, Faurisson's 'investigations' resembled those of Nabokov's literary critic in *Pale Fire*, who found the entire twentieth-century history of the imaginary kingdom of Zembla – coups, romances, gulag – in the most banal poem about New England domesticity. But unlike these essentially harmless delusions, Faurisson's errors were tragic in their implications. They were as bizarre as the flights of optimistic fantasy displayed by Pangloss confronted by the horror of the Lisbon earthquake. At their least obnoxious (and one was not disposed to be charitable after reading a few pages) they could be explained only by the absurd conviction that if things truly were black and incomprehensible, they could somehow, like Uri Geller's ridiculous spoons, be bent into a different, meaningless shape under the guise of rationality. That was all Faurisson had to say.

For there was no Allied 'conspiracy' to exaggerate the importance of Auschwitz, either before the war or afterwards. In wartime Britain efforts were made to minimize the significance of what was known to be going on lest the accounts seem like propaganda. There was a desire, perhaps laudable in its intentions, culpable in the event, not to repeat the errors of the previous war by giving an excessive airing to one group of victims of Nazism. Many people feared the arousal of wartime anti-Semitism on the Allied side. Some officials were themselves anti-Semites, like A. R. Dew, who noted: 'In my opinion a disproportionate amount of time of the Office is wasted on dealing with these wailing Jews.' When two witnesses finally escaped from Auschwitz, bringing details of the gassings,[22] they weren't immediately heeded, to the horror of those who wished the smallest gesture – a bombing of the camps, for instance – to be performed. It became almost impossible to explain what was actually going on. Arthur Koestler wrote an article in the *New York Times* in 1944 explaining that no one would listen to him when he gave lectures about the camps:

> Clearly, this is becoming a mania with me and my like. Clearly, we must suffer from some morbid obsession, whereas you others are healthy and normal. But the characteristic symptom of maniacs is that they lose contact with reality and live in a fantasy world. So, perhaps it is we, the screamers, who react in a sound and healthy way to the reality which surrounds us, whereas you are the neurotics who totter about in a screened fantasy world because you lack the faculty to face the facts.[23]

If you accepted the 'findings' of Faurisson and his ilk, the 'screamers' of our day – those who insisted that the truth should be told – were those who insisted that the Holocaust never happened. We who were certain that the worst had happened were tottering about 'in a screened fantasy'. Some day, Faurisson was saying, we would all wake up, and acknowledge that he, and not the rest of the world, was right.

It was a warm, late winter day when I went by train to Vichy, but the professor was wearing his topcoat and holding his beret. We climbed into a small Renault equipped with kiddie seats and drove around the town. I saw softish grey buildings, and I breathed an air of serious depletion. I could think of worst places to live, but they didn't at once occur to me. Faurisson explained that the locals were uneasy about the wartime role of Vichy, and that the spa had never recovered. He believed that a museum should be built, explaining what Vichy had stood for. 'There's another side,' he said. 'We should know about it.' With its faded awnings and carefully pollarded trees, the place was empty in the sickly heat. Forlorn, deserted, its shop windows filled with the sort of capacious brown lingerie that 1960s sexual radicals had wished to torch, Vichy felt as if a neutron bomb had fallen on provincial France in the 1950s, and no one had bothered to return.

Outside the peeling *Hôtel du Parc*, where Marshal Pétain lived during the years of his dreadful regime, Faurisson said he wanted to talk about Jews. Was I Jewish? I wasn't? There were Jews everywhere; Jews, unlike himself, had the money and the power. They controlled the French press and television, they now controlled everything. France was full of Jews – why look, the model Inès de la Fressange, who now represented Marianne, was Jewish. 'I'm poor, Mr Fraser,' he said. 'I have no power and no money.' Of course, Jews depicted themselves as victims, he explained; but it was he, Robert Faurisson – I noticed the same habit of referring to oneself in the third person as Irving had displayed – who would die poor. He said: 'My epitaph will be: "Faurisson told the truth about something important – and he died of it."' Grasping my arm, the professor told me the story of a Paris cabaret artist of the late 1940s, sacked for telling an anti-Semitic joke. He had pointed at the front row of the audience. 'Levin, Rothenstein, Cohen . . . you're all supposed to have died in the gas chambers,' the comic said. 'I don't believe these were gas chambers – they must have been incubators.' I noticed that every ten minutes, with the utmost regularity, Faurisson returned to the subject of Jews. Was he always an anti-Semite? 'Oh, I hadn't met any Jews when I started,' he said.

Stout old ladies with poodles chatted outside the Marshal's former *gîte*. We climbed the stairs to the third floor and went along a gloomy corridor. Faurisson explained to me that Vichy was chosen as the seat of government in 1940 because of its relative remoteness and the proximity of so many hotels, which were turned into embassies or government buildings. At one time sixty countries sent representatives to this diuretic capital of a fake state. Faurisson scraped at the brown paint on the door of a dentist's suite. In the 1960s, he explained, an identifying plaque had been present, but it was removed by order of the municipality. However, you could still see marks where the screws had gone in. We walked over to the grandiose war memorial erected in the 1920s and it was here, momentarily, that Faurisson stopped speaking about Jews. Instead he began to tell me about war. Many boys from Vichy were killed in the World War One because the farmland around was so rich, copiously supplying victims for the slaughter. He had concluded that all wars were stupid, no matter who fought them. Churchill was the same as Hitler. No distinctions should be made between degrees of bloodthirstiness. He had learnt these things as he got older, and also as a consequence of his research into the camps. I asked him whether that wasn't his real objection to the Holocaust – not that it never happened, but that it appeared to establish, definitively, that some things were worse than others. But he didn't appear to want to answer my question. Later, he asked me solicitously if I was feeling all right. 'You don't look at ease,' he said. Still later, he wanted to know if I had Jewish relatives. 'Yes, my wife and daughter,' I said. I began to say that this wasn't in itself important, but such distinctions were by now beyond me. 'We don't look at things like that in England,' I said.

The Faurissons inhabited a red-brick, fake-gabled bourgeois *pavillon* located in a nice suburban street of Vichy. Red and puce velvet chairs and sofas were carefully arranged around a wallpapered room with tasselled lamps. Mme Faurisson painted small provincial scenes of eerily empty streets, and these were displayed on the walls. She also collected porcelain images of the Virgin Mary, which were tastefully arranged in a small alcove. The professor began to talk about literature. He quoted to me by heart a passage from the anti-Semitic, paranoid genius Louis-Ferdinand Céline:

> The world is full of people who say that they are refined and who are not, I can say with assurance. As for myself, your humble servant, I do believe I am refined! The very thing! Authentically refined! Until recently I had trouble admitting it ... I was resistant to the idea ... And then one day I surrendered ... Let the worse happen ... But I am still a little bothered by my refinement ... What will everyone say?[24]

When Faurisson read out a literary text the whining instantly left his voice and he spoke beautifully. But his moods changed quickly. 'I don't know why my wife stays with me,' he said. 'If I were her I would have left long ago. Nonetheless, she stays with me.' While we talked, the telephone rang; the professor was being asked to speak at a revisionist conference in Istanbul. We sat down to eat lunch, which consisted of a *tarte aux légumes* and, after the cheese, a bottle of sweet Sauternes. Mme Faurisson was younger than her husband and nicely spoken. It was clear to me that Faurisson either censored his conversation for his wife's benefit or that, more probably, she had ceased to listen many years ago. I realized that I was feeling very ill, but I felt still worse when we went downstairs. For here were books about the Holocaust, hundreds of them, and stacks of scrawled-over papers. And here were photographs of Jews either dead, or about to be killed, or starving. Many of these photographs, or their likes, I had seen before; but their presence here, accompanied by the professor's soothing literary *commentaire*, after the *tarte* and sweet wine, spoke of some obscenity beyond my comprehension. I waited impatiently for the taxi to arrive, half-listening. At Vichy station I got to my hands and knees, vomiting into the antiquated and picturesque stand-up toilet.

But my nausea proved of short duration, and I began to feel better the moment the train pulled away from Vichy and its bland horrors. I was possessed by a feeling of lightness, even of elation. Previously threatening, Faurisson's views now began to seem wholly absurd. I unpacked a photograph which I had brought to show him. It was an aerial view of Auschwitz-Birkenau, taken from a great height, in which one could see the gate of the Crematorium II left open, and, approaching it, a file of people shortly to be killed.[25] You could make out the vent from the gas chamber, and the small garden built by SS men to lull those approaching their deaths. Not dissimilar to the views of mass graves taken in the Balkan Wars, the photograph was taken by an American reconnaissance plane after a raid on the adjacent Monowitz industrial complex. Those whose job it was to decipher evidence of damage didn't bother to process the part of the roll showing the camp at Birkenau, and the photograph lay undeveloped in an archive near Washington for thirty years. I held the photograph in my hands, thankfully.

I had hoped to interview Faurisson for television, but I wasn't entirely surprised to receive a letter at the last minute in which the professor begged off. No, it wasn't possible, the professor stated, in the pedantic, self-regarding literary style with which I was by now well-acquainted. It would be impossible for him to state what he really believed without an additional fine. In contemporary Europe, he was a Palestinian, living in occupied territory. His books were the stones of his own *intifada*. If he appeared on television, he would probably be beaten up. Less modest, Irving did agree to go to Auschwitz – but he ruined the effect by notifying the museum authorities to the effect that he wished to make use of their library. When they refused permission, as he might have predicted they would do, Irving posted his banning (and the BBC's) on the Internet. I was angered by this – but it was what I had expected, too. But I felt more sympathetic to Irving when I learnt that the London Imperial War Museum declined to allow him to be filmed there. For once the tedious business of filming for television appeared to have told me something about the contemporary state of freedoms.

It was a bright autumn day when I met Irving again, this time at Speaker's Corner in Hyde Park. He was dressed in brown brogues and an old mackintosh, and he looked like a retired officer cast adrift in the 1950s. By now our encounter possessed the predictability of a joust. But I began to wonder whether Irving hadn't known about his errors for some time. He had entered the revisionist fray for motives which he probably didn't understand himself, and he was now lumbered with his own history, a suitable punishment under the circumstances. Who would take him seriously if he now announced to the world that he had been wrong?

I had brought the board game acquired in Germany with me. I now asked Irving what he thought about the game. Would he ban such a thing? Would he play it? I told him that the same kids who had sold me the game had also, earlier in our meeting, been eager to deny the Holocaust. So what was I to believe – that he and they took the question seriously or not? For the first time in my presence he seemed to stumble. Perhaps the game was the creation of someone else, he suggested. It could even be a provocation. Perhaps those who profited from the Holocaust had made it. And who would they be, I asked. 'Oh, you know who they are,' he said. 'I'd be libelling them if I said.' But he was angry, and he really had nothing to say. 'Of course I wouldn't play it,' he said. 'I have better things to do with my life.' I sensed that he was still angry at the end of the interview, and he walked stiffly away without his so-British caricature handshake.

I realized that Irving had taught me something about free speech. I loathed Irving's views. And I now realized because of what had happened in places like Auschwitz, we would probably never make room for the equivalent of a First Amendment protecting free expression in Europe. Still, I continued to believe that it was in our interest to go as far in that direction as possible. Neither Irving, nor the game, nor the people who had sold it to me were without the power to do harm. However, we would learn from their hatreds – which, in any case, it was beyond our power to suppress. It hurt me to admit this, even as I was able to acknowledge what I had already learnt. I carried the board with me, in a large plastic bag, looking for a convenient receptacle in which to dispose of it. In the end I kept it, as a gross and timely reminder. Like Irving himself, like Faurisson, or the aerial photograph in my possession, it was something for our times.

It now struck me that Faurisson and the other deniers,

whether they liked it or not, had contributed to our knowledge. They had added to the scope of our interest in the Holocaust, making the construction of additional museums inevitable. One might mock the 'Shoah business', as Irving had done; but the character of the age imposed its own style of reclaiming truth from oblivion, just as it had bred its own, wholly distinctive, strain of stupidity or lies. Was it really so misguided to wish to tell more about the circumstances of so many deaths? And was it really the case that the Holocaust thereby belonged to the Jewish community and not to the rest of us too? I didn't think so. Bizarre as it might seem, the gross, unpardonable insult implied by denial had contributed to the revival of memory. In this respect, John Stuart Mill had been right – error, no matter how fully it was deployed, did produce a 'livelier impression of truth'. Nor had it proved possible, as the likes of Faurisson had wished, to recreate a world in which the Holocaust, having never existed, could therefore not influence the way we thought. It was just not possible to deprive us of what we knew had happened. Meanwhile, despite the airing deniers' views had received, their impact remained close to the margins. The Far Right had not yet benefited from any rehabilitation of Hitler or the Third Reich. One must worry, certainly, about the deniers; and one must fight them, in whatever way seemed most fitting – but their impact was as nothing in relation to the overwhelming effect of *Schindler's List*.

# HOW TO KILL AN ARAB

'In this way, everything began . . .'
Albert Camus, *L'Étranger*

Imagine a ritual execution at the end of summer, in deepest France. The killing takes place just after dusk in the hills outside Lyon on 29 September 1995, in Maison-Blanche, a picture-postcard hamlet where, alongside the two bars catering to weekenders or foreigners in search of *gîtes*, the charcutier, defying the enticements of fast food, displays a variety of stuffed heads, hocks and necks beneath a faded, reddish blind. A local farmer reports the presence of a young Arab, scruffily dressed and with a camper's belt around his waist, answering to the description of the fugitive holed up for four days in the vicinity of the nearby Col de Malval. And now the events can be described in slow motion, which is how French people still remember them. Sirens blaring in near-darkness, two vans carrying elite parachutist gendarmes draw up, accompanied by cars with television news crews. The Arab is standing just outside the plain concrete village bus shelter. He is small, and looks as if he is waiting for someone. As many as eight gendarmes deploy quickly in the small street, forming a semi-circle around the Arab. Commands can be heard, the clicking of firearms.

They tell him to give himself up but he doesn't, seeming to hesitate. He reaches into a pocket, raises a pistol and fires, missing.

On the blurred videotape, shown again and again on peak-time television, one can hear gunfire lasting several seconds. Then the Arab falls to the ground. After a pause in the action, two gendarmes walk over to him and one of them casually turns the body over with a boot. 'OK, that's good,' the gendarme says. But this tape is a censored version of the killing. The seconds of unshown footage tell a different story. They record unambiguously the order of a gendarme during a lull in the firing, when the Arab is on the ground, but still alive. '*Finis-le*,' the officer says: 'Finish him off' – and then the firing starts again.

Other than photographs of his dead body sprawled between the legs of gendarmes, only two images of Khaled Kelkal survive. These are the mug shots of which, in the weeks prior to his death, 170,000 copies were displayed across France, one in every police station. In the first, a photograph taken when he was first arrested for theft in 1990, aged nineteen, he is dressed in trainers, jeans and windbreaker. He looks quizzically at the camera, dignified at a bad moment. In the second, a routine identification a year later when he began his prison sentence, he is in profile. He looks somewhat older, and a lot less happy. One might conclude that he knows by now what life has in store for him.

During the summer of 1995 bombs were placed in a market, a public toilet, outside a Jewish school in Lyon and – most shocking of all, because it took place in the heart of Paris, killing seven and wounding ninety-two at the height of the tourist season – at the St Michel RER station on the Left Bank. It appeared that the police were caught by surprise. At the end of August, however, they found an unexploded bomb by the side of the TGV line from Lyon to Paris. The device was made from a propane gas canister, a style recommended in videos circulated by militant Algerian groups, and, more important, it had been held together with adhesive tape on which could be discerned fingerprints. The police announced they were now close to identifying a 'network' of terrorists organized from Algiers and stretching across France. They also said that they had a good idea who was the ringleader of this network. He was Khaled Kelkal, a 23-year-old petty criminal who had served a four-year prison sentence.

Something close to panic gripped France as the search for Kelkal began. In the course of the manhunt, which at one point kept 10,000 police and soldiers busy, Kelkals were spotted all over the country – in Northern France and Provence, in Paris and in Bordeaux. The lurid picture of a large, shadowy fundamentalist conspiracy of which Kelkal was the inspiration became the staple of police briefings and press reporting, and it was rehashed nightly on television. Long before he was tracked down, only forty kilometres from Vaulx-en-Velin, the suburb of Lyon where he had grown up and where his family still lived, Khaled had become something more than a planter of bombs. Instead, for most French people, he embodied the definitive image of the foreigner in their midst.

I kept track of the hunt for Kelkal as I tried to make sense of the European cultivation of what was known as 'difference'. White Europeans with EU passports talked ceaselessly about the distinctions between national cultures, even as these were disappearing. It was chic to be up on what the sociologist Ernest Gellner called 'secondary cultural pluralism' – things that maybe had mattered once upon a time, but now could be safely traded across a burdened table or in the banal circumstances of the endless multinational rencontres that were a feature of the already middle-aged new Europe. But the same Europeans were less forthcoming when it came to discussing how real foreigners were defined and, more important, what treatment they deserved. Statistics told a story of torchings of hostels for immigrants in Germany and incomplete police investigations. Elsewhere in Europe there were attacks – acts of violence committed by the non- or half-politicized natives. Polls revealed an indifference towards these events or a growing hostility to 'immigrants' or 'foreigners'. Always problematic, the question of who was a European could now be raised by simply stating who was not. Was Europe slipping away from enlightenment and reverting to its old ways? Many Europeans, looking at the 'ethnic cleansing' in Bosnia and Croatia and later, on a larger scale and proffering still more horrors, in Kosovo, believed that was the case. Many, I began to realize, didn't care one way or another.

'The entire effort of a civilization,' Zola wrote, 'must surely be to destroy the savage need to throw oneself at fellow human beings on the grounds that they seem a little different to oneself.' This was well stated in the robust tones of nineteenth-century humanism, but Zola's simple formulation appeared inadequate in the light of the contemporary scene. For there were nowadays so many ways of asserting difference or masking crucial foreignness with the assertion that almost everyone, one way or another, proved not to resemble each other. Racism in Europe was too large a subject for journalistic enquiry and too susceptible to easy generalization. Race difference was everywhere, and it came disguised as culture – no smallest piece of the European past was immune to the claims of imagined superiority or inferiority. In the old days major nations purporting to be great powers had spilt blood over the question. Now it was a question of whether Basques, Flemish or Scots could acquire parity with their past oppressors. But I noticed that the new 'nations' of Europe – those composed primarily or exclusively of recent immigrants – were left out of these ancient, over-rehearsed equations. Nobody was yet prepared to concede to them the right to ask admittance to the European funfair. And indeed such a right was vigorously contested by the growing importance of proponents of race politics.

The Kelkal story was interesting to me because it appeared to illuminate a small portion of the scene suddenly, and with startling brilliance. No great mystery surrounded the circumstances of Kelkal's last moments, and one must allow that heavily armed policemen, faced with a threat of violence, might be expected to respond in kind. Kelkal's death appeared to have provided French audiences with the sort of instant satisfaction they required. Perhaps, according to the new popular lawlessness of our time, being killed summarily by the roadside was all a young Arab deserved or got these days.

But I was to be proved wrong in the assumption that this particular death would be considered ordinary. Kelkal's brief career and his sudden end shocked French people – they responded with apprehension, much as British people viewed Irish bombings, Germans the activities of idealistic terrorists like Andreas Baader and Ulrike Meinhoff, or Italians the atrocities perpetrated by the Red Brigades. The apparent arbitrariness of Kelkal's actions, and their savagery, gave him a lineal connection to the solitary nail bomber who terrified Britain in the spring of 1999 by placing home-made devices in places frequented by blacks, Asians and homosexuals. To be sure, Kelkal was an Arab and his death could be read as another episode in the post-imperial French-Algerian struggle

– but it was significant that he was also *French*. Perhaps there were Kelkals throughout France – they lurked in one or another of the vile *banlieues* abandoned by God and Frenchmen. Any day, another Kelkal might emerge to shatter *idées reçues* of what Frenchmen or Arabs were permitted to do, and cause more bloodshed. The prospect of more violence bred fear as well as anger. Rapidly, Kelkal's life became a matter of consuming interest, as every detail of it was pored over or reinterpreted. Within hours of his death he had become an emblem for French people of all that was amiss in the troubled relationship between France and its Arab population, and a sign of whatever it was that had gone so wrong for 1990s France.

The day of his funeral was marked by a bomb placed in the Maison Blanche Paris *métro* station – the name of the village where he had been killed. Meanwhile, the censoring of the news footage came to light in a Swiss newspaper, though the news editor of M6, France's 'youth channel', insisted that he had acted not out of police prompting, but in the overriding interests of good taste. Newspapers like the left-wing *Libération* began to suggest that the police, in search of a suspect, might have exaggerated his significance – though there were others who believed that the entire official story was a fiction. However, a third group, including many French Arabs, believed that grand evocations of conspiracy were irrelevant. It was possible that Kelkal had been involved in some sort of terrorism, but he and his friends appeared to have been minor players. They had been manipulated – dead or held in custody, they were being used by the police. All these ideas came together in the generalized perception to the effect that there was something deeply, shamefully wrong in the manner of Kelkal's death. Not just his existence, but his murder did violence to the idea of what it meant to be French.

I was in France on and off that summer, during the bombings and the manhunt. Among the Arabs I met, I noticed a perceptible tightening up when Kelkal was mentioned. How did a young *beur* – slang for a French Arab – from Lyon become to be the centre of an international terrorist ring? Who was Kelkal anyhow? To pose such questions was to invite shrugs. Then I returned to London. Sitting in one of the new cafes that reminded Londoners that they belonged to Europe as well as themselves, surrounded by rich young Arabs with sports cars and white girlfriends, I opened the newspaper *Le Monde*. There, to my surprise, I read Kelkal's life story.[1] '*Moi, Khaled Kelkal*' consisted of a transcription of a very long tape recording made three years previously by Dietmar Loch, a German sociologist doing fieldwork on the question of what was euphemistically called 'social exclusion' by social workers and politicians and in posh newspapers like *Le Monde*. It was an astonishing document – not just as a consequence of its topicality, but because it was extremely moving, too. The Kelkal who spoke to me from these pages was an intelligent young adult, embittered but acutely self-aware – and familiar, too, with the mild ruses required to win over a sympathetic academic investigator perhaps over-concerned, in the best leftish way, with the matter of social context. I found Kelkal's narrative at times unbearable – and I also wanted to know more about his short life and death.

'I was born in Algeria,' Kelkal's own story began. 'At the age of two I came to France. I lived in Vaulx-en-Velin where I did well in primary school. I got reasonably good scores, even good ones. Then I went on the Noirettes College – and this is where I first got into trouble.' Kelkal's brother had been jailed for robbing a bank, but it appeared that his family was otherwise stable and law-abiding. Still, it seemed that these more or less favourable circumstances hadn't been enough. Without excessive self-pity and with few illusions, Kelkal recounted his career as a petty criminal. It was as if, offered some sort of footing on the steep French educational ladder, he decided, simply and without much heartbreaking self-enquiry, that in the end it just wasn't for him. Although he was a talented pupil, showing aptitude at chemistry, he cut classes, falling in with a boy who told him: 'There are interesting things to steal.' Kelkal began to make his own way by avoiding his respectable, exam-passing white school-mates, sticking to his own. This was not difficult to accomplish. He became an adept practitioner of the art of '*voitures béliers*' – the use of old, mostly stolen cars smashed into storefronts so that their contents could rapidly be stolen. 'In the afternoon, when everyone was at school, I had nothing to do,' he explained:

> A friend ['*un pote*'] is a friend, it's all a matter of sentiment, you don't judge him for having committed this or that act. I would say that 70 per cent of the kids here [in Vaulx-en-Velin] rob. Their parents don't have money when there are six kids . . . You need to buy blue jeans and there's no money . . . and I could see the difference in attitude between school and the atmosphere outside. I felt a lot easier. When you steal, you feel freer because it's all a game. As long as I'm not caught, I'll be the winner. It's a game: either I win or I lose.

However, one of his friends was arrested, and under questioning betrayed Kelkal to the police. He was convicted of stealing a BMW belonging to the president of the Lyon football club and using the car to rob a designer boutique. Sentenced to two and a half years in prison in 1991, he was advised by his lawyer to appeal. This turned out to be a serious procedural mistake in a field of which he could have little or no expertise. Kelkal was indeed released as an interim measure; but the judge who examined the case gave him a longer sentence. In the end, Kelkal remained three and a half years in prison. It seems that he was offered jobs when he came out of prison but they weren't the ones he wanted. Bitterness appeared to have overcome him. The training programmes seemed demeaning – they existed not to advance his prospects in the society which had so far defeated him, but to prepare him for an inferior life. 'It wasn't an apprenticeship that I now wanted,' he said. 'House painting or whatever – I couldn't have given a fuck. To do what? To lose my time? I no longer had the time to lose.'

Throughout France, and in the rest of Europe too, a fear of Islam led to lurid evocations of conspiracies conducted by bearded men wearing white robes. When it came to the depiction of serious deviance in France, armed young Arabs were prime candidates for hack TV shows. Speculating about his motives during the manhunt, the authorities had therefore made much of Kelkal's fundamentalist contacts – it was suggested that he had been recruited in prison, by an imam or a convicted terrorist. In his own account, however, Kelkal painted a somewhat different, less sensationalist picture. Put upon, lacking the means to succeed in the larger society, his family were thrown back on their pitifully slight resources. They lived in a small apartment in a block hastily constructed for immigrants in the 1970s. It seemed that they weren't specially religious and, like most French Arabs, they worried about money and jobs. A Muslim cellmate had taught him to pray, and he learnt Arabic; but he also insisted to his interviewer that acquaintance with the Koran had brought him serenity and reconciliation. 'All the rubbish in my life went to one side,' he said. 'And I can see that life, while it isn't simpler, is more coherent. Nowadays when I see things on

TV, I have a different reaction. I don't want to respond with violence any more. I'm sorry for people now.'

Kelkal was a member of the second immigrant generation. His sisters went out with white boys, marrying them; but for him the path towards integration appeared to be summarily barred. Like many of his friends, Kelkal decided that he wished to leave France. He did go to Algeria for six months, with his mother, but he sat at home there fretfully. He complained that there were no clothes to buy in the village. It was no good being rich in a country where money didn't get you anything. After that he returned to Vaulx-en-Velin which he knew and by now hated. Not much was known about him at this latter period of his short life, except that he had no work, played cards or football, hung around town and prayed occasionally at the mosque. It didn't seem that he was robbing designer shops, and those who knew him couldn't see a terrorist in the making.

Reading the piece I experienced a sudden shock of recognition, coupled with serious disorientation. Kelkal's narrative depicted him as a victim of circumstance, an unlucky adventurer in crime. It placed him within a distinctively French tradition, that of the educated outcast capable of lucidly recounting his removal from the bourgeois world. And it also made me think of the strange French relationship, halfway between admiration and fear, with the genuine social subversive, and how such figures – there were many fictional models, century after century, from Victor Hugo to Albert Camus and Jean Genet – dominated the French imagination. But there was also something new, and distinctively upsetting, about Kelkal's memoirs. In their frame of reference, and because of the language used, they were sub- or non-literary, coming from somewhere way outside the carefully tended, and by now obnoxiously restrictive, French cultural perimeter. They were utterly, frighteningly empty. It was not clear how much of the truth Kelkal was telling – and this didn't seem to matter much. Emphatically, through what he had become as well as what he had done, Kelkal was of our time. In his insouciance as well as his utter sense of hopelessness, Kelkal belonged to 1990s France:

> There was no place for me, because I said to myself: 'Complete integration is impossible, I can't eat pork.' And they had never seen an Arab in their class – 'Frankly, you're the only Arab,' they said – and when they knew me, they said: 'You're an exception,' But they always found it easier to talk to one another.

For Kelkal, the real problem about the idea of integration was that white French people didn't understand anything. They mixed up the idea of being an Arab and being Muslim. They just couldn't grasp that one might wish to read the Koran without becoming a fundamentalist. But the worst thing about them, he told the kindly German interviewer, was that they had lost belief in themselves and their future. They had ceased to want to live well, or even properly, and they didn't even wish (this was a ceaseless complaint, echoed, I discovered, by many young *beurs*) to have children. 'Our parents gave us an education, but in parallel the French gave us another one,' Kelkal said sadly and with some perceptiveness. 'There's no coherence in my life, just a little bit of that, and another piece of that. No, what I need is to have principles, even to respect something.' However, as Kelkal, admitted, there were no beliefs to be had in France. Of all his discoveries, this seems to have been the most distressing, and also the most important – that he no longer wished to belong to the society which had comprehensively rejected him.

I was stopped short by these words. I wondered how many anonymous European foreigners they could be applied to, those who didn't throw bombs and, as a consequence of the tangled immigration laws, failed in their quest to acquire some sort of a European purchase, let alone a piece of celebrated, widely exported civilization. But it was dangerous, though tempting, to read too widely into events; one could see the story as being distinctively European, but there were more local features, too. Confronted by the Kelkal affair, I wondered about what, reluctantly, I had come to think of as the strange seizing up of France. Something appeared to have gone badly wrong. The mood was very down – a plague of *morosité* (the glums) stalked the land, infecting everything. For posh Paris commentators, French discontents could be dumped at the door of 'globalization' – the process by which the world had inconveniently incorporated itself as a single unit, making the conservation of the French way in economics and culture highly problematic. But I was beginning to sense that the failure was deeper, consisting of a breakdown at the ailing core of French culture itself.

I began to rake over the few facts of Kelkal's life, returning to the files of cuttings which described the fear prevalent at the time of the bombings. I spoke to Dietmar Loch, who now worked at the high-sounding Interdisciplinary Institute for Conflict and Violence Research at Bielefeld. Was there anything he could remember that might have indicated what Kelkal would shortly become? The sociologist responded with caution – he explained that he hadn't liked the tone of much press coverage of his interview, which had been misleading. He had not been in a position to know what Kelkal would become, and he mustn't now give a misleading account of the importance of his research. In his discreet way, Loch was preserving the memory of Kelkal.

'It's hard not to want to draw conclusions, but as a professional I feel one should resist the tendency,' he said, sighing. 'Still, I remember he joked a lot – but then perhaps bright adolescents who drift into delinquencies often do. I would say that he was exceptional in a way, but very ordinary, too.' I wondered whether Kelkal's interest in religion had appeared serious to him, and whether his recruitment might have taken place in jail, as the press had suggested. Were French jails full of devout Muslims? Was that how the radical imams recruited their followers? The professor laughed at this idea. 'Oh, that's hard to say,' he said. 'I think he prayed, but it is possible that he knew relatively little. *Banlieue* kids go to the library, to read about Islam – that's the limit of their knowledge. It goes with beards and long shirts. It's usually no more than a fashion item. But I suppose that in Northern Ireland you could find many so-called terrorists whose knowledge of Protestantism or Catholicism is not deep. There are many different ways of justifying political action, and religion is one of them.'

Throughout Paris in 1997 the lids were still screwed on to receptacles for litter. The spring weather in central Paris was miraculous, and between interviews I picked up an old *Paris Match* from 1954 at a quai bookstall. A luscious Gina Lollobrigida was on the cover; inside a French soldier pointed his rifle at a skinny Arab bound hand and foot. The *fellagha* Djilani had allegedly killed three Frenchmen and a Tunisian. One might anticipate the summary punishment he would shortly receive, perhaps minutes after being made to pose for the photograph. 'A wave of terrorism crosses the frontier', a thick, black headline gloomily proclaimed, over an article recounting the non-progress of the ruinous French-Algerian conflict. Amid mildly salacious eighteenth-century engravings, and faded jokes involving dogs pissing against a wall, I also found a collection of pro-Vichy or collaborationist pamphlets, one of them containing an account of the notorious 1941 Paris exhibition warning the French against Jews in their midst. Here Jews were depicted as betrayers, agents of the plague. It was they who had caused the catastrophe of war. Swarthy, oriental, they couldn't be considered French.

In a cafe near the Châtelet I talked about Kelkal to Malek Chebel, an Algerian journalist living in exile in France. Chebel looked and sounded French, and he was wearing a leather jacket of the type made fashionable on the Left Bank. However, his anger was startling and wholly un-French in its lack of irony. He didn't accept the official version of Kelkal's death. Kelkal was a scapegoat, he said – the French needed their Kelkals; year by year, the police made sure that they got them, no matter what the circumstances. In France, if you were an Arab, it didn't matter whether you were guilty or not. Chebel was angry on two counts – not just because of what the French police had done, but as a consequence of Kelkal's own betrayal. He was too intelligent to want to make Kelkal into a martyr – or at least quick enough to see that this was not going to be acceptable.

I was surprised to see tears in his eyes as he explained why he had become disillusioned with France. Thirty years ago, he was proud to come here as a student; but he now despised the French permit of residence that he had been offered. 'They don't want us,' he repeated to me. 'And they lie to us. Rather than tell the truth about not wanting us, they tell lies – about how, in order to be accepted, we others must conform to their own very special ideas of universalism. But I'm afraid it makes no sense at all.' I thought again about this paradox. Most Europeans believed, one way or another, that their way of life was better. They might also think it had been worthy of export. But only in France were such ideas immodestly part of the country's official view of itself.

If they addressed such matters at all, most white French saw them through a haze of aestheticized distance, in TV programmes or through the lyrics of *rappeurs*. They certainly didn't visit the *banlieue*. On the advice of a Turkish friend I went to see Séverine Labat, an elegant woman who had done sociological research in Kelkal's home town, and was familiar with the workings of Algerian terrorism. Because she was dark-complexioned and usually wore a scarf, it had been possible for her to pass as an Arab – and she had consequently experienced the hostility of the police and, when they discovered who she really was, their evident relief. Séverine's views of the prospects for a multiracial France were bleak indeed. It seemed to her that integration had become a fetish word. In the past, Poles or Italians had come to France and fitted in, but that was through their relations with French people in the workplace. Now the problem was that there was no work – French and Arabs didn't even compete for the few remaining jobs. So, for most French people, racism had gone beyond being a matter of convenience. It was how they saw the world these days. Happily pregnant, sitting cross-legged in her Left Bank apartment beneath nineteenth-century prints filled with *képi*-wearing Frenchmen and happy Arabs, she sighed when I mentioned Kelkal. 'You have to look at French failures,' she said. 'The schools have failed, justice has failed. The old system is on the way out – only nothing is there to replace it. And all these things are somehow present in the Kelkal story. He may or may not be important for what he did, but for us all he stands for the French failure – and we talk to each other through him.'

I took the TGV through the portion of deep France where Kelkal's bomb had been placed. Cold and ornate, a large version of the Chabrol small town where erotic encounters or multiple murders take place discreetly, Lyon was filled with restaurants offering outsize pieces of *charcuterie*. I went by the sleek, half-empty *métro* to the bus terminus beyond the *périphérique*. An elderly white couple boarded the full bus with me, but they got off early. We drove along empty roads, among small tatty houses where the 'real French' – many of them now Front National supporters, as the posters in the windows told me – still lived. Passing a new civic centre that resembled a television station, we drove around housing blocks put up in the 1970s and through empty streets named after communist politicians, *résistants* or lyric poets. I had a map, which depicted the grid system of the small town, but it seemed shapeless to me. One architectural or social error had been repeated, almost to infinity. Set in concrete, this was an extreme version of what its critics scathingly referred to as '*la pensée unique*' – the strange French notion that in a proper world there must be only one way of managing or imagining things. I felt set down Crusoe-style in the midst of what I could only characterize as a breakdown, experienced on a national scale, and in relation to which the patient was still in what psychiatrists called denial.

There was a cafe at the bleak space called *Mas du Taureau* where I got off, but not much else. I walked around *La Rapinière*, where Kelkal's family had lived. I was surprised by how well-kept the cream or yellow towers were, by contrast with their English counterparts, but I also saw few unshuttered shops, no signs of a market or even a corner where people would want to linger. Unemployment in Vaulx-en-Velin was over 16 per cent – the 45,000 inhabitants were refused jobs as soon as a prospective employer discovered where they came from, and they found it next to impossible either to move or, if they owned their houses, to sell them and leave. Beginning in 1990, there had been riots, and the supermarket was burnt down. On a small scale, conveniently located, Vaulx had come to represent the French crisis of the *banlieue*, and I remembered what Séverine had told me. 'It's a complete desert,' she said. 'There's nothing there, not even a McDonald's, and only a municipal cinema – you could not be in France at all. And the place spells that out definitively to those who live there: it says "This is where you stay." After dusk the police stop every Arab at a roadblock.'

I recalled a scene from the movie *La Haine* in which a TV crew, too frightened to get out of their van, shouted questions at *banlieue* kids. At the best of times reporting in France wasn't specially easy; but in Vaulx I now found that it helped that I was British. Waiting at corners, passing from group to group, I did manage to meet friends of Kelkal, but I was aware of how their responses were garbled by hatred or mistrust. A latter-day, not wholly successful, aspect of French policy involved the creation of *associations* – officially sponsored youth clubs whose job was to inculcate civic virtues. The radicals didn't pay their phone bills or declined to answer journalistic enquiries. For members of 'moderate' clubs (i.e. those which were discreetly or half-heartedly Muslim) the Kelkal story had become yet another aspect of the burden of living in Vaulx-en-Velin. My meetings were frustrating, consisting of recollections of football matches or the various cars that Kelkal had stolen. Why did I want to know about these things anyhow? A complaint was that during the hunt and afterwards, the police searched and questioned many people. 'I don't know what he did or didn't do, and if he did anything he deserved punishment,' a young *beur* who had been to university in Britain said. 'But the worst thing was how he was killed, and how it was repeated so many times on TV. People said: "That's what they would do to me."'

That evening I walked around the centre of Lyon. In its emptiness and coldness, the city seemed more definitively and obtrusively white than before. I wondered how a young and clumsy Arab was supposed to make the great leap from Vaulx to Lyon. In a shabby street with tall shuttered buildings near an abattoir, I talked to Christian Delorme, the priest who had acted as intermediary between the Vaulx Muslims and white France after Kelkal's death and thus gained his own share of notoriety. Doleful and gangly, with the air of a medieval cleric out of *Monty Python*, Delorme seemed to complain about the role he had been forced into. He bemoaned the mistrust with which Muslims and French regarded each other. I asked him about fundamentalism, and he shrugged to say that it wasn't relevant. The families he knew had daughters who worked, and married white French boys.

The phone rang as we talked, and a variety of *soeurs* came in and out of the study to remind him of appointments. There was a smell of cooking from the other end of an enormous corridor. Père Delorme was a nice man, but he was also, it was clear to me, an accomplished church politician. He began to talk about '*banlieue* solidarity' – young men who had nothing and stuck together, helping each other. This might not be wholly admirable, but it was all that was left to such young people. Getting impatient, I asked him what Kelkal and his friends had really done, but he was not to be drawn. 'It's tragically simple,' he explained quickly. 'There was a conspiracy of sorts. Their hatred was used –

they were used. And they were dumped by whoever it was that used them. They amounted to nothing.' We were saying goodbye when he came back to the subject of French and Arabs. 'Kelkal's father died of unhappiness – he had cancer but he died early,' he said. 'And one mustn't forget the second conspiracy, the one among French people that consists of seeing Arabs as if they were not human beings. Sometimes I wonder if this is not the only important one.'

Many things still baffled me about the Kelkal story. How did he meet the people who recruited him? How did he convey his disillusionment to them? Did he offer to plant bombs – or did they tell him to do so? Lurid, filled with footage of thick beards and encounters in clandestine mosques, the journalistic accounts were not clear on this point. Nor did they attempt to explain why it was that anyone would have chosen him or indeed anyone from Vaulx. If there was indeed a 'Kelkal network', as the Minister of the Interior Jean-Louis Debré explained, its existence was short-lived, and it survived largely as a consequence of luck or police incompetence. Whatever its aims, it could certainly not be said to have been remotely successful, or to have posed any real threat to the French state.

On 15 July 1995 Kelkal and three friends in a Seat belonging to him were flagged down by police near Lyon. They drove through the roadblock, firing at and wounding a policeman as they pulled away. Whatever impression was conveyed to the public, it was clear that the police had no leads in relation to the bombings – they were lucky to find Kelkal's fingerprints on the TGV bomb on 26 August, just over a month after the RER attack in Central Paris. However, it took them another two weeks to match the prints to the existing ones in their records. Finally, they connected the Kelkal they already knew as a petty criminal to the bomb and the roadblock. *En masse*, abetted by gendarmes and co-ordinated by UCLAT, the unit of the Ministry of the Interior in charge of pursuing terrorists, squabbling among themselves, the police scoured France for two weeks without result. But once again, they were lucky. This was the moment when *cèpes* and *girolles* flourished in the autumn dampness. A mushroom picker scouring the woods near Lyon for choice specimens alerted them to existence of a campsite in which a number of young Arabs were living, and to which cars bearing provisions came at regular intervals. The police attacked at dawn on 27 September, taking Kelkal and his friends by surprise. Kelkal was able to get away, but his friend Karim Koussa, was badly wounded and captured as he attracted the gendarmes' fire. At the campsite, the police found a bag containing a copy of the Koran, some tins of food and, nearby on the ground, a Winchester rifle. After examining the spent cartridges the police suggested that the gun might have been used two months previously to kill the imam Sahraoui, a moderate Muslim with whom the Algerian fundamentalists were feuding.

This Clouseauesque sequence of events formed the basis of the case against Kelkal. It did, certainly, establish that Kelkal had wanted to plant bombs. But I felt that it didn't wholly encourage belief in the existence of a coherent network of which he was a major player. I resolved to try to see the case from the perspective of the French authorities. In France the reporting of criminal cases is governed by elaborate protocol. Journalists may not gain access to files, nor are they allowed to reveal their sources. But they may receive extensive briefings from examining magistrates or police, who have their reasons for wishing to release information. Defence lawyers, by contrast, may and do talk to the press on the record – it is for them to judge whether releasing information prejudices their case. All this explained the bizarrely coded nature of French crime reporting, and the way exposés veered between principled denunciations of injustice and shadowy, unsourced evocations of conspiracy.

The small piece of real or mock Gothic Paris adjoining the Châtelet was filled with cafes at which lawyers sat, often still wearing their robes, with their clients or mistresses; and it was here that I began to look at the police story. Among other titbits, the lawyer representing Karim Koussa told me that his client had a vivid recollection of the police talking to each other before he slipped into a coma. 'Shit, it isn't him,' one of them said. After twenty-six separate interrogations of the four suspects, the examining judges were unable to bring the most serious charges of terroristic acts. The young Arabs would be tried as an '*association de malfaiteurs*' – this proved to be the case when the trial finally began in June 1999 – a lesser charge of conspiracy carrying a maximum ten-year sentence. This was acknowledged to represent a failure on the part of the police. Even now those kept in custody were changing their stories. The witness who claimed to have seen Kelkal walk towards the TGV line carrying the bomb was now merely prepared to say that he had seen him taping up the device. By now no one really knew whether it was Kelkal who planted the bomb.

Familiar with the penal architecture of Paris from countless police films, I had nonetheless never been inside a courtroom or a judge's *cabinet*. I took a wrong turn at the ornamental lamps of the Palais de Justice, finishing up under portentous inscriptions in the vicinity of brass gratings from which recycled air was pumped into empty rooms. The police guides were from the provinces and they, too, couldn't find the anti-terrorist unit. Finally, in a remote suite lined with bulky files, I sat before one of the judges involved in the case, a polite if somewhat distant woman wearing an austere green tweed suit. Shrugging, parting her hands, she smiled and told me half-apologetically that she couldn't wholly clear up the affair. This was because Kelkal was dead, and no full investigation of his case had been needed. Whatever was known about him was now to be found in the hundreds of dossiers describing the activities of the other players – and because of the impending case their contents could not be made available to the curious. As she talked to me, however, sounding like a teacher, I began to sense a spirit of revisionism at work.

Kelkal, she now suggested, was somewhere in the canvas, but maybe not at the centre. His killing had been a mistake. 'We did want him alive,' she said. I told her that I didn't wholly believe in the official, 'fundamentalist' version of his motives. This aroused her pedagogical interest, and for almost half an hour, unprompted and with startling eloquence, she talked to me about religion and modern life. I must understand that Islamism was a movement for regeneration taken wholly seriously by the guardians of the French state. All religions, including Catholicism, had their quota of hatred, and there was nothing surprising in wanting a pure society. No one should be astonished by the phenomenon of fanaticism. We should learn to understand idealism, she suggested, even when it led to acts of terrorism – the implication was that we might also in certain circumstances come to admire it. I must have raised my eyebrows at this moment, because she spread her arms wide. 'It's a way of saying to hooligans: "Your actions are justifiable. You must be brave in a just cause," ' she said. 'And you really should hear what some of the others have said about Islam.' She paused, savouring the impact of her words. 'Just think of how Kelkal died – the morgue photos are extraordinary,' she concluded.

'He died a hero's death, on the way to the Garden of Allah. It was a terrible death, worse than anything either of us would be prepared to endure. Can you think of many people in the West who would be willing to be killed in that way?'

I had no answer to these observations. But I was inclined to think that the anger of Kelkal was simpler and more easily understood. I began to resent the French preoccupation with fundamentalist Islam. Among those whose job it was to define the way order was kept, it had taken the place of communism, as a shadowy, omnipresent threat. I went through musty cream Gauloises-impacted corridors of the Ministry of the Interior, adjoining the Elysée Palace. In an office, the walls of which were bedecked with fraternal greetings from colleagues in Oceania and French Canada, a casually dressed anti-terrorist operative provided me with an instant history of Algerian terrorism. It was a Saturday morning and there was time to kill before the lunchtime *onglet* and *frites*. My interlocutor proved to be as garrulous as the woman judge, and I had time to examine the numerous buttons and flaps on his leather jacket, worn in bizarre counterpoint with an orange shirt, in the cleavage of which one could see, nestling among well-tended silver hairs, a St Christopher's cross. When and why had the group been organized? Well, it seemed that operations in France began at the end of 1994, after French gendarmes killed four hijackers on board an Air France plane at Marseille airport. From Algerian intelligence sources, investigators discovered that the fundamentalist GIA, wishing to take revenge, planned to set up a series of networks in France. The money came from Algiers via London to Paris, thence to Kelkal in homely Vaulx. Elements of the network were located in Lille and Brussels, and the papers found in the belt that Kelkal was wearing included telephone numbers of contacts in an easily decipherable code. By now, it seemed, the network was broken.

Inspector X was courteous and helpful. But his astutely constructed organigram wasn't wholly convincing. I said that I found the neatness implied by so methodical a conspiracy hard to accept. For all I knew, revenge on France herself might well be the motive of Algerian fundamentalists. However, the motives of Kelkal and his friends, if not their behaviour, required further explanation. It was one thing to be angry, another to blow up the TGV. That required ambition of a sort, beyond the imaginative reach of most young Arabs. I felt it was too easy to shift responsibility for *banlieue* violence outside France. But there was also the problem of how little money Kelkal and his friends had at their disposal. Surely financial constraints had led them to the woods half an hour from home, where they were bound, sooner or later, to be detected. The official smiled indulgently. It seemed as if he was at last in a position to score a point or two off an ignorant Englishman. 'He was an Arab, and that's why he chose the woods,' he said. 'They go into the hills in Algeria when they need to escape. Anyway, you have to realize that this was terrorism on the cheap – these Algerian organizations do not have much money, and they don't need much. They enjoy enough support in France to do a lot of damage with limited resources.' Then he smiled and leant back in his chair. The morning hadn't gone so very badly.

On election day in 1997 I decided to go once again to Lyon. From the top deck of the TGV could be seen exquisitely assembled groups of very white cows and small belfries in the midst of heavy, rooted stone villages with orange roofs. Swilling mediocre Beaujolais from a plastic glass, it occurred to me that no one in 'official' France really knew why Kelkal might have wanted to blow a train such as this one to pieces.

What politicians euphemistically called the 'social fracture' was no doubt rooted in something approximating to reality, but it existed above all in the French mind. France was walled-off from comprehension of even the simplest aspects of French racism – by the habit of excess analysis, and the over-reliance on formal methods of deploying intelligence. A society that blocked out so much uncomfortable truth about itself, in the name of spurious clarity or by recourse to cherished, outdated notions of its own identity, was in bad trouble. But once again, I wondered if the same couldn't be said about most of Europe. How different, after all, were French people from other Europeans?

I supposed that I had always admired French rigour, which I contrasted with the underdressed sloppiness of Anglo-Saxon attitudes. In particular, what I thought of as the steadfast historic French refusal to countenance differences of race or colour impressed me. I admired the way in which French society expressed its determination to afford an equal destiny to each of its citizens, without either placing them at the margins or granting them unequal status, as the French believed 'Anglo-Saxons' – Americans, British, even Dutch – had done, acting in the name of the misplaced acknowledgement of 'cultural differences'. However, like other European powers, France had come down in the world; and French attitudes were changing. It was apparent that this French tradition, dating from the Revolution of 1789 and the proclamation of the Rights of Man, had by the end of the twentieth century ceased to be entirely convincing. It had been abandoned by many native French, who had most probably never taken it seriously, and it was now viewed with suspicion by those who might have benefited from it.

For the French still, against the evidence surrounding them, believed that they were different. They alone were capable of acknowledging the right of foreigners to become part of their universal culture – so long as the foreigners were prepared to become French. It seemed that the French perception of the rightness of their own enlightened attitudes was immovable. I recalled a frustrating conversation with a left-wing television executive, who maintained that the British Empire had consisted of plunder, while French imperialists, by contrast, had gone primarily to Africa or Indochina with the principal intention, not of stealing their rubber or taking them as mistresses, but of turning the natives into good French men and women. In the post-colonial era the sense of mission persisted. At its worst, it was just another feature of the national culture of narcissism. A 1970s report dealing with the prospects of immigration, expressed the matter thus:

> France must maintain the logic of equality between individuals that is to be found in her history, in her principles, in her own genius and which goes further, it seems to us, in the *enlargement* [my italics] of individual rights than the recognition of individual rights, of which we cannot underestimate the value and the need in other parts of Europe . . .[2]

These were fine if characteristically arrogant words, but they were unfortunately at odds with what happened each day in France. The French attitude towards race resembled what I had come to see as their least successful cultural products, such as derivative splashes of abstract art, the *nouveau roman* or artily obscure film essays. It was complicated, surrounded by fussy gestures, but at its heart was a charmless void.

In 1997 the television network Canal Plus showed a long and painful documentary which gave the first genuine account to a mass audience of the settlement in France of two and a half million North African immigrants. They had come not as individuals possessing inalienable rights, but as fodder for industry, which suffered from the low French birthrate. Recruited during the 1960s by French technocrats and their agents in the remote *bled*, where one villager was frequently chosen from 1,000 applicants, they were separated from their families and placed in barracks. They were not expected to stay, though it was convenient if they did so. The idea of French citizenship for such people came much later, in the 1970s, and it was granted grudgingly, against the expressed wishes of many politicians, when their families were encouraged to join them. Housing, usually in the new *banlieue*, was found for them. Many French people, in particular those with roots in Algeria, resented whatever acts of preference were granted to these 'new Frenchmen', and they were the first members of the Front National. From the beginning supposedly moderate politicians exploited racist sentiment by making speeches about alien cooking smells even as they piously expressed the wish that these no longer very new French would ultimately become 'integrated' and settle down.

One in every four French citizens had at least one grandparent who was not born in France, and for most of the twentieth century French immigration laws generously encouraged asylum and immigration. These were things of which French people could rightly be proud, but by the mid-1990s it seemed that they were being undone by a combination of economic recession and regressive national feeling. Although France hadn't reverted to a definition of nationality based on blood, during the first, right-wing phase of Jacques Chirac's presidency it became necessary for the children of non-naturalized immigrants born in France to apply for citizenship at the age of eighteen. Meanwhile 'sans-papiers' – illegal immigrants – were conspicuously removed from the fashionable churches in which they had taken refuge and sent home on charter flights. These measures did not presage a return to 1940s Pétainism, as many critics alleged; and indeed they were repealed during the later cohabitation between Left and Right, when Lionel Jospin became prime minister. However, they did diminish the validity of the French claim to be considered as the centre of the civilized, cosmopolitan world. More subtly, they bred an overemphasis on conformity among French intellectuals, who were now frightened of what they saw as a nativist white French backlash. Assertions to the effect that nothing could be done about racism were now frequently to be overheard in Paris.

In the past Frenchness had been grand and inclusive – though defined rationally, in terms of Enlightenment principles, it was experienced instinctively. Among the enlightened French, who loved their republic, one could no more resent the notion that the country should be considered as the last great place of asylum than imagine the Tuileries, the Louvre and every pack of Gauloises washed down the Seine into the unforgiving sea. But to its foreigners France had begun to seem like a separate, white European ethnic culture – and one often at odds with the world, clinging to its own Medusa raft of hatreds. France appeared to have fled its own tradition of universalism, abandoning it. In the 1990s the French retreat from cosmopolitanism was apparent in a tightened, somewhat defensive definition of Frenchness itself. Unlike its German counterpart, which was formed around the myths of race and belonging, French identity was a matter of culture. It rested on the presumed superiority of the language, the countryside, or the quality of manufactured straw hat, hairdo, sonnet, cheese, *crime passionnel* or high-speed train. For French *lycée* pupils and *annales* historians alike, there was still only one proper subject of study, and that was France herself. However, it seemed to me that France, so ardently pored over, was also in danger of losing elasticity and zip. Where other cultures welcomed collisions with the new global market of personal consumption the French impulse was to retreat. Sometimes, talking to French intellectuals, I felt that they believed that American popular culture had been invented in order to destroy their cherished traditions. They relied on their own idea of 'Europe' to save them from extinction.

Now the poison circulated wherever one cared to look. In 1995 I met one of the new-breed French-Arab community leaders in the North France port of Le Havre. Fawzi Gharram had film-star good looks and a highly plausible politician's manner. As we sat around the boxing ring, paid for by the Auchan supermarket from whose premises he operated, I was struck by how his criticisms were directed not at those whom one would have thought of as likely enemies, the Front National, but against French progressives. He reminded me of the celebrated 'scarf affair' in 1989, and the fact that many left-wingers had been opposed to the wearing of the chador at French schools. 'The words are a real problem,' he said. 'I'm fed up with the use of the word "integration" by intellectuals. It implies that the opposite – disintegration, if you like – is a danger. But the idea of separateness is dying in France – we can see that every day, in the number of white boys marrying *maghrébines*. However, sometimes you would think no one really wants that to happen.'

The polls depicting French attitudes to race gave contradictory messages. A whopping 38 per cent of French people declared themselves to be either 'very racist' or 'quite racist'.[3] This was twice the percentage to be found in Britain or Germany, and only Belgians displayed similar attitudes. It seemed that French people were also more hostile than other

Europeans towards 'non-European' immigrants. However, fewer people were hostile than ten years ago – it seemed as if the young French were beginning to learn acceptance. And the French outscored their neighbours in the conviction that, once immigration papers had been issued, they could not be revoked. Mysteriously, given some of their other attitudes, they also believed that France should be a country of asylum for foreigners. And a high proportion of French people – over 33 per cent – declared themselves to be 'anti-racist'. Sitting in the train, I wondered about these figures. Perhaps the French merely had become less capable of experiencing less shame in the matter of race or (it was nearly the same thing) were more honest than the Germans or British. Or maybe the French habit of polling everyone about everything had something to do with the result.

I returned to the matter of Kelkal. The most famous evocation of violence against an Arab came in Albert Camus's *L'Étranger* (*The Stranger*), and it began with sunlight trickling from a blade on a hot summer's day by the sea.[4] Blinded, the *pied-noir* protagonist shot the Arab once, and then, without excessive logic, four times. 'In this way, everything began,' he said. Meursault was unable to explain why he killed a man even when he might have saved his life by doing so, and we were half-encouraged to applaud him. Every French schoolchild knew this episode, and all the protagonists in this real-life story – the judge, the policeman, Père Delorme, even, most probably, Kelkal himself – would have been familiar with it. But I recalled that there was another way of reading the text, too; and this consisted of looking at what was left out of the story – what might have been included if the stylish perimeter of sandy wastes and perfumed seas had been drawn a bit differently. For the emptiness of the novel was perceptual as well as aesthetic.

Reading again and again, one was led to the conclusion that in Camus's novel, and in the French consciousness, too, Arabs didn't matter very much, except insofar as they were 'different'. If they stood on a street or an expanse of sand, appearing to threaten, one might end by killing them. I loved Camus's work; but I wondered whether, as a young *pied-noir* born in a white working-class community, he didn't share at least some of these attitudes. Later in his life, he was certainly at pains to disassociate himself from what might be considered to be callous. In the uncompleted draft of his last novel, *Le premier homme* (*The First Man*), set in the bloody days before independence, it was an Arab who, having learnt of the placing of a bomb in a crowded cafe, came to tell the whites seated there about it, thus risking his own life and saving theirs. But Camus was a truly exceptional man in every sense, whose painstaking desire to tell the truth, in all circumstances, got him into frequent trouble. In our time the views of his earliest protagonist Meursault were more common, and there were many Frenchmen who believed that they were worth holding.

I took the municipal bus to Vaulx through empty streets. It was a warm Sunday morning in May, and people were going to the polls to vote in the first round of the elections. In Vaulx the polling station was located in a large modern schoolroom with shiny floors. There were fourteen candidates, including Independent Greens and the happily named Union pour la Semaine de 4 Jours (Union for the Four Day Week) – but no Arab stood the smallest chance of being elected. I chatted briefly with the teacher – a communist voter in the old Vaulx style – whose job it was to collect votes. Outside it was getting hot when I sat on a low concrete wall, and the town was, as usual, empty, echoing with isolated footsteps and the occasional distant sound of *maghreb* music played at high volume. There was a strong smell of cooking, but it was welcome, speaking of something like home. Few Arabs were bothering to vote, and this must have been why I was attracted to the dark blue BMW and its two occupants wearing T-shirts. One of them was tall and strongly built, with the left side of his face covered by a series of makeshift bandages, and the other slighter and older, with dark glasses.

They were brothers, born in France, and it transpired that they, too, had known Kelkal. 'We were friends,' they told me. 'Oh yes, we were friends.' The elder brother Benal played cards with him ('he lost, usually') and Omar organized the security arrangements for Kelkal's funeral, standing bodyguard with his friends in the Muslim cemetery. As we sat together on the wall, in the sunlight, I heard a by now familiar story – the police, the pain of half-acceptance in France and the sense of deracination by the Benal family when they returned to Algeria. 'You couldn't buy a shirt there,' Omar told me. 'Nothing at all.' The brothers had given up on Vaulx. 'They should dynamite the town,' Omar said simply, scratching his bandaged head. They asked me if I liked African-French rap music and whether I had seen *La Haine*, Matthieu Kassowitz's cult movie about teenage *banlieue* gangs. 'It's just like the film,' Benal said. Omar explained that there were jobs if one struggled to find them. He worked as a bouncer in a nightclub, and Benal was a trained plumber. Instead of submitting to white bosses, they wanted to open a sandwich bar. I asked them about Kelkal – why in the end had it proved impossible for someone as bright as him? 'Kelkal is everyone,' Benal said. 'Everyone in Vaulx knows about Kelkal. He was someone that each of us might have become. But we weren't born in this shit here. We didn't grow up in Vaulx – and I suppose we were lucky.'

I said that I was about to go to Maison-Blanche, in order

to see where Kelkal had been killed, and they offered to drive me there. We left Vaulx and went through the centre of Lyon. Then we crossed suburbs, reaching open fields around small villages and, beyond them, steep hills. In the hamlet, we stopped the car and got out, walking around. I inspected the bus shelter, which was solidly built, with no bullet marks. I walked from the bus stop to the other side of the road, measuring twelve feet. In the noon heat, I tried to place the small convoy of police vans and press, hurrying up the hill to the appointed death. I tried to imagine the light at dusk when Kelkal died and the huddle surrounding him. Thinking of Westerns, or gangster movies, he told his academic interviewer that the *banlieue* would shortly erupt in violence and burn down, American-style. This wasn't wholly improbable, and it was what Le Pen believed, too. However, I was in Western Europe, and there were houses each side of the small village centre and small hedges over which open green fields could be seen.

The characters in *La Haine* talked ceaselessly of leaving the dreadful *cité* – it was called Les Muguets (Snowdrops) – where they had been dumped. But they never got anywhere, and two of them were killed returning from an ill-fated trip to Paris. The black gang member recited, over and over again, the experience of falling from a fiftieth-floor window. France was a place that told itself, while falling, that everything was all right. 'How you fall doesn't matter,' he repeated to his friends. 'It's how you land that matters.'

Kelkal stood before the semi-circle of gendarmes dressed in dark blue, with boots and flak jackets, carrying automatic weapons. He was exhausted by seventy hours of living rough, dazed by the past month spent on the run, hiding in friends' apartments or in the woods. At its simplest, which is how he expressed himself, he had played and lost – now there was nothing left to do but die. Colonel Vincent Coeurduroy of the gendarmes explained that his men had told Kelkal to give himself up before they opened fire, but it was possible that Kelkal did not hear them. 'I saw a man come out of the shadows carrying a gun,' someone passing in a car explained to the press. 'There were shouts and perhaps warnings, then a fusillade. When I got out of the car a man was lying on the ground.'

The emptiness of Kelkal's death flooded over me. Perhaps in the end he had wished to kill a policeman, but fatigue, or lack of competence with firearms, or indeed fear prevented him from doing so. Most probably, he had simply wished to do something – in the same way that one might want to blow up a train or destroy the entire hateful structure of contempt implied by the *banlieue* wastes. But we would never know, any of us, Omar, Benal, myself or anyone else. However, there were other things of which we could be more or less certain. No police ballistics report was available; but according to one newspaper twenty-three bullets were fired in response to Kelkal's single shot. As Omar and Benal reminded me, the gendarmes were marksmen, soldiers trained to supplement the firepower of ordinary police. They must have known what they were doing, and they wanted to be finished with things. As well as an act of self-defence, the killing of Kelkal was therefore an execution and, more important, an obliteration of reality itself. Rapidly, in a spirit of relative indifference and without excessive afterthought, this was how an Arab was killed in France.

# NOTHING IS THE SAME

'The ultimate future of these islands may be to the Chinese.'
Sidney Webb

I had come to Leicester in search of the reality of what in Britain was still known, using a terminology surviving from many dusty surveys, often obsolete the moment they appeared, as 'race', or, more euphemistically, 'community relations'. Depending on where the boundaries were drawn, over 30 per cent of the city's 300,000 inhabitants were classed as members of minority ethnic groups. One Leicester school boasted close to 200 Patels on its register. Already the city schools contained a majority of non-White British children, and when they grew up, it was implied, they would constitute a majority in the city. Would this make a difference? Did it mean that Leicester spelt out the future for many parts of England? But the city also interested me because of the not so distant past. It was one of the places where racist politics had first gained a toehold in Britain and then, for a long moment, appeared about to triumph. Throughout the lost decade of the 1970s, in the midst of economic depression and failure, the party then known as the National Front (later it became the British National Party – BNP – and, still later, during the Thatcher years, it vanished into squabbling factions, one of which became attracted to the ideas of Colonel Ghadaffi, another espousing a nativist, rubber-boot variation of Green consciousness) had improbably placed its hopes for national success in the revolutionary potential of Leicester.

Racists had twice come within a handful of votes of winning a parliamentary seat. Leicester became a place that attracted, near-fatally, the quality of national concern. It was presented as an image of what Britain should never be allowed to become – a place where white people were no longer welcome or, if the argument was turned inside out, where it was difficult if not impossible to be black and happy. In the way that these things tended to happen, TV coverage of riots and bigot utterances reinforced the idea of Leicester as an anti-Britain or battleground. I felt that I should already know Leicester through my acquaintance with similar places throughout Europe – in France, Belgium or Germany – over twenty years later.

Following immigration from India, Pakistan and the Caribbean, race hate and race politics infected the old white heartlands of the English Midlands throughout the latter part of the 1960s. What made Leicester special, and a place capable of arousing distinctive interest, was the arrival in 1972 of many Ugandan Asians. They were victims of Idi Amin's brutal and futile policy of Africanization which consisted of expropriating and expelling, with ninety days' notice (the number of days for which credit was habitually extended by Asian merchants, as the dictator helpfully explained), the country's entire commercial class, thus speeding the country's destruction. Most of the Ugandan Asians had chosen to retain their British passports at the moment of independence, thus forfeiting Ugandan nationality. No one had expected that these misfits of Empire would ever come to the mother country, but no other country of the Commonwealth appeared to be concerned about their imminent statelessness. Acting with what were presented as being decent impulses, therefore, but without much choice in the matter, the Conservative government of the day resolved to grant them asylum.

I had covered many of these arrivals as a young reporter and could remember the scene well. The Ugandan Asians went into exile with what they could carry, ferried by RAF or chartered planes, sometimes to remote bases in order to avoid demonstrations against their presence. They came from subtropical summer warmth, often disembarking into a cold English early winter morning. Notwithstanding these arresting images of plight, there was much opposition to their arrival. A sense of ungenerous disgruntlement characterized 1970s Britain, still struggling to abandon or forget the claims of its imperial past, and not anxious to shoulder what was perceived as an additional burden. Placid old white Leicester hadn't wanted the Asians, feeling (and expressing the matter often crudely) that the city already had its due, and indeed the local newspaper ran a campaign against their coming, pointing out that the city's already stretched resources would be further burdened. The council even took out an advertisement in a Ugandan daily paper, warning those who might be thinking of coming against doing so. 'AN IMPORTANT ANNOUNCEMENT ON BEHALF OF THE COUNCIL OF LEICESTER, ENGLAND,' read the advertisement in bold black capitals. It went on to say in the pompous style of officially sanctioned racism that things were not what they had been – a habitual English grouse, as old as the rain-slicked stones around Stonehenge or the ravens at the Tower – and that anyone coming to Leicester would encounter delays in being housed, finding education or receiving medical care. 'PRESENT CONDITIONS IN THE CITY ARE

VERY DIFFERENT FROM THOSE MET BY EARLIER SETTLERS,' the council declared, in an appropriate, though perhaps less than conscious, inversion of the familiar colonial idiom.

But the migrants had, it seemed, proved immune to these warnings. Many Ugandan Asians, thus conveniently alerted to the existence of Leicester, or seeking relatives already employed in the textile mills, or the factory making Imperial typewriters, had come nonetheless. Willy-nilly, the city had been launched on a hazardous path. It had been required to find jobs for the newcomers and, just as important, to create some sort of breach in the banked-up hatred or indifference that awaited them. This was the origin of the unexpected transformation of Leicester, from Middle England market town to cosmopolitan utopia.

I lived in a part of London once notorious for its race riots and then for its infant multiculturalism; but where the old shop fronts occupied by radical anti-racist groups now sold Italian handbags or offered pricey ethnic food. In some respects I found the problem of 'race' harder to define in Britain than the rest of Europe. As decades went, I had never specially liked the 1970s with its mixture of shabbiness and priggish, happily forgotten fanaticism. But this was the time in which changes, not yet for the most part occurring in the rest of Europe, had begun at home. It was the moment when one could first see the stirring of what Winston Churchill once disparagingly called the new 'piebald Britain' – and, just as important, the growth of opposition to it.

Looking in London at a 1974 piece of film describing a riot in Leicester, I was overwhelmed by the sense of having already been to this place. Over 1,200 police were present to protect 1,500 National Front marchers from 600-odd students and Asian activists. The NF marchers appeared to have been bussed in. but I reminded myself that in three of the city's ten wards they had won over 20 per cent of the vote the previous year. They carried Union Jacks and crude cheap banners. Most of them appeared to be old and angry, their faces marked by many years of bad diet. However, there were also young people, and some of them had begun to shave their heads. I looked in vain for the trademark Doc Martens, but all I could see were stout shoes. When it came to the slogans, however, there was nothing that might have seemed out of place in contemporary Europe, certainly not amidst the ragged armies I had frequented. 'There never was a coloured Englishman,' said a young demonstrator in an apparent echo of the words of the neo-Nazis I had met in Germany only a few months previously.

Mixed Gujarati, Punjabi, Bengali and Urdu signs bade welcome at the railway station, but I must nonetheless have taken the wrong turning. Instead of the anticipated multicultural metropolis, I found myself in the midst of a small market town. The old centre of Leicester was bricky and unassuming – the sort of half-sleepy, half-bustling place where George Eliot, who came from the Midlands, had located the beginnings of modern commercial England. There was a dull 1950s high street with half-abandoned shops, and a leafy close around the university filled with small nineteenth-century townhouses bearing the discreet brass plaques of legal firms or financial advisers. As elsewhere, some vague beginnings had been made in relation to the huge task of undoing the aesthetic depredations of poor 1960s municipal architecture. What I had taken for near-monochrome placidity came to appear as a cunning way of hiding things or finding handy compensation for disarray. It would be wrong to patronize Leicester – and I recalled that in Britain, just as one must never underestimate the prospects of underdogs, it was always a mistake to judge by immediate appearances. In the Leicester market there was a clock tower of sorts, telling what appeared to be real time. Here you could acquire iceberg lettuce, radishes or celery. Waxen lines of chipolatas were crowded into small display cases. This could have been taken to mean that the city was immured in its old provincial whiteness. In reality it probably meant the opposite – that such things, given the speed of change in Britain, and the confusion that had been created, spelt out a handy way of half-living in the past, utilizing it for comfort or consolation. Each time I saw the stacked piles of radishes I became more certain that Leicester was capable of standing for the contradictions of contemporary Britain.

I also began to realize that in Leicester (civic motto: '*semper eadem*' – 'always the same') even revolutionary change was depicted as if it were nothing much to get excited about. In Leicester, the literal accumulation of facts was taken to extremes. Everything could be made all right as long as it could be depicted as being for real. And yet, as elsewhere in England, not everything was easy to decipher. Approach the city by road, and you would be told how and where to leave the one-way system – but you might then be confronted by the fact that half the routes were closed for annual refurbishment. At the town's information centre a crinkly haired senior citizen guided me automatically to Leicester's rather modest Roman remains. When I told him I was in search of more modern relics he wrote in fresh markings for mosques, temples, synagogues, community centres, restaurants and jewellery emporia.

What had happened to the lost legions wrapped in the Union Jack? I called a number of former National Front militants, only to have the phone slammed down. No one wanted to remember failure on this scale, and there were no books written to commemorate what couldn't entirely, even within the multicultural Left, be seen as a victory. A former news editor of the *Leicester Mercury*, who had overseen the paper's genteelly racist support of the council, and then its equally genteel volte-face, told me that the Far Right, notwithstanding their apparent success, hadn't ever fitted into Leicester. A problem was that they, too, like the people to whose presence they objected, didn't come from amidst the ranks of those whom they purported to rescue. They were a collection of crackpots: white Imperialists, gun runners, halitosis-ridden child molesters, purple-veined vestiges from the sad past of Oswald Mosley and his not so merry men. The younger ones were on the way to the dole queue or the funny farm. And they were convinced that the cataclysm of race war was imminent – which had turned out not to be the case.

The pinched-faced, fastidious editor had been a Thatcherite and then a supporter of Sir James Goldsmith's Referendum Party. He displayed a hatred for Europe that was nearly pathological, and it was evident that his dislike for Tony Blair ('He's all over the place') was intense. But he also suggested that, in the end, British people didn't like the excesses of race politics. They hadn't gone for Sir Oswald Mosley in the 1930s, and the British aversion to extremes and uniforms probably explained the eclipse of racism in the late 1970s. This was an argument I had heard many times, but it was more bluntly put here. 'The National Front people weren't terribly intelligent people,' he said. 'They wanted to scare people, but it was they who did the scaring. Old ladies didn't like the boots and skinhead clothes.'

Paul Winstone had come to Leicester as a young Jewish socialist militant, in order to fight fascism, and he now supervised the multicultural utopia. At the city's renamed Customer Centre leaflets in five languages told you about housing rights, education and the reporting of harassment; and posters instructed you in the matter of seeking redress, getting attention or merely having a not-so-bad time. The reception area was painted in the light greens and orange of daytime TV. Winstone was a likeable big bear of a man, solid and enthusiastic, and we ate samosas in the back of a neighbourhood bar. His life had been devoted to the thwarting of those he still sometimes called 'the bastards'. Nothing that had happened in Leicester was inevitable. It could have happened otherwise – and in many cities it would have done. He didn't believe that the moment of race, or race politics, had passed. And he began with a class analysis of the failure of the Far Right. They hadn't understood that racism wasn't by itself capable of winning elections. By contrast, the Left, once work had been done among hostile or suspicious unions, had been capable of building an anti-racist coalition. Immigrants, it had been discovered, were capable of economic success. They were also good organizers, and the shiny new Leicester New Labour, composed of wealthy professionals, was evidence of this. It had been possible to leave the racists to wither on the margins.

But I was also struck, as we talked, by what I took to be a different, heretical strain. This came up whenever the achievements (or indeed the name) of Mrs Thatcher was mentioned. For Mrs Thatcher had belonged to the hard right of the Conservative Party where the matter of race was concerned. It was she who in 1978, shortly before the election which brought her to power and at a dangerous moment when the racists were still thought of as a menace, had declared that white fears of being 'swamped' were legitimate. And it was she, too, after the Brixton riots of 1981, in which 279 policemen and scores of the public were injured, who brusquely declared that such occurrences had nothing to do with unemployment.[1] Winstone didn't like Mrs T., but he was honest enough to acknowledge that she had helped kill off political racism – by securing the racist vote and ignoring the racists. Compared with the question of whether one was a believer in capitalism or not, skin colour hadn't been important to her. From the perspective of Leicester at least, the Thatcher years had coincided with the provision of lucrative inner-city grants and other incentives for small businesses. With the transformation abruptly wrought on the drowsy local economy by so many energetic Asian business-men, Leicester became a free enterprise showcase. Once the racists were removed, Tory politicians had discovered poten-tial supporters, coming to claim the new Asians as their own.

I told Winstone that I was in search of utopia, and I began to ask him about what appeared to be the Leicester ordinariness. The city lacked many of the stress indicators I had seen elsewhere. It seemed to promise a normal future of sorts. But I could also tell that these impressions were delu-sory. Winstone was familiar with the accusations levelled by French or Germans against what were considered to be the excesses of British multiculturalism. No French town would have wished to erect (or probably have been permitted to) signs in unfamiliar languages. You didn't find radio stations broadcasting in many odd languages in Germany. The idea that police forces should operate quotas (as they did now in Leicester, formally) or that political parties should seek, unofficially or not, to be more representative (a notion that had exercised the British Labour Party, admittedly inconclu-sively, for many years) was abhorrent in most of Europe. No black, Indian, Comoro Islander or Arab presenters graced the TV screens of Continental Europe. But I reminded him of how often I had been told in Europe that the implica-tions of allowing people the freedom to be themselves were dangerous. So many had assured me that this would either encourage local hostility, or lay the foundations for permanently separate lives. There was a terror of the British model of multiculturalism, epitomized by Leicester. In France such adaptability was perceived to mean the end of the world. In Germany people were still too scared to be excessively tolerant. 'You can't stop people living the way they want to,' Winstone said. 'A ghetto is a place where you are denied that choice – economically or through discrimination. We don't have ghettoes in Leicester.' Later, he said that it was possible for communities to coexist without merging. Did it matter that they didn't merge, I asked. 'Not to me,' he said simply. 'So it's live and let live?' I asked, wondering if it all came down to the language of the soaps. Winstone shrugged. 'You might say so,' he said.

It was hot, and I took a taxi to Belgrave Road. This was the showcase of the Hindu community – over a mile of brightly decorated shops selling saris, cooking utensils, spices and jewellery. Most of the restaurants were vegetarian, and some of them had added Indian-style pizzas to their menu. Sitting in the front window of a shop selling sticky cakes, I began with a yoghurt drink. In another restaurant I decided not to order the set meal. Instead I selected a wild variety of spinach, bean, dal, hot and less hot. It didn't taste like London Indian food. For one thing, it was less heavy and not obviously exotic. But I realized that this, too, was a delusion when I was dizzied by the hidden spice rush. How long would it take me to understand what was really going on here? Would it take me a year? Or two? Or more? A mother and daughter were sitting drinking tea at the next table. The daughter was talking about her university courses, and she switched in and out of Hindi with the speed at which my own relatives moved from English to French and back. On the face of it, Belgrave Road wasn't so different from many streets throughout Europe. There was nothing special by now about such intense concentrations of foreignness. People could live where they wished – and, as Winstone had said, they should do. But there was no place in Europe remotely like Leicester – and the city didn't feel like America at all. It was, in its new essence, definitively, inalienably British. Although I didn't feel at home here, I liked it very much.

The late afternoon light around the storefronts was golden. A long low street backed on to an industrial area which had contained the outsize textile works to which the Asians had first come in the 1960s. These were closed now, but a host of smaller workshops had taken their place. I could hear lathes and machines from the street, and it was possible to glimpse middle-aged women in saris working at benches. Between the renovated factories and the main road were long low red-brick terraces that seemed made out of one piece. The streets had British-sounding names: Kensington Road, Macdonald Road. Large four-wheel drive Toyotas and Mercedes were parked outside, and I noticed that most of the windows had been freshly replaced. From time to time a door was opened, revealing new stairways and a large kitchen at the back of the open living room. Usually the cable station playing Indian films was switched on, and there was a strong smell of spices and cooking. The children were neatly dressed, usually in matching dresses or shorts and T-shirts. From time to time large old BMWs filled with young men wearing sharp sportswear cruised up and down with the radio at full blast. I was struck by the fact that no one noticed my presence. I was also aware of the permanence of what had been this piece of exile in Leicester. When the Asians had first come it must have seemed a refuge of sorts. Now that the world had changed it was as if the phenomenon of globalization, so earnestly discussed by economists, had been implanted here. There was no going back for white Leicester – but the old categories implied by such notions as 'integration' were irrelevant, too. I didn't even know whether it was relevant to speak any more of belonging.

In Leicester, I visited members of the race awareness bureaucracy. Their offices had a scuffed look, and they were full of yellowing issues of defunct, consciousness-raising magazines. I found that people wanted to talk about Stephen Lawrence, the young black man stabbed to death by white thugs six years previously. One activist explained to me that unwitting or unconscious racism demanded perpetual vigilance. The definition of racism changed as we did, day by day. This meant that the sightings of racist acts or statements would vary according to where the onlooker was placed. I must have looked blank because he reached for a simile. 'It's like a moving staircase in the arrivals area of an airport,' he said. 'A sign will be different depending on where you're looking from.' He meant that there was no ultimate prospect of utopia in Britain, only the endless refixing of things implied by the ceaseless tinkering with the road system. I think he meant that in the end this was all that one must expect. Eating curries, I thumbed through the booklets I had been given. What were still termed, after so many years of supposed integration, Leicester's 'ethnic minority communities' were still overwhelmingly clustered around the centre of the city to which they had first come. The more significant the 'community' – Indians came first, followed by Pakistanis and 'Black Caribbean' Britons – the more dense proved to be the settlement. This seemed to indicate that people did indeed prefer to stick together, and that it was more comfortable in Britain to do so. No one, if they valued their own peace, should get too far out of line. A survey of reported racial harassment told me that 43 per cent of the victims were Indian, and only 13 per cent white. It seemed that racial abuse was the most common offence, with 41 occurrences over 18 months, but there were also 29 incidents involving an 'unpleasant substance'. Sticking together, I reflected, meant the more congenial aspects of schools, the proximity of neighbourhood shops. But it also lessened the likelihood that such petty assaults would go unnoticed, and indeed unpunished.

It was hotter in mid-summer and the gummy pavements were encrusted with bottle tops. I now learned to steer my way around Leicester by means of its competing shrines. Catholic, Anglican, Baptist or Congregationalist, the churches were decayed places, with forlorn, peeling posters advertising hope in the Redeemer, and blowsy red roses. The mosque was next to a large car park, alongside functioning workshops where cotton was being woven, and it was only a short walk away from the small red-brick synagogue with a greenish roof favoured in traditional Christian chapels or war memorials. Most of the temples had once been Christian places of worship, and they had been converted with great care and considerable expense, using marble brought from India and murals specially executed. Like the gods or seers whose images they contained, the Hindu temples appeared to be everywhere at once. In the lobby, next to the small shelves where one must leave one's shoes, were long lists of benefactors chiselled in gold, often with the sums (and they were large) which had been donated. Red carpets led to the bewilderingly complicated shrines. In back rooms were large photographs of emaciated gurus with helpful texts explaining in what, precisely, lay the degree of their holiness. In the Jain temple, the only one in Europe, as I learnt, there were murals in which skinny exponents of Jainism walked from one monastery to another. Strict believers in reincarnation, adamant in the matter of never killing, not even swatting insects; Jains, I learnt, believed in *anekantavada*, which meant, as my leaflet said, 'no one-sidedness, the principle that, as perception is conditioned by the viewpoint of the beholder, so reality must be seen from a variety of views . . .' In Leicester (and indeed in contemporary Britain) this seemed a sensible attitude, and I let the guide dab sandalwood on my forehead before I went out into the traffic-clogged street.

In small back rooms filled with filing cabinets, I drank Coke or ice water with those who were described as community leaders. They were proud of what they had done, but I noticed a degree of anxiety, too. The problem was that many of them had now outperformed the native English. Some of them expressed mild resentment at the lack of local initiative. Why didn't the locals save or rely on their own families for sustenance? Why did they imagine the state would look after them? Mr Morjaria, who was retired now and looked after the Jalaram Prathna Mandal temple, told me that his son had just bought him a new M registration car. 'My family won't send me to a home when I get old,' he said. 'They will pay for me. Because I paid for them, they will pay for me.' He told me how sad the churches had become in Leicester. '*They* don't care,' he said, meaning the British. For him, it was the British who still appeared to be foreigners.

The era of medium to good feelings had proved short-lived; now Asians worried about how to live alongside the British. Jaffer Karpasi was effusively (and it seemed quite genuinely) grateful for the welcome he had received over twenty years ago in Britain. 'The British really are tolerant,' he told me several times. 'They are surely better than other people.' But he now worried about the degree of conspicuousness of Leicester Asians. They had gone from old Ford Populars to Capris and Escorts. Now they bought big Mitsubishis, Mercedes or BMWs. By any standards, they had become rich – and they often found themselves employing those who, only twenty years ago, had been their employers. He talked of such people as familiar strangers whose behaviour was predictable but no more attractive for that. Once again, it was the apparent apathy of the native British that was worrying, and what appeared to be their dull resentment of success. But he would qualify such remarks even as he made them. 'They always know who we are,' he said. 'I suspect it would be easier for us if we were Jews. They, after all, can always pretend to be English if they want to.'

Karpasi was a successful accountant. His offices just off the Belgrave Road were packed with new hardware, and he had received an Empire medal for his services to the inter-racial cause. But Karpasi was also worried. When he had arrived in Britain as an adolescent, it was the indifference that affected him. He had been lonely and the acts of kindness were rare indeed. He remembered waiting in the freezing cold at a bus stop for half an hour, and how no one picked him up. An old lady spoke kindly to him. 'No one will stop for me because I'm old,' she said, 'and no one will pick you up because you're a foreigner.' Now he noticed more racism. The insults were more freely given these days; no one thought twice about them. 'They say "fucking Paki" – as if it were a relevant expression,' he said. 'But you also notice these feelings among the people who check my clients' accounts. "They've made a lot of money," these people will say – and the implication is that "you people make all the money, not us."' But Karpasi also thought that this situation might be a temporary one. The Leicester Asians, who had done so well, would in due course, as they merged with the rest of the population, cease to perform so remarkably. They would simply become more English. I didn't think that he believed that this would happen – or would be specially happy if it did.

That evening I drove to Oadby, a small postcard suburb of Englishness where the new rich Asians had begun to settle. The church was still neat, but women in saris walked up and down the pavements. Nearby a large black and white board proclaimed the existence of a private school (with 80 per cent of Asian pupils) but I noticed that the Oadby shops were owned by white British. Would Oadby acquire an Asian identity – or, like bits of Finchley for London Jews, would it ultimately remain the place you went to from the old centre of Leicester in order to seem as truly British as was possible? Later, I stood in the city centre outside the hotel that had been reclaimed from dereliction for the benefit of the Kosovar refugees. Two women in bright headscarves hovered about the entrance where small children played. Inside, a group of men sat around a scratched Formica table, talking. There was an anarchist bookshop just down the road, within the premises of the Leicester Secular Society, and a fraying, half-abandoned ABC ballroom. No churches stood here, and the street was run down, but not in an unpleasant way. The experience of Leicester (and Britain indeed) appeared to show that it was possible to set out without knowing much of what one was doing, or even wanting to do it at all, and end up in a strange, half-recognizable place.

After going to Leicester, I looked differently at the way in which differences were defined and arranged in Britain. Although many foreigners still purported to locate tradition in our archipelago, progressive disorientation was the motion I associated with being British. Britain had changed ceaselessly in my adult life. Had it changed for the better or for the worse? These were deep questions, and I had tended to leave them to one side, pleading my own half-ignorance or foreignness. But I now understood that the country in which I lived was both excessively familiar and dauntingly exotic. There were many forgotten tracts written about the likelihood of race war following on unchecked immigration. Despite intermittent upheavals none of the worst prophecies had come to pass. But neither, it seemed to me, had the liberal dream come to fruition. Liberals were divided over the meaning of such words as 'assimilation' or 'integration'. After such notions had proved hard to sustain, they had fallen back on the even hazier idea of 'pluralism'. In 1968 Roy Jenkins, perhaps the only British politician to have fully understood such questions, came up with a definition of multiculturalism, though he didn't of course use the word. Integration, he suggested, would occur 'not as a flattening process of assimilation but as equal opportunity accompanied by cultural diversity, in an atmosphere of mutual tolerance'. He might have added that this combination of factors was achieved with difficulty, and that it depended above all on the acquiescence of a native population, who, if they were told what was going on, were sometimes disposed to resist. But was this combination of half-virtues exactly what we had acquired in Britain? In response to this question, I began to compile lists of the half-truths or outright delusions which had come to mask or half-characterize the central matter of identity in Britain.

*Blood Without Honour.* In the rest of Europe blood ties or formal, legal definitions told you how you might became German, French, Belgian or Austrian. The ties of blood were deemed more important, but the contrary French tradition implied a situation where it was possible to choose a nationality (as was the case in the US, for instance) because it was specially valued. In Britain no one, even immigration officials, seemed capable of understanding the immigration laws. It seemed that the old, half-forgotten imperial tradition took precedence. It was your position on the vanished boat of Empire that mattered. Within the great degree of security conferred by Empire, and with the periodic obligation to get yourself killed on behalf of a country never visited, it had been easy to say that virtually anyone somehow belonged to the Britain of the imperial imagination. Now, if you were at all foreign, could you even say with any confidence that you were indeed British? Imperial social archaeology became an important subject in post-imperial Britain. The principal activity of the redoubtable immigration services lay in reconstituting lost and forgotten passenger manifests, making nice distinctions between the spaces behind the air shafts and the ones beneath the lifeboats.

*All Change.* Originally, the status of British citizen was extended to any subject of the king or queen emperor. No sooner were the ends of Empire in sight than the changes began. Further alterations were introduced as more territories were shed, becoming part of the new Commonwealth or elected to go it alone. Thus arose from the extinct near-universal category of *Civis Britannicus* the high-sounding (but in reality lesser) citizenship of the United Kingdom and Colonies. I could score these momentous changes with a soundtrack from Elgar to Andrew Lloyd-Webber. The new dispensation stated that within the grandiose but meaningless notion that all imperial subjects had political rights lay other, henceforth more important distinctions. Not so implicitly it carried the promise that things wouldn't be delivered.

*Fear The Natives.* The imagery accompanying the soundtrack on this old imperial epic contained an element of menace. Fear of the foreigner came rapidly to white Britain, well before it took root in the rest of Europe – and it acquired political importance as a result of the activities of the anti-immigrationist Right, and those (they were to be found among Labour supporters in the trades unions as well as the Conservative Party) to whom the rise of bigotry appeared either threatening, or to present an opportunity for electoral success. There were race riots in West London and Nottingham; white hooligans received stiff sentences from stern judges while buildings were still smoking. British people looked across the Atlantic at the burning ghettoes, taking fright. There was a noise of gates closing in Britain as the liberal, laissez-faire tradition of Empire was extinguished. In 1962 immigration was first made dependent on the availability of jobs in Britain, with the introduction of a voucher system. Five years later, with the flagging of the economy, the right to come to Britain was denied to those who didn't have a connection with the mother country through the circumstance of their birth and that of their parents and grandparents. The gates were finally banged shut in 1981 with the notorious piece of legislation that put an end to remaining shreds of generosity. This meant that the old, half-abandoned minorities of Empire couldn't any more assume that a home awaited them under duress. It reflected a resolve that the Hong Kong Chinese wouldn't easily be able to come to Britain, and it spelt the end of the Empire as a living piece of civilization, capable of affording sustenance to its members as well as the odd fancy dress visit on the part of a distracted monarch.

*Little England.* The lesson appeared to be that, appearances to the contrary, everything changed in Britain. The multiple pressures of 'race' and 'immigration' altered Britain definitively, narrowing the scope of Britishness even while the vestiges of Empire were imported, transforming the old mother country. To those of my generation who had lived through these times, it seemed incredible that at any moment any one of the millions of imperial subjects scattered throughout the world could have claimed political rights. But that 'liberal moment' had existed, and one could judge its importance by rereading the debates that surrounded its extinction, and the installation of a 'Little Englandism' based on convenience:

> This was when the British government decided on grounds which were quite openly those of expediency rather than principle, that it could no longer protect certain of its citizens because of the colour of their skins. Unlike the Dutch, we were not prepared to accept the responsibility for winding up our past imperial role. At that moment the liberal rhetoric with which ministers clothed their policies finally ceased to convince . . .[2]

For *The Times*, the changes imposed in 1968 were shameful beyond any measure so far proposed in Britain. They exceeded even the Munich sellout of Czechoslovakia as an index of national disgrace. 'The Labour Party now has a new ideology,' the newspaper declared. 'It does not profess to believe in the equality of man. It does not even believe in the equality of British citizens. It believes in the equality of white British citizens.'[3] In the House of Lords, Lord Foot suggested that British passports should henceforth read 'not to be altered in any way, except only by the British government'. Nonetheless the changes were accepted without excessive protest.

*This Far and No Further.* The attitude of grudging, disdainful superiority lingered, in part defining the new

Britishness to white Britons. It was apparent through the
various attempts to dissuade asylum-seekers from coming to
Britain, and punish them when they did so – in 1999, in a
new piece of legislation, by providing them with a special
scrip (the 'asylo', as it was nicknamed) with which to purchase food, and only 70 per cent of the income support
afforded to indigent native British. Slovak gypsies and Bosnians were put up in slum boarding houses at seaside towns;
and a military camp, used in the 1930s to accommodate
Jewish refugees, was reconverted for the new asylum-seekers.
Diligent British officials scoured the Eurostar for cheats who
booked double tickets to elude the inspectors; they placed
pressure on the French police at Calais to stop stowaways,
causing the eviction of vagrant foreigners from all-night
shelters. By European standards the British were mean in
their treatment of asylum-seekers. In the 1930s, France gave
refuge to many more Jews than Britain; and in the 1990s,
Germany and France as well as Denmark and Sweden were
to prove more receptive to the plight of Bosnians. However,
the presumption of special, easily abused generosity persisted. The British knew that everybody was out to do them
down. These attitudes persisted in press reporting. In 1900,
for instance, a *Daily Mail* reporter saw 'Russian Jews,
German Jews, Peruvian Jews; all kind of Jews'[4] devour the
free refreshments laid on by the Mayor of Southampton.
'They jostled and upset the weak, they spilled coffee on the
ground in wanton waste,' the reporter noticed. In September
1998 the *London Evening Standard* reported that the children of 'bogus asylum-seekers' from Kosovo (by now they
were no longer called 'so-called refugees') were begging outside Tube stations, 'repaying (British) kindness with crime'.
Teenage Romany gangs of pickpockets had even worked

their way through the crowds watching the Changing of the Guard.

Perhaps we were all now, to greater or lesser degree, foreigners in Britain – though of course some of us were more foreign than others. Somewhere, beneath so many reports and so many high feelings, all this added up to the central mystery of the Britain of our time. 'Swamping' – Mrs Thatcher's aptly evocative word – was still feared in Britain. Despite interdictions of petty racism, the aversion to foreigners wasn't extinct. The British presumption of generosity was not altogether ridiculous, to be sure; but the old embattled nativist consciousness was still present, not so latent indeed, and it would be naïve to assume that the attitudes that had lent support to a large racist movement had simply vanished. And yet it was difficult to reconcile this with the new openness that had come to Britain with a large brown-British and black-British population, and much intermarrying. At a time when the makeshift identity of Britain showed signs of disintegrating or reforming into its older constituent parts, the newest Britons – those from the old Empire – appeared most loyal to the idea of union out of difference. They had experienced few problems in calling themselves British. Their problems had consisted in getting others to accept that they were indeed what they said they were.

Was Britain really a multicultural society or not? Was it a successful mixed-race place? The question of what it now meant to be British was too complicated to permit easy paraphrase. It wasn't so much the statistics that mattered, but what people felt and who they had become. And in this respect what one might consider to be the 'reality' of race and identity was complicated indeed. For the stories told by black, white or Asian Britons were often far from unflattering

– it appeared that they did think that so much uprooting, so many difficulties in self-installation, had in fact been worth it. That was how the matter of integration was presented in public anyhow. And then, suddenly, catastrophically, the national plot took a different turn. There were riots or murders. Perhaps a fresh set of statistics revealed the feelings that were hidden beneath so much normality. Something close to panic gripped the great and the good in Britain. At that moment (and these occurrences were frequent, coming every year or so) it appeared that so many years of careful indoctrination in race relations meant nothing. At that moment the 'panic and emptiness' apprehended by E. M. Forster – the nothingness that underlay so many totems of good feelings, and so many accumulated illusions about national solidarity – became suddenly and brutally present.

In April 1999, a nail bomb was placed next to a stall in the crowded Brixton market, injuring many. The next week a similar device went off in Brick Lane. A third bomb destroyed The Admiral Duncan, a crowded pub in Soho frequented by gays, killing two people and mutilating or badly injuring dozens. I was in the area that evening, on the way to a drink; and I found myself near the smoke, the police barriers and the anxious crowds. One might have imagined that Londoners would be inured to carnage as a result of the experience of the long IRA campaign, but they responded with incredulity. They were in shock – no one had told them that an explosion within an enclosed space was capable of causing so much damage. Anonymous phone calls had attributed the blast to extreme racist groups such as Combat 18, but these proved to be hoaxes. For weeks the press sought a comprehensive explanation of the outrage. Stories were printed about the National Front and its links to newer, marginal white racist groups. There were calls from politicians and anti-fascist campaigning groups for the banning of extremists, and the familiar arguments about freedom and self-protection were replayed. The existence of individuals or cells capable of doing so much damage posed questions about whether the recipes for bomb-making were received from the Internet and whether the idea for such outrages came from the German neo-Nazis, or the American crackpot right, or some tradition closer to home capable of sustaining such acts. As it happened, the assaults turned out to be the work of a 23-year-old solitary from Farnborough, Hampshire. He had a good education, no record of racist acts and no apparent motivation. All that was known about him was his respectable family and the fact that he had worked as a ventilation engineer on the new Tube extension. Like all news stories, the nail bombings passed rapidly into oblivion without excessive ceremony. But they had proved to be a pretext and an occasion. They showed how the British were far from finished with the ugly presence of hatred in their midst. If one were disposed to deconstruction, it was possible to say that the chief characteristic of the new multicultural Britain was a pervasive uneasiness – but one that lay just short of shared guilt. Wisely, perhaps, British people appeared more concerned with the identity of the perpetrator than the obscurely tangled misconnections that must have led to his actions.

On 22 April 1993 five white adolescents attacked a young black at a bus stop, in Plumstead, a suburb of South London. Despite the presence of eyewitnesses, the police failed to arrest any suspects in the days after the murder and, notwithstanding a lengthy investigation, which included bugging members of the gang thought to have murdered Stephen Lawrence, got no further in the succeeding months. No doubt things would have been left there, but for the energy and persistence of the parents of the murdered boy. In 1995 they initiated a private prosecution against the suspects, but this proved to be unsuccessful – which meant that three of the suspects could never be tried again. Not deterred, the parents of Stephen Lawrence complained about the quality of the police work which had led to the murderers remaining unpunished. The result was a document clearing the police officers. Still less than satisfied Mr and Mrs Lawrence secured a second inquiry, this time organized by the Home Secretary. In 1999, after the interrogation of eighty-eight witnesses and hundreds of thousands of pages of transcripts, reports and documents, the results of the inquiry were finally published.

The transcripts were turned into a play and a television programme. They became a pretext for many statements about the British condition. But they also interested me as a narrative. It was the way in which Britons had told and retold the Lawrence story that gripped my imagination. As a heroic record of the efforts of two loyal and finally defeated parents, the document made painful reading. Was this really how murders remained unsolved? The police errors were gross and easily explained. Undermanned, the Plumstead police force had moved too late in its investigations, allowing time for the white suspects to construct their story and dispose of any pieces of clothing (if they were indeed the murderers) that might have incriminated them. Incompetence of this kind was probably not so rare as people liked to think, but it was here displayed in awful detail. But the police had also proved painfully remiss in their handling of the Lawrence family. They hadn't known how to comfort the parents, or even supply them with adequate information about their own lack of progress. They were trapped in their own story, which consisted of saying that these things happened and that they were anyhow very busy. Under pressure police officers let slip faux pas about 'coloured' people. To begin with they had been convinced that Stephen Lawrence had died in a fight, and under interrogation they still appeared to believe that his death wasn't the consequence of race hatred. When it became apparent that the parents wouldn't accept their son's death lightly, employing their own solicitor and seeking the assistance of various 'anti-racist' pressure groups, they were not so subtly classed as a problem best dealt with as little as possible. And many of the policemen interrogated appeared deficient as human beings.

Opponents suggested that the police had merely proved to be incompetent, and that the sort of treatment meted out to the Lawrences would have been the lot of any white family. But these versions of the story (they occurred among nostalgics or those who felt without wishing to say so, because it would be interpreted as being impolite, that such failure didn't matter) failed to draw any general lessons. All the critics could do was suggest that in their zeal to make amends those in charge of the inquiry had disregarded rights in the cause of vengeance. They had turned their activity into a show trial in which not just the gang, but Britain itself was judged. These critics didn't feel that so evident a malfunction of the judicial system warranted (as the inquiry recom-mended) the removal of the principle of double jeopardy, which would have permitted the retrial of the suspects.[5] They weren't even sure that additional 'racial awareness training' of the police (the words held unfortunate Orwellian over-tones) would accomplish much. Their contention, ultimately, was that a Britain in which everyone behaved as the writers of the report wished would be sorrily inhibited. The enemies of multiculturalism yearned for the old days when no one paid much attention to race differences. But those days had not been innocent, and they were dead and gone

At times the report read like the academic analysis of a TV cop-show script. But this too, the further one ventured, proved to be a comforting delusion. For it was the voices of the participants that lingered in the memory and the degree to which, going over the same subject again and again, they failed to fit in relation to the relatively simple events. The Lawrence story belonged to all of us and also to no one. It seemed as if everyone involved, given time to examine the death of one young man, had concluded only by saying that no language or perspective existed in common whereby such an event could be understood.

So here, on its way out, was the old voice of liberal Britain, rattled but eager to find the least insecure ground from which to uphold public morality:

> The group of white murderers then disappeared down Dickson Road. We refer to them as murderers because that is exactly what they were: young men bent on violence of this sort rarely act on their own. They are cowards and need the support of at least a small group in order to bolster their success. There is little doubt that all of them would have been held to be responsible for the murder had they been in court together with viable evidence against them. This murder has the hallmarks of a joint enterprise.[6]

Here were the befuddled and defensive police:

> Throughout his evidence he made it repeatedly clear that he refused to recognize that the attack was purely racist. He accepted that there was a racist shout before the attack and that one essence [sic] of the attack was racist. But he added that 'because these lads had attacked whites before, very very similarly with a similar knife, I believe this was thugs. They were described as the Krays. They were thugs who were out

to kill, not particularly a black person, but anybody and I believe that to this day that was thugs, not racism, just pure bloody-minded thuggery.'

And here, far more shocking than they could ever seem in TV interviews, bugged by the police, were the gang members who got away:

> We stress that the sentences used are only part of prolonged and appalling words which sully the paper upon which they have been recorded:
> Neil Acourt. Sequence 11. 'I reckon that every nigger should be chopped up mate and they should be left without fucking stumps . . .'
> David Norris. Sequence 50. 'If I was going to kill myself do you know what I'd do? I'd go and kill every black cunt, every Paki, every copper, every mug I know . . .'

And here finally, speaking in the Coroner's Court, was Mrs Lawrence:

> 'My son was murdered nearly four years ago; his killers are still walking the streets, when my son was murdered the police saw my son as a criminal belonging to a gang. My son was stereotyped by the police, he was black then he must be a criminal and they set about investigating him and us. The investigation lasted two weeks, that allowed vital evidence to be found, my son's crime is that he was walking down the road looking for a bus that would take him home. Our crime is living in a country where the justice system supports racists murderers against innocent people. The value that this white racists' country puts on black lives is evidence as seen since the killing of my son . . .'

Was Britain indeed a 'racist country'? Was there such a thing as 'unwitting racism'? You could only answer yes but add that these definitions no longer possessed any generally held meaning. You could wish, too, that it might be possible to start again, scrapping the way in such matters was approached and indeed talked about. Britain had its own long history, not just of racist acts or laws, but of the way British people thought of themselves. 'Racism', a word that existed for the purposes of simplification, had been exploited for propagandist reasons. Analysed into extinction, covered with reprobation, it returned ceaselessly, often serving no purpose. Over time the tone of racist utterances was subtly modified, becoming banal. In the oldest meaning of the word, the Lawrence murder was banal. That was the real tragedy – and the one not alluded to in all the hours of transcriptions. That was what Mrs Lawrence correctly understood to be the significance of her son's death. Not generosity, but a refusal to acknowledge what was going on was the real British contribution to the question of how people who thought of themselves as different could rub together. I recalled that E. M. Forster, speaking of democracy during the 1930s when goodwill as well as tolerance was in short supply, had acknowledged this strange quality with two cheers. Perhaps, judged not just by what it might have become, but on the basis of what elsewhere was on offer, the British way wasn't quite so bad after all. Or was that not saying very much?

# TO THE FRONT AND BACK

'Personally what I felt most often during those years was a sense of sorrow and pity.'

Marcel Verdier, *The Sorrow and the Pity*.

The woman dressed as Joan of Arc, wearing fake chain mail and a papier-mâché breastplate covered with fleurs-de-lys, struggled with her horse. She couldn't explain what she had to do with Joan or indeed what Joan was doing here, among the Front. 'I don't want to say anything,' she repeated. Meanwhile marchers assembled somewhere near the Hôtel de Ville, gathering momentum down the Rue de Rivoli. By the time they passed the makeshift stand opposite the golden statue, where they deposited purple and white wreaths, they were in full throat. It was a beautiful day, but I noticed how a spirit of hostility dominated their slogans. Everyone had something to complain about. There were grizzled Scotsmen in psychedelic kilts and young Belgians wearing Celtic crosses. Oldish, poor-looking participants sported berets and medals or strange items of headgear that appeared to have been left on shelves for many years. A priest standing in front of me was wearing shorts and boots. Although few women marched in the parade, those who did were wrapped in tricolour sashes, and dressed garishly in purples or bright reds. The chants were raucous, old-fashioned, expressing old or traditional enmities. '*Juppé, foutu, le peuple est dans la rue!*' cried the young frontists, referring to the balding, insignificant centre-right politician who was then Prime Minister, but sounding like extras playing street thugs from the 1930s.

On the stand, a pallid, hungry-looking man in his early thirties intoned what appeared to be a liturgy. He identified the banners of each delegation, linking them to a topographical, ancient France of corn and wine, rivers and hills. '*La Beauce s'approche!*' he cried, or '*Allez, Dordogne!*' Each time a delegation passed he raised a skinny wrist, causing the crowd to applaud, and I thought of that ancient-seeming French institution, the *colonie de vacances*, the state-funded summer camps endured by every middle-class French child. Prizes were dished out in a *colonie* for any form of good conduct, sporting or otherwise. Among the Front, it occurred to me, you got a prize for the miracle or privilege of merely being there.[1]

I hadn't experienced the Front *en masse*, and a sharp whiff of despair entered my nostrils. You could be grumpy in France – indeed, disaffection was part of the national birthright – but the state of enragement was what I felt around me. In the phrase of the novelist Albert Cohen, the Front were 'the sort of people happiest hating together'. I could have been in the large open wing of an asylum called France. The Opéra was plastered with immense female figures borrowed from Michelangelo on which the names of the four southern towns held by the Front – Marignane, Orange, Vitrolles, Toulon – were inscribed. It was hot by the time Jean-Marie Le Pen began, and at first I had trouble following his speech, until I became habituated to his archaic style. Le Pen was dressed in a too-tight suit, wearing a huge Tricolour sash, sweating and grimacing through bridgework. He spoke ponderously, moving his arms like a less than competent swimmer. Overweight, with a blotched, sick-looking complexion, he was like a waiter who has just performed the feat of balancing a tray of coloured liqueurs. In between huge assemblages of sentences, he paused, showing his teeth and I noticed that he couldn't smile. On the vast images reproduced by monitors or face to face, I tried unsuccessfully to spot his glass eye.

But I had little or no problem in understanding the music behind his scattered observations. By his use of grotesquely chosen words, standing on the creative edge of malapropism, Le Pen flattered his listeners. Meanwhile it wasn't excessively hard to pick out the enemies. He worked his way from the vicious left-wing press to the venal French political elite, passing through the remote, malign cartels of international capitalism, owned by America or, more vaguely, a Jewish-dominated Anglo-Saxonism. As well as Jewish lobbies, free-masons had their place and so of course did the reviled brown- or black-skinned immigrants, always knocking at the castle gate when they weren't inside, stealing the wealth, the maidens and the identity of France itself. Foreign influences were everywhere, from rap music to fast food and street violence. A Frenchman had nowhere to go in order to be himself. The Maastricht Treaty put in a regular appearance; and so did the Euro, ultimate symbol of national self-extinction. And then there were the 'socialo-communistes' – the old enemies of the French people, who hadn't changed, despite appearances, and who still, with their alien ideology of 'Judaeo-Marxism', encompassed the destruction of France. All these horrors, great and small, could be amalgamated within the governing threat of 'mondialisme' – 'globalism' was the best translation, though it was significant that the word had a somewhat less malign meaning in English – a process whereby France, if she wasn't already parcelled up and sold off, would mysteriously be destroyed. It was late, late in the day, Le Pen was saying. Soon it would be too late and France would be gone. This was the fate awaiting the people of France in the era of globalism. They would cease to be themselves, becoming instead puppets of all the forces which they most hated. Shortly – we were never told how this would happen or what France would look like – they wouldn't exist at all.

Nothing was new about the speech, which might have been delivered at any point in the last fifteen years, but that, I realized, was the point of demagogy, to reassure by the constancy of depicted threats. And Le Pen's oratory was formidable, relying on what the American historian Richard Hofstadter, referring to Senator Joseph McCarthy, called 'the paranoid style'. He had created a contemporary music of defeat and despair. Where most over-educated French politicians spoke the language of index cards or memos, Le Pen was familiar with nouns and verbs. Lengthy subordinate clauses scrolled through his interminable speeches like the fields of *la belle France*. He didn't disdain the subjunctive, even in its rare pretrerite form, and he parodied the grammatical authority of those he despised by using the third person indefinite with a future tense. Stopping, switching mood, growing suddenly alert like an old tabby cat, he played on his audiences. I found it hard not to be moved by Le Pen, even while I hated or despised everything he said.

He made the same speech at each rally with little or no variation, except that he sometimes walked about the stage, waving his arms or extending them, in the kitsch-intimacy style he had borrowed from American televangelists. Recently, a team of researchers had fed a sample of Le Pen's

speeches into a government computer. 'The speeches of Le
Pen are not dependent on rationality or on the analysis of
facts in a Cartesian manner,' they concluded, perhaps stating
the obvious.[2] Nonetheless, Le Pen did appear to believe in an
old-fashioned society with its roots in custom and biology –
he still adhered to the totems of old France. Among the
'enemies' of this society Jews (59 per cent) were cited more
frequently than immigrants (34 per cent) who beat freema-
sons (only 6 per cent) into third place. But Le Pen also
insisted that he was, despite the observations of his
opponents, a democrat. According to him, France had come
adrift as a consequence of what he took to be the failure of
politicians to heed the popular will. In a France of which Le
Pen was the leader there would be frequent scrutinies of
popular feelings, particularly on such pressingly emotional
questions such as the death penalty or whether immigrants
should be sent home. It was clear that the citizens of Le Pen's
France would be encouraged to give expression to whatever
it was that bothered them so much.

Meanwhile a rich infusion of paranoia was to be found
bled into every utterance of Le Pen's. Sometimes, indeed, he
spoke of himself in the third person, as if he were a cherished
pet taken away to be put down:

> Put to death. Banned from TV. The victim butchered and cut
> up in pieces. A Le Pen who has become archetype of the racist
> (or Frenchman) and must be consumed by everyone. Everyone
> from the artistic, media or political world is morally obliged
> to strike out at Le Pen and incite others to do this.[3]

Uniquely among contemporary politicians, he evoked the
prospect of despair as something wholly desirable. Nothing
could be done, he repeated, over and over again. He was

saying that catastrophe was imminent, and that it would propel himself and his followers to power. *Nous sommes foutus* is what he repeated. Meanwhile he communicated to his followers the pleasures of failure. No one would end by blaming him if he achieved nothing. Whatever they did or thought, no one here was at fault. Le Pen's appeal rested on a presumption of his own importance. He alone was capable of saving his country in this hour of need because he, Jean-Marie Le Pen was the only remaining link to the real past of France. Who but himself, pouchy and red-faced, was worthy of the tradition of the Maid of Orleans? Who else could chase out the newest wave of invaders currently occupying France?

One of the FN's most famous posters said: 'Three million unemployed, that's three million immigrants too many!' – a no doubt conscious echo of Hitler's observations about Jews in 1930s Germany. Another depicted a jet silhouetted against the setting sun, promising, with the crude hilarity beloved by frontists: 'When we get in, they go out!' The FN controlled four major towns in the south of France. It had eleven delegates in the Strasbourg Parliament and thousands of elected representatives throughout France. The FN had created its own trades unions, most successfully among police officers and prison workers, but it could also boast recruits in high schools and in the army. Nowadays there was a FN private security force, FN soup kitchens, frontist newspapers and publishing houses. It was sometimes possible to imagine that France itself belonged to the FN.

These were the 1997 elections for the National Assembly, called on impulse by President Chirac in a rash and, as it turned out, ill-fated attempt to forestall the implications of slipping popularity. Under the current dispensation parliamentary elections were conducted on a first-past-the-post basis, with two rounds of voting. Uniquely among European democracies, the system encouraged second thoughts. It was introduced by de Gaulle during the Fifth Republic to keep the Communist Party at the margins of national life, with the additional hope that recalcitrant individualistic French voters could be induced to abandon their hopeless loyalty to small parties. But de Gaulle's efforts to create stability in France had worked rather too well. Nowadays the system favoured parties that either were geographically concentrated or were capable of forming coalitions – and it discriminated against the Front on both counts. At best Le Pen could hope to pick up a handful of seats. He had to hope that enough would be achieved in order to secure the momentum of disaffection on which he depended.

No democracy could boast more than a makeshift set of rules capable of ensuring that a half-representative set of politicians were elected to office. However, Le Pen was right to complain that the system discriminated against him and his followers – for many people that had become its primary function. He could even legitimately depict electoral failure as the triumph of thwarted rectitude over corruption. FN activists believed that French democracy, being rotten, could offer them no satisfaction whatsoever. Among the many, often foolish or contemptible messages delivered by the FN, this was the one I began to take most seriously.

Carefully, I began to stalk Le Pen. You could often catch his good eye and manoeuvre through the dense crowd of journalists. I arranged to collide with him after each meeting, when sweat was drenching his suit. I discovered that he enjoyed aggression and that he was easily flattered. Only the unexpected appeared to cause him problems and, like most politicians, he reacted badly to the notion that his dignity might be on trial. 'I don't disagree,' is how he responded stiffly when I asked him whether his followers didn't come to hear him speak in search of a religious experience. He told me that he understood the French soul through the experience of having addressed so many meetings. When I told him I wasn't sure whether the French soul was full of love or hatred, he didn't reply. Instead, he said that he didn't mind if he was hated or not. Once, surrounded by over twenty cameramen and journalists pushing their microphones forward, I asked him when and how catastrophe would strike. 'I'm not Madame Soleil,' he said, referring to a famous astrologer. It was significant that he told me about the collapse of France in 1940. Look how easily the French state had fallen to pieces under pressure. It would take only the bankruptcy of the Renault car company or a torching of the *banlieue* to bring him to power. Tactlessly, I reminded him that he was now sixty-nine years old. Was he not too old now to benefit from catastrophe? Oh no, he said, recalling Churchill's example. Oh no, it wasn't too late. I noted a flicker of anger and a grimace when I asked him how he would feel if the long-awaited catastrophe never happened, leaving him with a life wasted in the futile pursuit of hatred.

After the floodlights and the ranting, as a crescendo came the 'Marseillaise':

> *Marchons, Marchons! Que le sang impur*
> *Abreuve nos sillons!*

By now, hearing it at each meeting, I hated this refrain, wishing France could find a less uncongenial anthem. Among the people I was with, I noticed signs of fraying. We were, each of us, melancholy; then we became angry. One night it was raining, and we struggled through the crowd carrying bedraggled banners as if returning from a funeral. I remember sitting afterwards at a restaurant table close to tears. 'What's wrong with these people?' I asked. 'What is wrong with France?' I realized that I would have to find out for myself. So I drank too much and, even as I did, regretted it. Over dinner or next morning on the Eurostar, feeling lost, I indulged in the sort of baffled hand-wringing I associated with a younger self. For I had no idea what to do with all this hatred. All I knew at this stage was that it would be folly not to acknowledge that I, too, was touched. There was something I had to do with myself now. At the very least, I told myself, it wouldn't do to remain some sort of caricature of the impartial English journalist.

I tried to put myself in the place of the clean-cut, muscular stewards, dressed in blue sporting blazers. Why were they here? What would they consider to be a 'good' meeting? If I asked such questions, they would smile or nod warily. The journalists shrugged when I asked what it was like to follow Le Pen for months. 'You get used to it,' one cameraman said. 'It's less awful outside Paris because one can eat better.' With stained fingers, wearing a rumpled suit, the man from the left-wing daily *Libération* succinctly explained to me the problems involved in reporting the long march to nowhere of Le Pen. The real problem was that Le Pen had been around long enough to become a part of French political life. He and his ideas had become thoroughly banal, and for that reason alone they were in danger of seeming unexceptionable. This presented a special set of problems to journalists, who didn't know whether they should depict him as unacceptable or acknowledge that, by now, he was indeed there to stay. In French television, reporters were faced with an acute, and probably unresolvable, dilemma. If they gave airtime to Le Pen, they were adding to the vote-getting potential of the Front. If they didn't, like Ann Sinclair, who was Jewish and had been insulted by Le Pen, they were passing over the opportunity to criticize him. Zolaesque rudeness came easily to French journalists, but the tradition of polemic was at its weakest in relation to Le Pen. For it transpired that the frontists wanted to be insulted by journalists – they didn't expect fair coverage, and didn't appreciate it when they got it. Persistently, they reiterated how unfairly they were treated, in particular by television. But the Front were more than capable of outmanoeuvring their adversaries in press or television, using the legal, regulatory framework to complain when they didn't get coverage. And they had been extremely successful. Le Pen himself, in his many TV appearances, showed that it was not so difficult to use the institutions of a democracy in order to increase the quota of hatred.

For years now, I'd seen caricatures of frontists dressed in jackboots and carrying truncheons – depicting Le Pen's uniform, the austere *Le Monde*, wary of colour, even went so far as to use brown and red on its dense front page. Over-familiar, never very witty, these cartoons weren't specially convincing. Was anyone dissuaded from joining or voting for the Front by the news that they might be considered to be a fascist? It didn't appear so. By now Le Pen had become a ready made object of reprobation for the enlightened bourgeoisie. After so many years it was only too easy to identify him as a fascist, and one risked little by so doing.

For the correctly leftish, indeed, 'anti-fascism' was part of the civic religion. Now that the Club Med was totally commercialized, and education had passed into the hands of left-wing lobbies, anti-Front demonstrations stood in for more traditional expressions of Republican solidarity. They also hid what its most intelligent proponents by now acknowledged to be the deficiencies of French socialism. Among ageing *soixante-huitard* French ex-radicals (I loved the self-consciously antiquated adherence to lost causes implied by the tag) my interest in Le Pen was greeted as a strange Anglo-Saxon foible when it wasn't presumed to go, *à l'anglaise*, with a penchant for black leather. But these same people appeared unable to admit to the definitive Frenchness of Le Pen; and they also ruled people like himself out of the Europe they hoped to inhabit. If I suggested that Le Pen, far from merely representing the unpleasant past, appeared to be a portent of the European future, they stared at me without comprehension.

I could appreciate the size of the crowds that gathered in churches to protest against the expulsion of *sans-papiers* and I was touched by the ability of such organizations as Ras-le-Front (Down with the Front) to mobilize young people. But I didn't feel such gestures came near to confronting the Le Pen problem – which was that he alone, crass and dangerous as his ideas might be, represented the only remaining opposition to the orthodoxies of progressive France and Europe. Le Pen was able to express solidarity as well as hatred, and this what I found terrifying about him. Didn't Le Pen feed off the failures of democracy? Didn't he alone represent the accumulated rage of so many of the shut out and lost? Didn't he somehow speak to us, as Europeans as well as French people, of our failings? Such messages, I discovered, were not well-received. After one less than conclusive conversation, held in the sunshine overlooking a quai, I scribbled on a paper tablecloth:

| LE PEN | ANTI-LE PEN |
| --- | --- |
| Identity | Internationalism |
| Nation State | 'Europe' |
| Lost Past | Bland Future |
| Anti-capitalist | Tame Business |
| Anti-elite | Meritocracy |

| Xenophobe | Cosmopolitan |
| Racist | 'Anti-fascist' |
| Moronism | Culture |

The real trouble (and it was now the trouble with France) was that the FN had ultimately found its comfortable *gîte*. This was in part the work of François Mitterrand, arch-cynic and grand master of manipulation. By the mid-1980s, after his unsuccessful attempt to introduce traditional socialist policies, Mitterrand was faced with flagging electoral enthusiasm. He dismantled the unofficial system of censorship which had kept Le Pen from addressing TV audiences. He also fiddled with the electoral rules, introducing proportional representation in national as well as European elections – which allowed the FN to win a number of seats in the National Assembly as well as the European Parliament. As Mitterrand had anticipated, his opponents were faced with an ugly and unresolvable dilemma, which thenceforth dominated French political life. Should they ever appear to ally themselves with the Front? Was it appropriate for a democrat to accept the votes of racists? Never specially energetic, additionally depleted by the effort of dealing with such questions, the so-called 'classic' or old French Right faltered and then declined into near irrelevance. In Germany, as I was learning, any sign of nationalist extremism evoked panic on a national scale. But in France the elite still affected to believe that the effects of Le Pen need not be damaging to democracy. It shouldn't matter that more than 15 per cent of French voters were squandering their votes in a hopeless, racist cause. Rarely alluded to was the fact that, for so many years, the same system had been used to keep out the communists.

I took with me to Le Pen meetings *Le petit dictionnaire pour lutter contre l'Extrême Droite* (*The Little Dictionary of the Extreme Right*), a slender volume from the word processor of Martine Aubry, the daughter of Jacques Delors, and a prominent member of the elite Left. Ms Aubry, it turned out, believed that the revival of nationalist feelings justified the installation of some form of censorship. 'The time has come to abandon the unreal purity of libertarianism or the ultra liberal complacency whereby it is forbidden to forbid,' she suggested.⁴ She prescribed a civic code of correctness involving participants in selected gestures of activism. If a taxi driver or drunk expressed racist sentiments, one must reprove him personally (the offender was presumed to be male) even if this meant stopping the cab and getting out. Citizens should take to the streets and, lest they seem too serious, strive to inject an element of play ('*le ludique*') into their anti-racist protests. As exorcism, I reflected, or as a means of tidying up after Le Pen's ravages, these measures were fine. But they left untouched the problem of what should be done with those for whom race hate was attractive. These were not the sort of people likely to be impressed by the likes of the film-star Emmanuelle Béart shedding Christian Dior make-up to lead another demonstration. I got the feeling that Ms Aubry, like the good schoolteacher cadres who appeared to make up the bulk of the Socialist Party, would rather the people standing in front of me, screaming for Le Pen, didn't exist. Perhaps it was they, rather than the foreigners, who should be sent back to wherever it was they came from.

Those most painfully affected by Le Pen's presence were France's tribe of secular intellectuals. Many of them had spent a great portion of their thinking lives in an effort to efface the stain of collaborationism, only to see a revival of the spirit of Vichy in Le Pen's success. For such people – courageous, not necessarily wealthy, left behind in the corruption of French socialism – the existence of the FN was the real tragedy of their time. Among the bric-a-brac of busy, productive lives, and in the sunshine of Parisian spring weather, I encountered the real measure of Le Pen's destructiveness. In his cramped, book-filled Left Bank apartment, the historian Pierre Vidal-Naquet threw up his hands when I said that I was shocked by the fact that 15 per cent of the French electorate had voted for Le Pen. 'Of course it's awful,' he said. 'The man is either a cynic or a lunatic. He believes the moon is made of green cheese. And his triumph makes nonsense of our belief that man is a rational creature.' Vidal-Naquet had investigated Le Pen's past in Algeria, bringing to light documents that appeared to implicate him in the torture of Arabs, and he had been among the first to identify the anti-Semitism implicit in Le Pen's dismissive remarks about the Holocaust. In his seventies, alert but stooped, he bemoaned the loss of French moral prestige caused by the FN. When I asked what could be done about Le Pen, he smiled. 'Oh, I'd happily kill him,' he said, smiling. 'Or at least abolish him. Abolish unemployment or abolish Le Pen – one or the other. But something has to be done.'

Were the FN really fascists? I recalled the reason I liked to come to France. It wasn't just the food, or the architecture, or being half-French. Despite its failings I really did believe in the universalist tradition of French democracy. Those things which we had learnt to call rights did exist, I was sure of it, and in a half-decent world they should belong to everyone – which was why, every time I came to Paris and had time to spare, I walked to the deconsecrated church known as the Panthéon near the Boulevard St Michel, went down to the musty cellar and stood before the tombs of Voltaire, Rousseau and Zola, inhaling as deeply as I could. This was the only form of religious observance left to my perhaps excessively laicized existence, and it explained my distress in the presence of Le Pen. One evening at the Palais des Sports I became sickened by the procession of candidates, each expressing their aggrieved hatred of foreigners or their slavish loyalty to Le Pen. I let go in front of my colleagues – these people, I said, overcoming many years of perhaps excessive journalistic scruple, *were* fascists. I hated being in their presence. There was really little or nothing to distinguish them from their antecedents. But I felt uneasy after my outburst – as if I, too, had been overcome by the same epidemic of polemical oversimplification which bothered me when I read the French press.

Then I noticed a wide-eyed, forty-year-old activist dressed in a yellow windbreaker by my side, who began to take me to task for my English incomprehension. He was from Corbeil-Essonnes, he said, but he added, speaking impeccable English, that he might have come from 'any fucking *banlieue*'. I wouldn't understand anything, he said, because I didn't have to live 'in the shit, with this *ramassis* of dirty people – a pile of rubbish'. He had nothing to do with the world of Hitler, Mussolini or Pétain, and my strictures were irrelevant to him. I must understand that one could have grounds for hatred. France was ruined by the arrogance of its ruling elite. No one cared about the fate of ordinary people, who lost their jobs to foreigners; and France didn't exist for many French people. 'My life is shit,' he repeated, over and over again.

The Front HQ was located in an old brewery in the suburb of Neuilly, and one could mingle with the party brass, *en famille*. Here were survivors of the Vichy government and their offspring, professors of harmony from the Sorbonne, glint-eyed journalists who had half completed doctorates on such subjects as Auvergnat folk music, and lost-looking families from the aristocratic *seizième*. Sometimes, the conversations came straight from a *Tintin* album. I once found myself discussing the role of physical education in modern life. To an animated seventysomething wearing a twinset and pearls I was obliged to explain that I had no views about the validity of the traditionalist mass.

Among the many unfortunate notions sponsored in Marshal Pétain's time was the obnoxious *francité* – the idea that an immortal France existed independently of the contemporary world. Pétain and his people wished to eliminate the idea that France was defined by laws embodying liberty and equality. They proposed their own version of a cultural revolution – by excluding Jews and other enemies, by diminishing or even abolishing democracy. During the 1940s, many traditional French symbols, ranging from the humble beret to the fleur-de-lys, were used to convince people of the desirability of the past. The family was exalted as a measure of social coherence and the paraphernalia of traditional Catholicism made a comeback. The young French, when they weren't being encouraged to get themselves killed on the Eastern Front in German uniform or packed off to Germany as *gastarbeiter*, providing fodder for the war effort, were sent on endless, character-building *randonnées* in remote mountain ranges. These ideas had been used to hide from French people the reality of German occupation, and they disappeared from sight after 1945. But they had recently made a second comeback, and they were present, bizarrely, in this room.

It was 1968 that appeared to offend these people most of all. This was apparently the moment when authority disappeared in a trail of anarchic slogans during the revolt that brought France to a standstill. In America and Britain the 1960s were these days remembered mostly for the burning of bras, but in France the year of revolution spelt for these militants a radical break between the traditionalist past and a modernity composed in equal parts of dogmatic arrogance and socialism. Intellectuals of the FN hated their counterparts of 1968, who had taken to the streets and were now rewarded by posh jobs in the media. In opposition to what was perceived as this New Class, the FN, like other right-wing parties, set their own distinctive version of family values. 'I like my daughters better than my cousins, my cousins better than my neighbours, my neighbours better than strangers, and strangers better than enemies,' ran Le Pen's slogan. For its members, the FN was above all a large family. It looked after its own passionately and diligently. To listen to so many propagandists one might assume it was the only true French family left.

Le Pen's second wife Janny was here, dressed in a sleek black suit, so were two of his jut-jawed, handsome daughters. (In the best family tradition of the FN, another daughter had stood as candidate and she awaited the results in her *circonscription*.) As the evening went by, Le Pen came and went, giving interviews or addressing cameras for the benefit of the studio shows on each channel. As the results began to come in, however, I noticed first a fraying of tempers, and then (it was a pronounced FN trait) the waning of optimism, followed by the re-occupation of old positions defined by resignation or cynicism. Early in the evening, the party appeared to be over. To be sure, the Front vote had held up at around 15 per cent, but it was clear, too, that appeals to shift votes away from the old right-wing parties had not been successful. Once again, the FN had ensured a victory for the Left at the expense of the old Right. But it had not benefited from the debacle.

I watched Le Pen stand on a small dais talking to a TV camera. Of course, he claimed that everyone had lost, most of all the French people, but he didn't even convince himself. From the middle of a dense crowd of reporters I suggested he should step down or, alternatively, accept that his own function in France was that of a jester or *provocateur*. And I wondered how much he really knew about France, and whether French people, whatever he liked to say, weren't ultimately hostile to his extremism. For a moment, I thought he might lash out in my direction, but he didn't. Instead he treated me with weary familiarity, as if the exchange had been part of an argument between us lasting half a lifetime. '*Monsieur*, I do know my France,' he said with mock courtesy. 'And after forty years of struggling I have got to this. Do you really call this a failed career?'

To be sure, judged by the most conventional criteria, Le Pen was a failure; and he would certainly never exercise power in a government. However, as the months went by, and I went around Europe, it occurred to me that things were more complicated than I had anticipated. The existence of the European Far Right, which Le Pen had done much to create, didn't depend on such minimalist equations of power and influence. These days, politics in Europe consisted in part of abrupt shifts of mood or sudden reversals. A politician could gain power, like the ex-crooner Silvio Berlusconi, and vanish. Or it was possible to enjoy the outward forms of power year after year without achieving anything – this appeared to be the fate awaiting the affable but ineffectual President Chirac. So it followed, too, that, like Le Pen, one could fail, and through repeated failure bequeath a tradition of mistrust, both of parliamentary institutions and of the idea of democracy itself. In this horrifying respect his failure must indeed begin to count as something like success.

There were many books about Le Pen,[5] testifying to the strength of the French obsession with his long and eventful life, but few of them touched on the degree to which he could be seen as an exemplary character, the sort of figure who graced the pages of French novels before they came to resemble plumbing manuals and ceased to be read. Re-translated into the nineteenth century, where it perhaps properly belonged, placed in ruthless order, Le Pen's life consisted of a number of startling episodes that would have delighted Hugo, Balzac, de Maupassant or even Alexandre Dumas. As I set these down, it often occurred to me what a hammily satisfying epic, transferred to the screen, Le Pen's life would make – perhaps played by an ageing Gerard Depardieu.

*The Fabulist.* Le Pen was born in 1928 at the edge of France, in the Breton fishing village of La Trinité sur Mer. He was an outsize, demanding baby. In 1942 his father's boat was blown up by a German or British mine. Although the death was descibed as a simple accident, the young Le Pen was given the privileges due to those whose parents had died in combat. For years thereafter he lobbied to get his father's name carved on the war memorial, and he continued to depict himself as owing a special debt as a consequence of being an orphan of the state. So was born, out of a small lie, the idea, ceaselessly canvassed by the Front, that Le Pen had some special claim on Frenchness. But Le Pen was less successful in his efforts to convince people that he had taken part in the battle between retreating German troops and the Resistance; or that, given the assignment of transporting German shells, he had pitched them into the water. Did anyone care whether he told the truth or not?

*The Soldier.* Le Pen's adolescent acts of heroism consisted of breaking other student heads. But France was fighting the Algerian war, and he was quick to sign up. He arrived in Saigon too late for the humiliating defeat – it was among the worst in France's history – inflicted by the Viet Minh on

French troops at Dien Bien Phu. 'I missed the last *métro*,' he told biographers. In Saigon, Le Pen behaved like the sort of adventurer described in Graham Greene's *The Quiet American*. He acquired the illusion (it would later be shared by many of his contemporaries, becoming a motif of his movement) that he possessed some special insight into the destiny of so-called native peoples. Back in Paris, the 27-year-old veteran sported his veteran's green beret, warming to themes of glory and betrayal.

*The Tribune.* The lost France which he came to represent was forming before his eyes. For it was in these years that the great French move away from the land and to new cities began. The old activities of *commerçant* or small farmer no longer afforded much of a livelihood or, just as important, conferred status any more. A new class of state administrators presided over the crash modernization of France, herding its reluctant citizens into the *banlieues* or the new *grandes surfaces* – the supermarkets that were destroying peasant livelihoods. Mostly forgotten these days is the brief, unsuccessful revolt known as Poujadisme after its founder Pierre Poujade. Taking members from every party, Poujadisme appeared briefly to be about to supersede the existing parties. Like the FN thirty years later, Poujadisme blamed France's contemporary ills on a combination of foreigners and capitalism. In French terms, where such distinctions still carried weight, the Poujadists were xenophobic rather than racist – they appreciated the loyalty of France's dark-skinned citizens (still part of the Empire) while viewing with opprobrium what they regarded as the predatory activities of the Parisian Jewish *grande bourgeoisie*. Poujade bequeathed to Le Pen a florid rhetorical style and the conviction that protest politics, practised far away from Paris, could prove of determining influence in the fate of the French nation. He knew how to whip up large crowds by the simple exploitation of disgruntlement. When Poujade's movement gained 9 per cent of the vote, Le Pen became the youngest parliamentary deputy in France. But there were differences between the two men. Poujade, who was a milder man than Le Pen, believed that the real function of his movement was to return France to its agrarian petit-bourgeois past. He didn't want to take sides on such great issues of the day as Soviet communism, and he didn't want to be involved in the debate over the fate of Great Power France. He was happiest denouncing the Jewish Prime Minister Pierre Mendès-France for drinking milk at a diplomatic reception, thus betraying the interests of wine-growing *France profonde*.

*The Torturer's Apprentice.* Le Pen believed that a great betrayal was taking place in Algeria. In the Assembly he spoke up for Empire, attacking the perpetrators of terrorism without offering the smallest prospect of reforms to alleviate the lot of Algerians – and in 1956 he finally quit Poujade's movement to rejoin the French army as a paratroop officer. Perhaps Le Pen, without knowing it, had been looking for the final, humiliating act in France's colonial history. If so, he was lucky. He served during the ill-fated Suez expedition, when France and Britain were forced by America to abandon their punitive mission against Nasser. Then he was posted to Algiers itself, where he scoured the streets for terrorist suspects under the authority of the notorious Colonel Massu. Many allegations were made to the effect that Le Pen had tortured or been present when suspects were submerged in filled baths and electrocuted. Le Pen always insisted that there was nothing wrong with torture, in circumstances where it could be justified, and that the use of such methods in Algiers had been very effective in combating terrorism. However, he insisted that he had not himself been a torturer

– all he had done was warn Algerians, not of their rights (for they had none) but of what would happen if they persisted, and what future awaited them if they resolved to abandon violence, confess their ways, and inform on their comrades. Le Pen was always proud to have served in the company of real torturers. He made it clear that he would have become a torturer if he had been asked, and circumstances had been right.

The Anti-racist. The white French settlers insisted that they would govern on behalf of the entire population – Arab as well as ethnic French – and they called their political movement Algérie Française. Like them, Le Pen took the idea of a French Algeria seriously. However, it appears that he also really did believe that, given time and opportunity, it would be possible for Algerians to become 'integrated', acquiring the rights and obligations of French citizens. This hope – it was never grounded in reality, because so many Algerians did not wish to be part of France – lay behind his belief that the nationalist FLN should be fought by any means. But it also explained his unyielding hostility to those who could see that the great colonial adventure was finished. In his view, they were traitors who had betrayed the most fundamental values of France. Algeria was the defining lost cause for Le Pen. He became identified with the most extreme attacks on the Republic, in and out of Parliament, leading processions of veterans through the streets of Paris. When the clandestine OAS was formed, with a policy of assassinating French politicians prepared to abandon Algeria, Le Pen offered it some support. Just before the final exit from Algiers, he made a speech in which he suggested that the French army should take matters into its own hands, and 'liberate' France.

The Exile. Like his arch-enemy de Gaulle, Le Pen experienced many years in which his talents were neglected and his availability to the Republic ignored. He made a living by reissuing, and sometimes pirating, military music (he was fined for over-enthusiastic sleeve notes praising the tunes of National Socialism). But so much isolation left him embittered. Bored, he even returned to university at the age of forty in order to complete the equivalent of a Master's degree, writing a thesis on the subject of the tradition of French anarchism.

'1968 was nausea,' Le Pen wrote in his autobiography. 'It was a gesture of despair . . .' Once again the authentic Right had failed, and was left on the margins of life. But 1968 also saved Le Pen, for it was shortly afterwards that he was approached by the far-right student militants of the Left Bank. They felt outperformed by the various Maoist or Trotskyist *groupuscules* of the Left – and they were looking for someone capable of bringing them together. Flattered, Le Pen agreed, and in 1971 the Front National was formed.

*The Revolutionary.* Among analysts the current long French crisis is thought to originate in the 1970s, but the phenomenon is hard to account for. France is not the only European country to have experienced rapid transformation, becoming urbanized, or to have accumulated a sizeable proportion of the population confused by sudden change. Other European countries experienced a slowing down of growth or saw their institutions called into question after terrorist attacks. Still others saw their welfare systems altered out of recognition or destroyed without a comparable malaise. But in France, perhaps because the crisis lasted longer or did not seem capable of resolution, it assumed different, perhaps more deeply menacing, configurations. Neither the application of socialist policies, nor neo-liberal ones, nor finally the 'Europeanism' of the governing classes appeared to be a remedy. Abandoned by other parties, many voters came to believe in Le Pen. 'I am like you,' he would tell them in speech after speech. 'There is no difference between us.' But what was the real relation between Le Pen and his supporters? The polls revealed that not everyone who voted for the FN liked or trusted him – except on the matter of immigration, where, it seemed, there was a genuine identity of vision based on fear. Over the years, the FN gained ground among the new disenfranchised – disgruntled former voters from the Socialist Party and even the communists. Le Pen also proved attractive to the young and poorly educated. Young men in particular found something in his postures of revolt and his violence. Many said they would be attracted to his ideas if it wasn't for his personality. Many also said they would vote for him although there was no chance of his ever coming to power. These attitudes persisted, year after year.

*The Statesman.* At a moment when dullness appeared to be the principal quality required of European politicians, he began to look like a real leader. Le Pen liked to imply that he had lost an eye brawling with his enemies (weak eyesight was the real culprit), but he now traded in his Moshe Dayan patch, replacing it with a glass eye of which a spare was carried by his loyal wife Pierrette. The Le Pens had lived a frugal life, but they began to mix with the *haute bourgeoisie.* Le Pen became friends with the ailing heir to the Lambert industrialist dynasty, visiting him at the family home at St Cloud and taking him to the horror films he liked. With the assent of his mother, Hubert Lambert changed his will, making Le Pen his sole legatee. The dispossessed Lambert relatives sued Le Pen, claiming that the dying man had not been in possession of his faculties. A long moment out of Balzac ensued when the Le Pens found themselves sharing the family seat with those who had sued, bumping into them in the marble lobby. Finally, Le Pen settled with the Lamberts, and the orphaned fisherman's son and college dropout acquired a fortune of close to £20 million, some of it conveniently secreted in a bogus foundation created by the Lambert family in Switzerland.[6]

*The Majestic Cuckold.* Le Pen was hampered in his drive to respectability by an ugly scandal. In 1982, his wife Pierrette, tiring of her husband's loud mouth and interminable absences, went to live with her husband's ghostwriter. It transpired that Le Pen had kept her at home against her wishes and he now denied her any part of his recent inheritance. Le Pen was outraged by Pierrette's defection, and his conduct during the divorce was vindictive – the Le Pen daughters signed a public letter in which they accused their mother of dishonouring the family name. In another bathetic event, enlivening a dreary moment in French public life, the exasperated Pierrette Le Pen posed for the French edition of *Playboy*, wearing an apron and carrying a feather duster. If her ex-husband wanted her to work, she said, she was prepared to do so. 'She dared to do that!' Le Pen said admiringly when he was shown the pictures.

*The Sublime Hooligan.* The great French novelists would have wondered what made Le Pen run. To a degree I hadn't encountered yet among politicians, he posed the question of why people wasted their lives in search of power that never came to them. What had he ever really wanted to achieve? Was it enough, to enjoy the pleasures of prominence, merely to wish to spoil the country that one claimed to wish to save? Amid busts of Napoleon and family photos in a small suburban villa near Cannes, I sat down in the small study of Colonel Jean-Jacques Girardet. Tall, with his greying hair cut *en brosse*, the Colonel was a not unsympathetic figure, the sort of man you might expect to be mayor of a small French town or village. In his long career as a soldier and a police-man, it had not been his lot either to organize or perform acts of torture. Instead he had supervised the Garde Républi-caine in their daily duties at the Elysée Palace. However, on retirement Girardet joined the Front and managed Le Pen's security arrangements. Recently he had fallen out with Le Pen, and only three months previously he had received a curt letter of dismissal. Girardet had said that Le Pen was unreli-able, and that he shouldn't be leading the party. I wanted to know what had caused him to change his mind – surely Le Pen hadn't changed at all. All Girardet could say was that he had enjoyed Le Pen's outrages because it had been possible not to take them wholly seriously. He told me a story about a visit of Le Pen's to Guadeloupe, where the presence of so many (mainly black) demonstrators made it impossible for him and his cronies to get out of the plane. 'They were happy to fly home,' he said. 'Air France was giving free champagne. And that, ultimately, was Le Pen – free champagne and racist jokes.' Was that all Le Pen was about? The Colonel looked at me and nodded.

*The Ultimate Nihilist.* Those looking for a modern anti-hero could also find one here. On 13 September 1987 Le Pen appeared during an electoral campaign on an RTL radio show. Asked about Holocaust denial, he replied thus:

> I have a passionate interest in the history of World War Two. I don't say that the gas chambers never existed. I ask myself questions. I haven't seen any of them. I haven't devoted any special energy to studying the question. But I feel it's a detail in the history of World War Two . . . Do you want me to say that [the existence of gas chambers] is a revealed truth in which everyone must believe? I tell you that historians are still debating these matters.[7]

The word 'detail' in French was ambiguous but Le Pen's voice made it clear in what sense it was used. '*Un détail . . .*': he wanted to imply summary indifference to the question of whether anyone had been gassed or not. His cynicism was accomplished – breathtakingly so. Le Pen gave me reason to find the words for what I hated in him. Over the years, it seemed that political rhetoric had ceased to reveal, or indeed even to conceal, ideas. Spin doctors had appeared to render political speech more accessible, but they had increased the blandness. If there was a crisis in contemporary politics its origins lay in the progressive decay of political speech, and the likelihood that henceforth politics might tell us nothing about ourselves or our destiny. Meanwhile a politician like Le Pen could, through his revolt against the rules of the game, depict himself as an honest man. You might not agree with him, he was saying, but you could at least acknowledge that he believed what he said. And yet Le Pen's real message was somewhat different. He was telling people that it didn't really matter. You could believe whatever you wanted to about gas chambers, just as you might feel free to entertain the thought that blacks were inferior or that the moon was indeed made of cheese. The truth was that nothing mattered very much.

*The Enemy.* I now wondered whether and how the Le Pen and the FN were indeed different to the rest of us. I concluded that it had to do with the fact that they, almost alone among Europeans, still believed in the transforming power of politics. Most of the rest of us spent our lives in search of pleasurable experiences. The FN loved pamphlets and public meetings with a passion I associated with old-style communists. But unlike the latter, who believed in the certainty of success, the Front's political religion revolved around failure. They themselves usually failed – and they wanted or needed things to become worse so they could come to power. But they, and certainly Le Pen, understood that this was never going to happen. If conflict animated the Front, it often took place between themselves. The frontists were like members of a strange tribe who periodically left their own territory in order to slay enemies only to return to the real business of destroying themselves. They knew they would never get anywhere; but they persisted nonetheless. Meanwhile, as Le Pen realized, they were capable of doing much damage to us all.

It was drizzling at Charles de Gaulle airport and there was a strike of *pompiers*, delaying my plane. The papers were full of outraged accounts of the exhumation of Yves Montand, whose remains were to be sampled for a posthumous paternity suit. The latest scandal consisted of the gift to a socialist politician from his mistress (a lobbyist working for the publicly owned oil company Elf) of a 12,000 franc pair of loafers. In the south, a cold Mistral wind was blowing, bringing earache and a sharp, pinched feeling around the nostrils. As I drove along the *Autoroute du Soleil*, vestiges of frustration and anger returned to me and I realized that I had come back to the Front.

For tourists, and indeed most French people, Provence spelt out the memory of holidays to which a postcard of Cézanne was affixed. It was the pretext for films cannily revisiting the heritage folksiness of Marcel Pagnol and starring Gerard Depardieu, or narcissistic books (they were usually written by expatriate English) attesting to the surviving quaintness of the French way of life. But Provence had been the object of much misguided governmental social engineering. Starting in the sixties and seventies, the olive groves were cut down. Around *zones industrielles*, new towns were created in a gimcrack architectural style familiar to anyone who had endured the canned music and totalitarian accommodation of cut-rate French motorway hotels. Designed for driving through without pausing, the landscape, like the celebrated light of Provence, had thinned; and one could catch sight of the polluted sea only fitfully, through facades or pylons, beyond the occasional moribund palm tree.

I parked at the edge of Vitrolles and walked around. There were pinkish, grubby blocks in every direction; this was a style of building that, but for its dinkiness, would have seemed more appropriate in Odessa or Brno. In 1983 the population of Vitrolles was 20,000; but now it had climbed to 40,000, with 40 per cent under the age of twenty-five, many of them Arabs. Unemployment was more than twice the national average. The town was empty, and I walked past half-empty shopping centres to the Sous Marin nightclub, sole multicultural meeting place of the town, recently deprived of funds and shut down. I paused just outside the *mairie*. Here the local Ras-le-Front activists unfurled for me a large poster depicting a blue-eyed baby and its equally blue-eyed mother. 'Welcome! A bonus: 5,000 francs for French families,' the poster read. In Vitrolles the *mairie* was offering money to those who were able to establish that their babies were authentically French, and not 'foreign'. The programme had caused much anger, and at least one of its beneficiaries had returned the money.[8] However, the mayoress was at pains to recount that, appearances to the contrary, the programme was not racist. All they wanted to do was redress the balance in favour of those who were French.

Bruno Mégret had won Vitrolles for the FN, but he was obliged to place the town in his wife's hands after an investigation revealed a number of campaign irregularities. This gesture to French babies was part of the FN policy organized

by Mégret and known euphemistically as National Preference. It was anticipated that the best houses, jobs, social
services, education, would go to French citizens. Private
companies would likewise be encouraged by law to employ
French people rather than foreigners. In the meantime, the
records of recent arrivals would be re-examined – with a
view to reclaiming their precious passports where this was
deemed appropriate or possible. This was a measure which
had its precedent in the behaviour of Marshal Pétain and his
government, who in July 1940, merely twelve days after
coming to power and way before any German pressure on
the matter was even thought of, passed legislation removing
citizenship from those (they were mainly Jewish) who had
become French in the past decade.[9] Mégret's initiatives, it
was clear, were more ambitious than Pétain's and better
thought out. With the stress placed on second-class citizenship, they amounted to nothing less than the desire to impose
a form of apartheid in France.

Among FN militants, Bruno Mégret had the reputation of
a *dur*, a hard man – they meant that he was serious when he
talked about his extreme policies – and they would contrast
him, often admiringly, with Le Pen, who was all hot air. At
the same time it was evident that he wasn't really one of
them. For Mégret came from a middle-ranking (these distinctions were still important in France) bourgeois *fonctionnaire*
family. He was a *polytechnicien* – a graduate of the most
posh engineering school – and although the frontists were
proud that someone so well educated had strayed into their
midst, they mistrusted so much conspicuous excellence. The
problem was that, unlike Le Pen, Mégret was not an imposing man, bearing a close resemblance to Mr Bean. It was easy
to lose him among crowds or to forget his presence on a dais.
Next to his colourfully dressed wife Catherine, who was the

granddaughter of Russian Jewish immigrants, or the thugs who usually surrounded him, he seemed nearly invisible.

In contrast to his mentor, Mégret acknowledged that the Front, in order to get to power, would sooner or later be obliged to do a deal with the so-called 'respectable' Right. This would happen, not because the views of the FN had become acceptable, but because there was no choice. He was at once a caricature of respectability and, in European terms, a wholly new phenomenon. Around him, even more than in Le Pen's proximity, I sensed the force of malignity. It was nearly impossible to catch him out, almost as difficult as it was to get him to smile; and one was meant never to be able to imagine him telling an off-colour racist joke. Years spent designing motorway exits had taught him the value of adroitly managed evasion. He had organized Le Pen's campaigns brilliantly, and he was the author of most of the FN's policy documents. Of course, France's posh schools turned out many Mégrets each year, and they staffed every ministry and most private companies. Their chilly absent demeanour indicated that, within their own definitions of reason, they would be capable of anything; that was the impression such people were trained to convey. But Mégret had left this closed world behind, casting his lot with people who were at best unreliable. He represented the new revolt of the 1990s.

Mégret canvassed in a natty green loden topcoat, which made him look like a middle-ranking employee of a Swiss bank. It was bright and cold, and the Mistral made me cough ceaselessly. We went to instant towns dumped on the edge of marshes where vast refineries had been erected. We shivered outside *mairies* while Mégret performed his methodical round. In cafes I noticed that he wasn't afraid to talk to Arabs, so long as they were vetted by the group of advance men accompanying us. We stopped in smoky cafe after cafe, and Mégret sniffed fastidiously. Each time I came close to contact it was as if a sheet of clean plate glass came down between us.

Mégret had spent a year studying in California.[10] He told me that America was decadent – the usual qualifying adjective to the effect that, yes, the place was also vital, was absent. Of course, he said primly, it was up to Americans to decide what they thought of Michael Jackson, but these things were not for France. Acquaintance with posh dining clubs over the years – he was a member of the Club de l'Horloge, where businessmen and *fonctionnaires* gathered to debate their bureaucratic versions of the unthinkable – had, he told me, convinced him that the problems of foreigners could not be resolved. There must be a new approach to the problem, voluntary if possible, but involving expulsion, too. He was not himself a racist, though he did acknowledge that there were racists among the FN. All he believed was that the foreigners were different. Primly, he expressed the view that such differences were best expressed elsewhere, but not in France. To say that he was power-obsessed was perhaps accurate but it didn't explain much. When I looked at him I saw the Richard Nixon of *Six Crises*, a man who would court any form of humiliation in quest of power because he had no private identity; or Clerici, the repressed, hyper-respectable and half-buried hero of Alberto Moravia's novel *The Conformist*. I wondered whether Mégret wasn't a man whom unacknowledged passions – the swirling clouds of anarchic feelings emanating from his most loathed decade, the 1960s – had pushed towards a shut-off singleness of vision. Perhaps he carried a device that punished him for each indiscretion, or indeed had come to regard my own presence as equivalent chastisement.

Among low-grade *fascisants* of the 1990s, I'd heard views

like his expressed many times. But Mégret performed the number more than adequately – he might have attended any Paris dinner party without (as his mentor Jean-Marie would surely have done) disgracing himself. However, it occurred to me that one could have made a similar observation about Vichy civil servants like René Bousquet or Paul Touvier. They, too, believed in the cultivation of order as a substitute for the messiness of democracy; and they also considered themselves to be humane. They were as good at attending dinner parties as they were at rationalizing the dispatch of *sans-papiers*, and later French-born Jews, to their deaths.

I realized that Mégret and I had begun to hate each other when he called me an Anglo-Saxon. I was the sort of person who let the rot into his tidy constructs, and he must feel that I would end by washing away France in a tide of ill-considered liberalism. But I felt that the flaw in his arguments was that neither France nor French culture was homogeneous any longer. The separation of authentically French from half- or non-French, if it was ever attempted, would be violent and protracted. Mégret talked as if it could be achieved peacefully, without destroying the idea of individual rights. This was impossible – a National Front France would need to tear up the Constitution and charter every spare plane in Europe. Like most frontists, Mégret detested the EU. In his case this was not primarily for sentimental reasons or because he was attached to the past, another way in which he differed from Le Pen, but because it would be impossible for France to remain part of a civilized Europe while implementing his programme of apartheid. And Mégret, I was certain by now, was intelligent enough to realize this.

We were in the Marseille flower market when I reminded him that he planned to impose a code on journalists. They would no longer have the right to 'undermine, by provocation or derision, the values of [the] nation'.[11] I pointed out that, Anglo-Saxon or not, I certainly wouldn't share his view of what constituted French values. Did this mean that I, too, would be silenced? His smile was thin and awkward, and I noticed that he tried to hide the rodent teeth. 'I suspect that, like most journalists, you suffer from moral laxism,' he said, attempting a joke. I pestered until he became uncomfortable. Recently, Mégret had been one of the few frontists prepared to defend two billsticking activists accused of killing an immigrant. I understood that he really was without shame. Laxism, he finally told me with the closest I had seen to passion, wasn't the same thing as freedom. It meant letting the thugs who attacked old ladies go free. 'That's what laxism is,' he said to me.

It seemed that in 1968 Mégret had tried to get his *lycée* class to pass a resolution condemning the upheavals. As a student in Paris and America, he had hung around the edges of pot-smoking contemporaries, and he was remembered as a prim, over-earnest youth. The first blonde to be seen on his arm was his wife, and he had met her late, at the age of forty-one. What, exactly, did he find so horrifying about the contemporary world? What was so awful about multiculturalism? We passed some Benetton posters featuring a black nude and I asked him what he thought of them. What would be the fate of Benetton in the France of the Front? 'Oh, they'd be forbidden,' he said quickly. He smiled again, lowering the glass between us, so that the many flowers around us suddenly seemed made of plastic. 'But only in public. In private, people would be allowed to do what they wanted with them.' No sooner had he said this than a cab driver got out of his car and barged between us. He didn't realize who I was, and he began to reassure Mégret: it was all right here, and he should feel at home; no Arabs were allowed here; if they came their heads would be broken. I watched Mégret nudge the man, silencing him. Not a flicker of embarrassment was to be read on his face.

Leaving Mégret, I walked through the market. There were astonishing colours everywhere, and I felt as if a missing, under-appreciated faculty – perhaps the ability to combine the sense of mid- or wide-focus with that of smell – had suddenly been restored to me. Looking around the market of Marseille, I was perplexed. There were Arab stallholders among the French. For centuries Marseille had been the recipient of immigration from all over the Mediterranean. One might assume that here, above all, the existence of a European melting-pot might be acknowledged. And yet I knew, too, that more than 25 per cent of Marseillais, most of them former communists and socialists, voted for the Front. By now they must know exactly what as well as who they were voting for. Indeed demographic studies demonstrated that they knew only too well. In a 1993 poll not a single Front voter agreed with the proposition that France, by reason of its tradition, should be considered a place where those persecuted in their countries might find refuge.[12] Over 85 per cent of the same sample expressed hostility to Arabs, 58 per cent towards gypsies and 49 per cent towards homosexuals.

I bought the newspapers and flipped through the commemorations of 1968, reflecting how remote the preoccupations of Parisian commentators seemed from this perspective. But I remembered an experience of my own from those days. On the advice of a friend I had gone to a small Left Bank cinema where, for four and a half hours, I sat before a series of grey images interspersed with interviews. Marcel Ophuls' film *The Sorrow and the Pity* had been banned by the anxious bureaucrats who presided over French television in those days. It recounted the real story of collaboration: the degree to which so-called 'ordinary Frenchmen' went along with the views of the authorities. Sometimes, the film implied, the occupiers' zeal had been exceeded by that of policemen, professional informers, or those merely eager (and there were indeed many of them) to be helpful.

In those days, as a consequence of the official myth of the Resistance[13] propagated by de Gaulle, the idea that French men and women had collaborated was a fresh one – and since then many books had appeared each year recounting in increasing, first humiliating and then tedious, detail, how this had been accomplished. But I now viewed Vichy in a somewhat different light. For the anger experienced by French people in 1940, I now understood, wasn't solely a consequence of defeat. Most French people had viewed the regime of Marshal Pétain as an opportunity to be left alone – they would be able to escape the Germans, through the pursuit of neutrality, no matter how absurd that notion might seem in 1940, but they would also, finally, be able to do without the foreigners who had infested France. Most important, they would finally do without Jews. Now what was striking about the film was the degree to which it demonstrated that for many being French had always been inseparable from the idea that one must refuse the presence of others. Many of its participants sounded very like the people I'd been interviewing. Over the years I'd hoped the old France of Vichy would somehow be extinguished. But now I felt less certain that the old France of hatred and bad toilets could be put to one side.

Two months later, I drove once again along the ugly scarred strip of Southern Provence. Toulon was the largest city of the Front, and the one that had been longest in their hands, but as a port, formerly the arsenal and principal base of the French Navy, it was also a place that spelt out, in its own history, the extent of French decline. Toulon was about as appealing as a used condom, and its godforsakenness was truly apparent in the sliver of building works connecting the *mairie*, the port and the street where the hookers' bars were clustered for the benefit of sailors whose ships no longer docked. Here one could stroll through empty, foul streets, past bars called the Caravelle or the Nevada, crossing the evil-smelling four-lane highway to the half-abandoned port where empty souvenir shops sold ashtrays and cushions for loved pets in the shape of pom-pom hats.

On my first day in Toulon I took a boat trip around the *rade* from which Napoleon departed in 1799 for his defeat in Egypt and at the edge of which the Vichy-supporting admirals of the French fleet sunk their ships in 1941 to avoid their falling into British hands. The catamaran loaded with pensioners went slowly past dismantled hulks of Empire: aircraft carriers like the *Foch* and the *Clemenceau*, cruisers, destroyers, boats for carrying troops, barques for wine and hookers. A grey, oily sky pressed against piles of rusting metal and weeds. Here the hopelessness of much of the French past was apparent. Whatever had been its absurd pretensions to civilize the world, defeat was the real motif of the French Empire, both its raison d'être and, as Le Pen had realized, its ultimate destination. A cheery young guide in white shorts explained to me that French ships were now serviced in Croatia because it was cheaper. When I asked what could be done for the city, he shrugged. 'They say they try,' he remarked of the local politicians, meaning that it appeared they did not.

Toulon was a biggish city, with the tradition of corruption shared with more fortunate places like Marseille or Nice. Because of the Navy, it had once belonged to the Gaullists, but successive mayors were caught with their hands in the till,[14] and the city passed to the FN. Jean-Marie Le Chevallier, the mayor, was, unlike Bruno Mégret, the image of quiet emollience. Provençal-style, he offered the policies of the Front without ideological pain, and to this end he always appeared in public with his wife Cendrine, a mother of three and an ardent Catholic whose gaffes were the cause of jokes among local reporters. But the '*pépère et mémère*' style of the Le Chevalliers was resented by many people. As anyone might see, the town had not prospered in the past years. All the mayor had done, it seemed, was hire a few extra police-men and shut down the local avant-garde cultural centre, putting up instead an ugly statue of Raimu, the Toulonnais star of Pagnol's films. Disaster had struck when the Le Chevalliers interfered with the local book fair, trying to make it more representative of frontist authors, with the result that most serious publishers withdrew their sponsorship. In last year's elections, the mayor had won the only parliamentary seat for the FN, but (this was becoming a tradition among the FN) he was disqualified. Now, in what was another FN tradition, his wife Cendrine was standing in his stead; and reporters had come from all over Europe to see the fun.

The first night I witnessed a near-fight between counting officials, an ex-admiral from the Front and a socialist retired schoolteacher. A similar acrimony was evident in the blank green room of the *mairie*, where the votes were announced. Civic traditions of order notwithstanding, one had only to ask the simplest question to be surrounded by an angry crowd. The frontists were loathed by the rest of the Right, who felt that Toulon had been stolen from them; and the emotion was amply reciprocated. But Cendrine polled adequately on a low turnout, and now she was pitted against the socialist candidate, the flamboyantly named but colour-less Odette Casanova.

I accompanied Cendrine to pet shops, thalassotherapy centres and *foyers* for old people. I watched her kiss babies and gamely dance the tango with toupéed old roués on stiff legs. Cendrine looked as if she might, long ago, have wished to play Joan of Arc or even Eva Perón in a school pageant. My favourite outfit of hers was a stab at a miniskirt in the shape of a toga, with the words 'irony, eclecticism, style' mysteriously inscribed along the hem. I asked her what this meant, but she wouldn't say. Cendrine's squeaky voice, her cold handshake and her stiff, declamatory manner made her ill-equipped to canvas, but she was game, and livelier than her anodyne husband. She told us that she represented not just the FN, but all right-wing voters. The Front, she declared, was moderate, not extreme. When we told her that this was not the view of the other defeated candidates, who had not told their voters to side with the Front, she repeated what she had just said. Like Perón in the company of Evita, Jean-Marie hovered solicitously behind her, scented handkerchief in his right hand, in search of gaffes.

But why were we here? Was Toulon really important in the story of the FN? We picked out a restaurant owned by a conspicuous anti-fascist, a Rugby coach, where my colleagues were poisoned by bad seafood. I was luckier – or perhaps by now immune. Each evening the reporters gathered at the port cafes to swap notes. I enjoyed the company of the unsuccessful centre-right candidate, a civilized local doctor in his thirties who liked good red wine and had a sense of humour. 'They're terrible,' he said. 'Don't be deceived by the notion that they are moderate. These people are an utter disgrace.' I asked how important Toulon was. The man from the very conservative *Figaro*, a white-haired *bon vivant* veteran of the Falklands war and many African conflicts, who still used a manual typewriter, shrugged. 'The little people vote for characters like the Le Chevalliers,' he said. 'But there are many little people in France.' Toulon was, appearances notwithstanding, important. If the catastrophe hoped for by Le Pen ever happened, it would be through such places. It didn't matter that the Le Chevalliers were ridiculous so long as they won elections. It didn't matter how old-fashioned appeared to be the language or the methods of the FN, so long as they commanded loyalty.

And the Le Chevalliers had been able to build what appeared to be a real political machine. One could meet the stupidest, most gross racists within their entourage but there were also highly intelligent people. None of them conformed to the image of Provençal jollity so earnestly commended by the boring mayor. The following night I went to the offices of *Jeunesse Toulonnaise*. Here were banners, photocopying machines, posters. The members of *Jeunesse* were clean cut, hair *en brosse*. Because they resembled the arrogant provincial young I had known as a pre-1960s child, playing indifferent tennis at various French seaside towns, I was drawn to them. But they proved just as hard in their opinions as anyone I had met in the Front. They, too, believed that French salvation lay in sending foreigners home and reconstituting France. I hated their pretentious magazine, with its foolish attempts to restore the reputations of anti-Semitic gurus from the 1890s. I loathed their immodest evocation of the war dead of France in the name of opposition to the European future. I despised what appeared to be their wilful ignorance, and the way in which much of what they said might have been lifted from the speeches of Le Pen and Mégret. I suppose I also resented and hated the fact that young and intelligent people should be thus wasting their time. Still, because they were intelligent, I couldn't bring myself wholly to walk away from the long shouting match between us. Although they told me that they didn't belong to the past, that they had nothing to do with the stains of Vichy or the closed, resentful nationalism of the more distant French past, I didn't believe them.

In Toulon an official had told Dalilah, a French citizen born in Algeria who operated two red-light bars, that she wasn't eligible for the principal municipal cemetery. 'Get buried elsewhere,' he said. In its isolation, grotesquely, this anecdote spelt out what the Front had done to France. But how were such attitudes best fought? One afternoon I drove up to the hills outside Toulon, through olive groves and small roads. I walked around a stone amphitheatre with Gerard Pacquet, director of the Châteauvallon Centre. Mild, speaking in long sentences, wearing a worn tweed jacket, Pacquet resembled a Parisian intellectual. But he had built Châteauvallon himself, with his own hands, turning it single-handedly into one of Europe's most important centres of contemporary dance. When the Front came to power, he felt an instant chill, and he was told that it might be better if he regarded the entire matter of culture from a less elitist perspective. To his credit, Pacquet refused to put on performances of Provençal dances and declined the financing he had previously received from Toulon. He was convinced that the Front were behind the withdrawal of regional funds which had bankrupted the centre.

Pacquet told me the story of the arrival in Toulon of a rap group called Nique ta Mère (Fuck your Mother). He had anticipated that their presence might cause problems, and declined to allow them to perform at Châteauvallon. But others had taken the band's side, and accused the mayor of censorship when he declined to let them perform in a municipally operated space. 'Sometimes our intellectuals can be very stupid,' Pacquet said. He agreed that the Front's success was tied to the limits of democracy in France. Perhaps in France the idea of a cosmopolitan culture uniting everyone had been badly formulated and it was necessary to return to basics. He asked me if I found France a specially racist country. In spite of my experiences at the Front, I said no, not necessarily. Part of the problem was that French people were more honest in their expressions of distaste for foreigners. Nonetheless, I felt much healing was required. It would be necessary somehow to establish that in contemporary France it was possible to be both very French and wholly cosmopolitan, just as one could come from another country, retaining many original values, and contribute to the totality of Frenchness. That was what France had always meant to me, and that was what it should mean for the rest of Europe. The FN notwithstanding, I hadn't given up hope yet.

On the night the votes were counted a second time it was raining, and I caught sight of Cendrine getting out of the mayor's car. She, too, looked as if she had eaten a bad oyster. I was standing in front of her when she was obliged to concede defeat, by the margin of thirty votes. I hadn't expected grace under pressure, but her venom stopped me cold. With her loyal husband standing anxiously behind her, she screamed that her defeat was due to the biased press or the betrayal of her campaign by the rest of the non-FN right wing. She proposed to appeal against the voters' verdict. Although I knew this wasn't yet the end of the FN, or indeed of Cendrine, I was surprised by the degree of pleasure her defeat afforded me. I did hate the Front as much as many French people. Like them, I needed to know the FN could be defeated; and to this extent, Toulon had been important to me after all.

I did return to Toulon once more, in late summer, to find that everything was much the same in the soap world of the

FN. Dalilah had finally secured her space in the cemetery by the cunning expedient of threatening to give more press interviews (including one to myself). She even won a court case against the offending official. Le Pen had been stripped of his civic rights for two years, which meant that he wouldn't be able to take his seat as a European MP. But Cendrine had appealed, successfully, to the Constitutional Court, and another election would shortly be held in Toulon. Wide-bottomed frontists ambled past the brothels of the port, but the girls told me that business was bad. The most important event of the past months was the victory of France's World Cup team composed of Frenchmen of many ethnic origins, but this was pooh-poohed by those attending the portentously named Summer University. They were concerned with the battle for the succession between Mégret and Le Pen, now reaching its climax.

Mégret had made a misguided early lunge for the succession, but the old man had reciprocated, all but destroying him. It was clear that Le Pen overwhelmingly retained the support of the Front militants, even if many officials preferred his suaver deputy. The atmosphere was thick with rancour. Now no one was talking to Mégret, and he looked like a small, badly bullied boy, smirking with shame. Le Pen was wearing a blue and yellow Rugby shirt and yachting shoes. He looked rested and happy. I told him that I had read the books about his life. 'They're lies,' he said expansively. 'Imagine a biography of Vercingétorix the Gaul composed by Romans.' When I asked if there was one book that I should read he sniffed. 'You could try the one my wife's lover wrote,' he said. 'We paid for that book to be written, so there are fewer lies.' I had come to see Le Pen in the hope of experiencing, by way of farewell to the Front, an additional outburst of his. I could see that he knew that this was why I was here and was of two minds as to whether he should satisfy my desire. We shuffled around the usual questions, but he kept turning away from me, indicating that I didn't matter much. Why would he want to do anything for an Englishman? But a ribald, gamy tone crept into our conversation. Told that Bruno Mégret had wished to censor Benetton ads, Le Pen burst out laughing. 'Next time you interview me you can come in your *slip* (underpants) for all I care,' he said. We talked about Clinton's misadventures. 'France used to be quite famous for *la pipe* [blow jobs],' he said with satisfaction. 'It didn't seem to do our reputation any harm.' But I persisted, as I had learnt to do. Why was no one convinced that he wasn't a racist? Why was his movement described as racist in every edition of the foreign press? And why did I, too, feel that despite professions of frankness, his own speeches weren't wholly honest? (Of course, I might have said, but didn't, that the trouble was that they were so honest.) Suddenly, he responded in the style of an animal unexpectedly deciding to share a juicy bone with a rival. Of course, the international press was dominated by a Jewish lobby, he said. And what did he have to do to convince people he wasn't a racist, he asked, throwing up his hands in what did not appear to be mock exasperation. Would it be enough if he married a Negro (*'un nègre'* is what he said) and one dripping with AIDS (*'sidaïque'*, the word he used, was his own coinage, with echoes of the insulting *'judaïque'*, an appalling Vichy-era phrase implying the malign, conspiratorial ideology of Jewish interests)? Well, it would be some sort of a proof, I said, spurring him towards outrage. Now he became intoxicated, repeating the insults, and I could see that he had passed into a trance of non- or half-control. Even if he did that, he continued, yes, married a black man, people would say that the man was merely a token – *'Le Nègre de*

*Le Pen*' ('Le Pen's Nigger'). And if he went to Washington, taking Monica Lewinsky's place, everyone would still say he was anti-American.

These *mots* would certainly cause him trouble – maybe they would even lead to another race-hate court case and an additional fine. It occurred to me that Le Pen must know this but that he didn't care. The goodish Front champagne went to my head in the poor air conditioning, but I went on drinking. There really was nothing to be done with these people, I now knew. In fact the FN had passed its peak, and it would henceforth decline, splitting in two, with Le Pen and Mégret struggling against each other for the title to the movement amid growing disenchantment among frontists. Although I couldn't have known it, within six months many of those before me would have left the FN, joining Mégret's unimaginatively titled MN (Mouvement National) on its road to obscurity. Some, like the Le Chevalliers, tried to save themselves by calling themselves independents of the Right.

But this didn't necessarily mean that the poison of the FN was any less toxic, or indeed that the movement had failed in its real objectives. The frontists would never come to power, but it would be hard to efface their negative achievements. Racism was legitimate in France now, and nobody need apologize for its existence. Everyone understood this clearly. If the FN was no longer a threat that was partly because, as Le Pen grasped, the damage implied by its existence was already done, requiring many years of reparations, and perhaps an entirely new vision of France not at present much in evidence among the timid, unimaginative political class. Meanwhile the best revenge to be taken on the cosmic bad taste implied by frontists' existence lay in a spirit of derision. For they were dangerous but also tragically stupid. Nothing could come of their activities except more stupidity or more hatred. Noble phrases wouldn't prevail against them, nor would the exercise of reason alone. Still, I wondered whether I or, more importantly, those whom journalists called misleadingly 'ordinary voters' would always have the stomach to do battle with the banality of racism. One day another Dalilah would meekly accept a plot in a non-French cemetery – or the local journalists wouldn't write about her efforts to gain her due. By that stage the Pacquets would have quit the stage in despair or boredom. People like myself wouldn't get on and off stuffy planes in order to bait the next Jean-Marie or harass Bruno's heir. And at that moment we would all be threatened. I paused in the hall, with the FN anthem in my ears. '*Avec Jean-Marie, tout est bien*,' the singer repeated, over and over again. Deeply, with mounting panic and nausea, I hoped I could do something to postpone or definitively forestall that day.

In the late summer of 1998, like many hundreds of thousands, I came to Paris for the final of the World Cup. I didn't know much about football, but I suppose I had come as a belated homage to my French grandfather, who was a wheel of sorts in French football and whose exasperation I remembered fondly whenever the team lost, as it usually did. Some hours before the match started, sitting in a Left Bank cafe, I began to think that something might have changed in France. Tricolour flags were stuck through every car window, and there were honkings and bursts of the 'Marseillaise' at each traffic light. In the summer heat, walking slowly towards the Seine and the Champs Elysées, it became possible to understand what it must have felt like to have been in the city on 21 August 1944, the day of liberation. As I walked around the crowds, however, I noticed something else. There were many Arabs and blacks in the crowd, and many of them were carrying tricolour flags. Groups of white fans honked and shouted at groups of Arabs. '*Allez la France*,' they cried, or '*Allez les bleus*.' When I heard the astonishing 'aah' that greeted Zinedine Zidane's second goal, I knew that nothing in France would ever quite be the same again.

But the French newspapers were divided in their views of the importance of the *Mondial*. Some conservative commentators praised the coach for having known how to instil in his charges (the idea was fatuous as well as patronizing) a lost, provincial tradition of French team-playing. Others did believe that the victory signalled a real change in the French attitudes towards their foreigners. I decided to see for myself; and shortly afterwards, when I was in Marseille, I went to Les Tarterets, the 1960s *cité* where Zidane was born and where his relatives still lived.

It took an hour by bus from the centre, and I was conscious, as I had been so many times before in the past year and a half, of passing through one of the frontiers of the new Europe. I had to walk through wasteland to get to Les Tarterets. There were graffiti around the building where the Zidane family lived and teenagers pretended to be his cousins. Recruitment for the football team was up and, as one might have expected, everyone was still excited by the great victory. It did for a moment seem as if football was capable of bringing French people together in a way that politics, or social planning, had failed to do. And perhaps in time football would help to give a new dimension to the Frenchness in relation to which France's foreigners could gain no purchase. Zidane would become a model for the *banlieue* kids, and he and his team-mates would be remembered long after any number of mediocre politicians were forgotten, as true French heroes and not as foreigners. However, the more I walked around the *cité*, the more ambiguous this message became. Here in Les Tarterets, it was clear,

*Antillais*, African blacks, Comoro Islanders, Portuguese and Arabs lived together – but they were separated from the white French by bus routes, by schooling, by jobs, by what they ate or believed in, by who they were or, more pertinently, were not.

On the return journey, I found myself standing next to a middle-aged couple. The man was an Arab in his late fifties, probably from Algeria or Tunisia, neatly dressed in a frayed suit and a white shirt with the collar buttoned. His wife, who wore a chador, was, I suddenly realized, white and French. She looked tired, and she obviously wasn't well because he had to ask for a seat on her behalf. And nobody, Arab or not, wanted to give her one. The man asked around and no one moved. I did the same and I even asked the conductor but to no avail, and the three of us stood together, without talking, for the rest of the one hour bus ride. I tried to imagine his feelings of shame, anger and disappointment, but I realized that an impenetrable frontier lay between us.

# THE NEW LOST TRIBES OF EUROPE

At Saarbrücken on the German-French frontier one summer morning in 1998, I was confronted with what appeared to be a miniature version of the new Europe. Small, massed armies of anti-fascists and the Right faced each other across a cordon of German police in riot gear. But it was the context, and how it had altered, almost unrecognizably, that interested me. Saarbrücken was the capital of the Saarland, which was taken from Germany in 1919 and administered by the French, under an international mandate. In 1935, the third year of Hitler's rule, when a plebiscite was held, the Saarlanders chose freely to be German, and to belong to a dictatorship, by an astonishing margin of 91 per cent. They thus resolved their own future according to the familiar outlines of the past – we would now call it an ethnic one – with which they were happiest. I stood on the road in the sunlight, watching the long column of green VWs packed with riot police. To one side were the remnants of a small concentration camp and, not far away, Germans killed in the 1945 fighting were buried. But it was the old frontier that caught my attention. Beyond the already half-derelict German customs posts there was a French roundabout and, by its side, a supermarket advertising cheap *primeur* wines. In front of it, holding a flimsy piece of plastic, stood a lone gendarme. He explained that he was here only in the mild expectation of trouble, in case a complementary demonstration of French rightists wished the join their German equivalents. Otherwise he and the plastic wouldn't be needed at all.

All over Europe, it was easy to find people who believed that the old frontiers had gone and nothing any more separated Europeans from each other. 'Only on the football field,' a Danish friend explained. 'These are the only places the old ideas matter – and merely for the afternoon.' But it was also possible to discern new boundaries in Europe. They separated the rich parts of a country from a poor one, or they lay athwart the definitions of race or difference. Europeans weren't so much united as rethinking the matter of what now should constitute the divisions between them. Not all of them wished to exist in a frontierless state and, for many of those who did, the experience was sometimes unsettling. It was thus, beginning on the margins of European life that one could start to see a new movement, the purpose of which was to restore or recompose the sense of difference that had characterized European life for so many centuries.

In the most important, least geographical sense, this movement existed somewhere between the rival and complementary realms of racism and xenophobia. It began just where the boring ordinariness of most European politics left off. But it was not to be neglected – it, too, would form part of the European future. I caught sight of this future early in 1997, when I saw Mrs Thatcher standing in a clump of evergreens, in the midst of a garden centre in Dorset. Beneath the familiar spun-sugar helmet of hair, she looked older and stooped. She walked lightly amid her ageing fans as if she were playing a favourite role of Bette Davis or vice versa. We moved on to the sunny playground of a Church of England school where a youngish Anglican cleric with a neat beard awaited her, along with a class of six-years-olds. Listening to Mrs Thatcher's by now familiar over-emphatic sentences, watching her bend, dutifully, over one child after another, I stood in Tory heaven. But I was also aware that day of a transformation of sorts, and not just because of Mrs Thatcher's age or the certainty of the Tories losing the election. Trying as I did to look at my own country from a non-insular European perspective, I believed that things had changed definitively. I was present at the moment when the Tory party ceased to be the old coalition of rich and less rich that believed it had the right to administer Britain. A newer party was being born. It was misshapen and without evident promise – more bizarrely, given the circumstances of its creation and its views, it had much in common with other recent European creations. I found that I understood the Tories the more I knew about Europe.

For Mrs Thatcher didn't want to talk about what the Tories had done or might do. She didn't want to encourage us to enjoy the early spring weather or bask in the picture-postcard image of her British people, saved from collectivism and delivered safe and sound for the end of the century. Instead she had a consuming grievance to air. It had been the cause of her ejection from office in 1990, and it continued to plague her mind. It was called Europe. She passed before an 89-year-old veteran with medals covering his breast, pausing with practised ease to form a tableau for the benefit of photographers; and I heard her talk about nation states and how Britain needed to recover control of its laws, its parliament and its economy. 'Recover,' she repeated loudly in the veteran's ear. 'RE-COVER.' When I tried to ask her what she really thought about the then mooted Single Currency, or the apparent triumph of wicked people in Europe who wished to see the Continent further integrated, she reacted in the latex-puppet style of herself, wagging her index finger at me. 'I have already said everything I'm going to say,' she declared in the same very loud voice.

I remembered Mrs Thatcher's famous parliamentary exit line. 'No, no, no,' she had cried, jabbing her hands over the dispatch box, when she was finally obliged to confront what she considered (most of it she had sponsored, inadvertently as she claimed, during the previous years) as the enormity of the Maastricht Treaty. Of course she had always been motivated by the habit or the desire to fight, but the object of her disapprobation had changed. In the end Europe had consumed her and her brilliant career – but it had also diminished her party. The Tories, I now understood, were not the same people. How would deep nationalists react to the age of the Single Currency? Could they survive at all in the new Europe? In denial at the prospect of removal after eighteen years of power, they not surprisingly didn't want to address such matters. But I found that I could make some headway by hanging around the edges. The party was ageing alarmingly, and at meetings I felt that I had never met so many old people outside the precinct of a home. It wasn't the real Europe that they disliked, the place with good food, newish trains and bossy, leftish politicians with patronizing latinate syntax and no misgivings when it came to holidays in places like Tuscany. No, what they hated was the obscure, uncomprehending force field which had drawn Mrs Thatcher, whom they loved passionately, into its orbit, destroying her and themselves. This was their Europe, and it had already proved incompatible with their Tory England.

At this stage, I wasn't able to make any firm connections between what I saw here in England and what I was beginning to encounter elsewhere in Europe. All I could do was establish the fact that under pressure the Tory Party was narrowing its appeal. In the past it had combined many sorts of half-believers but it was now drifting into sullen ethnocentrism. This wasn't to say that it was like Le Pen or the other monsters I was encountering, but the family resemblance, faint though it might be, was nonetheless there. The same music was to be heard on either side of the Channel, and it filled Flemish bogs, Bavarian or Austrian Alpine pastures, echoing across the populous plains of Northern Italy. I was witnessing a set of discontents, resumed within the idea of 'Brussels' or 'Europe'. What these people hated was the idea that they, or at least what they believed in, might disappear. This was a hatred deeper than ordinary politics, but the problem was that in Europe it could only be expressed through the old paraphernalia of parties and flags – which had in any case already let their proponents down. It could take different forms, confusing the observer. Most of the people misleadingly known in Britain as Eurosceptics had changed their minds,[1] passing (like Mrs T. indeed) from a qualified, half-suspicious admiration of 'Europe' to outright hostility. Some of them had changed their minds more than once.

Elgar was still played for the Tory faithful, and Union Jack plastic hats grew like mushrooms around every hall. But something, it seemed to me, had changed. The occasion had become what a German friend called 'Nuremberg for old people'. 'Hatred is like a blow-flame,' wrote George Orwell in 1940. 'It can be turned in any direction at a moment's notice.'[2] He was referring to the mass hates of his day, brought into being by propaganda. But hatred these days appeared to have a different basis. It could be switched in many directions or attached to many causes. It could even appear skittish. Much hatred in Europe was directed towards the foreigner – in France, of course, 'Anglo-Saxons' with their hated 'globalism' fell conveniently within this definition – but in Britain it could be turned in the direction of 'Europe', a place filled with foreigners. Following the maxim, once again, that it was best to know one's enemies, I set out to become a connoisseur of the many ways in which 'Europe' was capable of unhinging the minds of, or otherwise destroying, people once considered to be capable.

To this end I attended many of the richly absurd meetings of Sir James Goldsmith's Referendum Party. Goldsmith was an Anglo-French billionaire who had invented his own political party for the express pleasure it gave him to attack the enemy in Europe. I knew that he would get nowhere (he knew that, too, as it turned out, for he was dying of cancer) but I was interested in what appeared to drive him. It didn't appear to me that Goldsmith was a racist. Nor could one readily call so cosmopolitan a man a xenophobe. However, the hatred, which he displayed at each meeting and with equal intensity, regardless of the number of people present, usually twenty or thirty, exceeded anything that 'Europe' might have done to him and us. Goldsmith had perfected a version of the Grand Tourer conception of politics, pushing archaism to art-form status. He arrived on time, with a disdainful, unhurried air, and entered perfunctorily as if obliged to descend from his automobile in a place known not to be worth the visit. After a brief speech, in which he rubbed his hands, he affected to take questions, but instead he talked. Strident, spitting out at us over the lectern, he sounded like a cleaned-up, patrician Le Pen. For reasons known to himself, he pronounced the name of the small and innocuous Dutch town *May*-strict, giving it the accents of bondage and imminent enslavement. Packed with images of decay and excrement, shouted out to diminutive audiences, his speeches were filled with allusions to the mendacity of politicians. I shouted questions at him over the backs of the small crowd. Goldsmith I had met before and I had admired his brilliant mind, at least where matters of business were at stake. But, alas, Sir James had now undergone the identical savage process of comprehensive self-deconstruction as Mrs T.; and the ranting, barking figure before me each night was proof of Europe's power to diminish. I felt disoriented by the experience of Sir James. But I also began to recognize that this music, coming from the noisome past, would also echo through the European future. We developed a strange relationship, shouting at one another across empty halls. On the last occasion I saw him, in a grubby, paper-strewn Ashford town hall, after his family had one by one delivered their tributes, I cupped my hands. 'What's the biggest danger to Europe?' I bawled. 'Chauvinism,' he roared back. 'Bigotry. Have you seen Le Pen?' I nodded that, alas, I had. 'Well then, imagine a place with twenty parties like his. That's the kind of Europe the bureaucrats are bringing into existence. That's what they'll do to us.'

I was perplexed by this remark, because of the degree of self-knowledge it revealed. Was Sir James a portent, perhaps, like one of Shakespeare's historical tableaux, entitled *The Horrors of Maastricht*? Or did he mean that *he* had become like Le Pen? In the event Sir James failed comprehensively, gathering only a handful of seats in the election and dying shortly afterwards; and the Tories went down with him. But I found that I wouldn't accept that what he had done was meaningless, despite his apparent lack of accomplishments. In Europe, one should look for the future in the past, above all. No one should be taken in by the current triumph of progressive, 'pro-European' ideas. And no one should rule out some variety of national revivalism. The new dividing lines in Europe were not being constructed to separate classes, nor were they explicitly about race; they stood in relation to how much of the old national past, real or not, one wanted to conserve. For it seemed that in Europe the idea of *heimat* – a place which belonged to oneself, as a member of an ethnic group or a nation – was still for many people a fundamental, far more significant than religion, ideology or the fleeting allegiances conferred by possession of consumer goods. Some Europeans wished to live in snug ethnic homes from which foreigners would be excluded. Others merely wanted to retain the right to their already existing countries – and this meant being loud about the presumed virtues of what remained of the vanishing native land.

I began to look at the new tribes of Europe as they grappled with the idea of extinction; but this proved to be more complicated than I had imagined. To begin with, not every nationalist party in Europe was necessarily opposed to every particular implied by the idea of 'Brussels'. Some of them indeed – the ones whose origins lay in suppressed nationalities, and who were eager to see the righting of perceived wrongs – could envisage some sort of advantage to be drawn from what the others denounced as 'Federalism'. It was helpful to think of Europe as a map existing across time and even space, which was changing shape unpredictably, expanding or shrinking, depending on the perspective from which you examined it. If you were young and energetic, and came from a place previously neglected by history or which had been oppressed by a larger, more intrusive national culture, the freedom of Europe was a gift the likes of which had never been seen; and one could see how, from the perspective of Ireland or even Finland, the changes in Europe were unquestionably a Good Thing. But the same map looked different from the lost provinces of the FN or from the neo-Nazi badlands of East Germany. Here one would recall what was being lost, above all. It would be easy to think of the future more sourly, as if one was being stuffed, along with a number of unwanted, old, soiled articles, into a large, anonymous laundry bag. For the losers, it didn't matter who was doing the stuffing or who and what else went into the bag. I discovered that identity wasn't ultimately something you could argue over much. People either felt lost or they didn't. It was what they felt, obviously, that counted. And in parallel, never wholly explained, came the sudden disruptions implied by the prospective or actual losses of livelihoods. There were ghost towns all over Europe. No distress was on the scale experienced around the mid-century, before or after the terrible wars, no one was pushing cartloads of marks about the streets (as they appeared about to do in the former Soviet Union) or scrabbling amid the rubble; but it was bad enough to make people start. Many of them ditched their old parties in favour of people who spoke to them more clearly. This was how the new politics of race and identity came into being in Europe.

What would it mean to be French, Danish or Finnish in twenty years' time? Federalists presented the future as if we Europeans would shortly belong in a large lighted shopping mall in which all that remained of the past were the labels attached to the various countries. They tended to depict the new currency as if it were a privilege card you got with a magnetic swipe entrance device. Overwhelmingly, in Federal writings and speeches, Europe was depicted as a matter of convenience. It was something the rest of us were presumed to want – or which we would in due course come to accept, however reluctantly. Above politics, 'Europe' was thus in its terminal reasonableness also happily placed beyond discussion. Meanwhile, political scientists examined the opponents of 'Europe' through the phenomenon of 'populism'. They meant by this some form of direct appeal, visceral in nature, and bypassing reason. Populists weren't necessarily racists, socialists or anti-Europeans, though they might be any or all of these things.[3] They might (though this would seem to be ultimately a disqualification) not actually be very popular. Nonetheless, populists were menacing and obnoxious to those who wrote about them. The populists took old and half-buried resentments, dressing them up in new language. Like the so-called 'hard' Far Right, they bred in an atmosphere of hatred. It was taken for granted that they were not real democrats. This was their real, unavowed link with the fascist past, and it was why they, too, were dangerous. The term 'national populist' was now used by progressive historians to express disapproval of these opposition politicians – and it was supposed to describe the danger of the new orientation, somewhere between little-nation snugness and black leather.

Should the likes of Sir James and Mrs T. be called populists? Did the word describe Jean-Marie Le Pen? My own memories of populism were hazy, referring back to the brief pre-eminence of the Panama-hatted Huey Long, who was thought during the 1930s to be an American fascist, but who, before he was murdered, did a lot for the State of Louisiana and its white poor, building roads and football stadiums. Otherwise the word had passed into the slang of marketing, coming to mean the sort of crudely effective TV shows or ad campaigns of which their perpetrators felt mildly ashamed. But I could see that the word was useful when it came to describing the patchwork of attitudes that characterized the battalions of the legal, constitutional Far Right in contemporary Europe. It was certainly better than other current formulations, like that of post-fascism. So I unpacked a new set of maps as I went back on the road. I was interested in the relationship between the old forms of hatred and the new. But I also wanted to see how the idea of a nation might fare in the new European laboratory. Who were the populists – or, just as important, *what* were they?

It was raining the summer day I arrived in Antwerp, and I remembered that it had rained, too, on the previous day I had come to see the Vlaams Blok.[4] Two overweight knights circled around each other carrying outsize shields and medieval weapons while a small crowd looked on. At stalls, yellow and black stickers proclaimed the motto of the movement: '*Die Belgium!*'. I dodged flapping tent sides, and kept out of the rain as I asked the Vlaams militants – the *blokkers*, as they called themselves – what they thought about foreigners. I'd come from Brussels, where I'd attended a press conference of the *blokkers*' latest hope, a stern law and order policeman sacked from the force for not having revealed his fascist past. There I'd been told that the movement was trying to change itself, giving at least the appearance of altering its racist past in order to take its place on the new Europe. 'You'll see,' said a young journalist specializing in the Far Right of the Low Countries. 'We Belgians may not be quick to take up the latest fashions, but when we do it's a serious gesture. But don't be taken in. Nothing has changed, and the same hatreds are there.'

I looked around the dripping tent. Happily, like Flemish Belgium itself, the movement was small, and I could find representatives of every generation within hailing distance. I spoke to the founder Nazi sympathizer Karel Diller, who was in his eighties, stooped and white-haired. Then I went over to see Roland Raes, the Party ideologist, a bulky Poirot-like figure with a guttural delivery and a rumpled suit. Finally I talked to Gerold Annemans and Filip Dewinter, the current leaders. In their Boss suits, with bulky shoulders, and their blue shirts with polka-dot ties, they looked like any other centre-right or centre-left politician in Europe. The Vlaams Blok was created in the 1970s, shortly after the National Front. For the older generation it was a means of reviving the pro-Nazi Flemish nationalism. For younger members it fulfilled two complementary functions. It gave voice to the desire for Flemish separatism that arose in the 1960s as a consequence of the various linguistic reforms in Belgium, and, just as important, it began to explore the hatreds implicit in the presence of a number of immigrants, most of them Arabs, in Brussels and Flemish Belgium. Throughout the 1980s, the Blok gained votes steadily until in Antwerp it now polled 26 per cent of the vote. However, the party had now reached some sort of a fork in the road. The more astute *blokkers* wished to cover, if not leave behind, hard-core racism. They believed that Belgium was going anyhow, and that they should be beneficiaries of its collapse. But they could only hope to triumph if they cleaned themselves up.

In the old days you needed muskets and uniforms to create a country, but nowadays in Europe a new set of maps and a slogan would do. I suppose it was the scissors-and-paste certainty of the *blokkers* that appealed to me. They believed that Hitler couldn't be wholly bad – because he had espoused, briefly, the matter of Flemish language rights. It had been wrong to persecute the Flemish Nazis, because they were only expressing the submerged national sensibility which was theirs by right. Everything was so simple – you just had to boot out the decadent Royal Family, clean up Brussels, carve up the map and *voilà*! – the kingdom was done for. In their false simplicity the solutions resembled those propounded by Sir James; and something of these accents of righteousness I now found among the older generation. But certainty was going out of fashion. Its place was being taken by a less hard-edged style of expression. Whereas, on my previous visit, I'd been treated to accounts of Muslims killing sheep in their bathtubs, everything now came scaled down to the amiable notion of cultural differences. I must understand that multiculturalism had failed. The Rushdie affair demonstrated that Muslims, whatever liberals cared to affirm, *were* different. They didn't fit in at all. It was possible for an Englishman like myself to become Flemish – I would merely have to learn the language, which, they assured me, wasn't too difficult – but not so for Muslims. However, the Blok acknowledged that force-feeding those who were to be deported, gagging them or tying them up, wasn't the best way. They must be convinced of the need to go – and Blokland would give them money. Finally, they would want to go. And the same was true of the Belgian Royal Family, who in any case spent most of the year in Switzerland and Monaco. They too, given the choice, would wish to leave ex-Flemish Belgium to its snug devices. Why would they want to stay? I asked them about Europe. Surely the EU would view with discomfort a separatist ethnic state controlling what was in effect its capital. Oh no, they said. In due course, the EU would change. It would have to change in order to take account of the new nationhoods. And I mustn't worry too much about that.

For the moment I took their advice and didn't worry. You could look at Europe as a place which was suddenly, not altogether unhappily, experiencing the attractions of chaos. For more than forty years the claims of ideology had dominated the Continent. The presence of barbed wire on one side and American bombers on the other had ensured that a kind of clogged high seriousness survived. Meanwhile the appalling European past of genocide had made the wearing of sackcloth mandatory. And yet such comprehensive sobriety couldn't endure. Perhaps these outbursts of obscure national or local feeling, coupled with a project designed to render Europe rational and uniform, merely showed that we were now witnessing an outbreak of European levity. But I felt that it would be wrong not to take these folk seriously.

Chain-smoking, keeping an eye on their children struggling within the outsize heaving dragons of the adventure playground, the Vlaams Blok wives beat time with their feet to Flemish bluegrass. The *blokkers* appeared to be more stolid and practical-minded than their mentors in the FN. They lacked the passion of the sectarian Far Right or indeed of the British Tories. Not everyone here, I reminded myself, was a member of a strange and vicious tribe; and they didn't seem to indulge in the sort of infighting between rival Führers that frequently characterized the Far Right. Unlike the FN the *blokkers* weren't animals of a kind that the programmers of nature programmes would not have seen fit to display on prime time. But their apparent desire to change themselves posed a number of questions. Nor did it resolve the question of how and whether racist parties, given the chance, could so modify their policies that they ceased to be racist. Whatever they might say, I didn't feel that the *blokkers* were yet ready for the new Europe.

It was grey the day I went to Venice, and there were bright flags sticking out of the windows of the *vaporetti*. Among the gold, reds and yellows was a bright green banner with a white, three-pointed symbol at its centre that resembled the one adopted by the British campaign to legalize marijuana. They were wearing green shirts, often with matching caps and scarves, and they shouted to each other and sang. They were supporters of the Lega Nord, a movement dedicated to the overthrow of the Italian state. They called themselves Padanians – the name given to the rich portion of Northern Italy each side of the river Po, composed of the old kingdoms of Lombardy and Piedmont and extending right the way down to Bologna and Florence. More animated than the *blokkers*, the Padanians were nonetheless just as adamant about the uselessness of the nation state in which they claimed to be oppressed. And they were also xenophobes. The only difference appeared to be that, for Padanians, the outside threat came not from dark-skinned chador-wearing Muslims, but from the feckless and corrupt Southern Italians in their midst whom, it seemed, they desired to send home.

I followed the Padanians over wet flagstones and through echoing *piazze*; now I was in the midst of a rival movement to Garibaldi's, forgotten and now revived for our times, but rescored for the benefit of a TV commercial. The Padanians did indeed dislike Calabrians. They talked about how boring Sicilians were, and how all Neapolitan women, far from resembling Sophia Loren, had moustaches. I might have been in a crowd of Scottish football fans trashing the English. But I should not assume that just because they were ridiculous, the Padanians would get nowhere. Indeed, I recalled that at one moment the Lega Nord had run Milan. They still polled around 15 per cent of the vote in Northern Italy. We paused before an old palace, recently purchased by the movement. This, I learnt, was to be the parliamentary building of the new state. The dignitaries who now appeared on the balcony, waving their arms at the crowd, were functionaries or politicians who had thrown in their lot with the new state. I elbowed my way into the building and found myself talking to the Minister of Ports and Fisheries. Later, my head lightened by Padanian *prosecco*, I had a long conversation in very bastard Italian with the Deputy Prime Minister. I must have been impressed by what he said because my notes tail off at this point. For his part, he was delighted by my suggestion to the effect that there should be a Padanian football team. He went out on the balcony and shouted at the crowd. There would be a Padanian football team, he said. Not only that, it would win the World Cup. And, thanks to the BBC journalist present, Padania would shortly put itself forward as host nation.

Gusts pushed clouds in our direction across the Rialto, blowing the banners of the Padanians to and fro like Chinese dragons. Sirens and bells filled the air with bland, friendly noises. You could buy Padanian banknotes, passports and even blood-donor certificates in a series of stalls grouped along the rainswept Riva degli Schiavoni. They were inscribed with the likeness of Umberto Bossi as well as the three-pointed green marijuana-like emblem. What I by now acknowledged to be the fancy dress of the Far Right – chain mail, lances and halberds, funny hats – were in evidence as well as green shirts. I picked up a 50,000 *scudi* note, examining the likeness of the founder of Padania. Hirsute, with oversize aviator glasses, poorly suited in a way that seemed perverse for an Italian, however reluctant a one, Bossi looked to be an entirely unconvincing founding father. He had dropped out of medical school, coming to politics as the circulation director of a local paper. He knew about special offers and the value of sponsored events. These things, as his opponents never failed to point out, were just as important to him as policies. Indeed, the record showed that Bossi wasn't always a separatist. Like his ex-coalition partner, Silvio Berlusconi, ex-crooner and media magnate, whose government he destroyed, Bossi wove in and out of positions according to the expressed whim of his supporters, shedding whatever proved to be inconvenient or unattractive. But he was consistent in expressing virulent distaste for the corruptions of Rome. It was Rome that had stolen the wealth of the North, Rome that sold his stout supporters into bondage. Rome and Brussels were part of the same tightly woven chainlink of bondage hooping in the poor Padanians and depriving them of their birthright.

A large pontoon held a dais for dignitaries and well-wishers, and I stood behind a noisy group of Padanians who were swaying tipsily. Suddenly, I was half won over. What was so silly about the desire to spend one's Saturday afternoons wearing a green shirt? As I became habituated to the football chants, however, I caught a refrain. 'Don't jump if you're an Italian,' the crowd shouted; and they were jumping. And now I was alerted to a change of mood by the swelling chords of Verdi's chorus of slaves and the waving of many small pieces of paper. This was the celebrated oath of loyalty, sworn on the sacred honour of the crowd, and it pledged the huddling masses not to tolerate the existence of Italy but to fight for a free Padania. I looked around for signs of invasive irony and realized that these were real tears. Many were sniffling into their green handkerchiefs or conspicuously striving to overcome the growing lumps in their throats. At 4 p.m. Bossi began to speak. He told us that the love affair between Italy and its people was over. He treated us to a lengthy (and probably inaccurate) disquisition on the origins of the word *Italia*. According to Bossi, it was a Southern dialect word from Calabria meaning *vituli* which was the same as *vitelli*. Italy was a country of *vitelloni* – playboys and idlers, as they were so memorably described in Fellini's comedy of the same name. And now it was time to stop being useless, and start being Padanian. As he said these words, a giant cruise liner passed behind Bossi and the others gathered on the dais. On its many decks stood happy Italians, waving their hands and handkerchiefs at us. The boat was sleek, new-looking, and it might have been a prop from a movie. Its passengers were far enough away not to be able to hear what Bossi was saying, or indeed tell why we were there.

Not long after, I talked about Padania with a young professor from Bologna University who specialized in post-war financial history. We were flying over the Alps and the separate peaks were clearly visible in the sun. I told him that I couldn't understand how serious it all was – and not just because this was Italy, and Italian politics were identified, not always correctly, with histrionism. If so-called 'real' nation states were indeed redundant in Europe, then the creation of fake ones was quite logical – and, it might be argued, about as dangerous as the newly mooted European football league. Padania might indeed take the place of a piece of Italy without doing any harm. But Bossi's desire to eject Southern Italians from Padania was real enough and, like the Vlaams Blok, he would require a police force to do this. In the end, therefore, there was nothing virtual about Padania – one did, finally, require the contemporary equivalent of muskets in order to form a new state. The professor sighed, scratching his head. It wasn't easy to study politics in Europe these days. Twenty years ago things had been somewhat simpler. In those days people blew up railway stations because they wished to destroy the Italian state – and it was the idea of money that appeared uncertain or abstract by comparison with real life. Now he was glad to be studying the creation of Bretton Woods or the fate of Eurobonds. Even the soon-to-be-extinct lira seemed real by the side of Bossi. Shrugging, he contemplated his paper cup. 'It would be better if we could be absolutely certain that Bossi, and people like him, mean nothing,' he said. 'Unfortunately, that is not possible. In politics you can never be certain of anything.' He began to tell me about the transformation of Italian fascism, and how it had finally passed into the mainstream of Italian life, becoming wholly banal. 'You can never say how these things happen in Italy,' he said. Then he began to talk of the excessive simple-mindedness of what his colleagues called populism. It was possible to see how appalling things like fascism could happen merely by examining the dreadful array of stupidity inherent in democracy. 'Look how stupid television is,' he said, echoing a refrain voiced by every Italian I had met. We were silent now, looking morosely at the Alps beneath us.

In communist Bologna one side of the main square was decked with an enormous banner. It was a gift from Benetton, and it covered the restoration work funded by the company. Four enormous faces of half-Chinese or African teenagers were there to proclaim the virtues of multiculturalism. They didn't smile, indeed they bore no expression whatsoever. They would have seemed less out of place in Brazil or New York. I thought of Bruno Mégret with his pathetic cut-price antidote to the Benetton spirit, and I recalled being in Sarajevo just after the siege, seeing a plaque put up by the company in memory of all the reporters who died there. As multiculturalism or as a primer to contemporary civilization, Benetton wasn't enough. Nonetheless it was what we had – and I was grateful.

Next day I drove through vineyards and past apple orchards. In Italy a feud had broken out within the ranks of the old fascists, splitting the movement in two. On one side stood the brand-new Aleanza Nazionale, whose leader Gianfranco Fini now polled around 20 per cent of the vote. A passable orator, well-suited, Fini looked and sounded like a democratic politician – there was no reason to doubt him when he said that elections were here to stay and that the old-style corporatism, relying on the wisdom of the state as incarnated by its ranks of bureaucrats, unchecked by democratic institutions, was dead. Although he proclaimed Mussolini's greatness, it was to the Duce as a historical figure that he paid homage and not as a model. Like his fellow populists Fini didn't like the idea of a Federal Europe, but he liked even less the racism of the Front National; and he had broken conspicuously with Le Pen. Not entirely convincingly, Fini told reporters that he became a right-wing militant as an adolescent because a demonstration had stopped him going to see John Wayne in *The Green Berets*. Now he liked to quote from Camus and Gramsci. So Fini infuriated both the Left and the old fascists, who regarded him, respectively, as a fraud or a traitor. Nonetheless he appeared to have proved that it was indeed possible to tread some of the path between fascism and some form of democratic practice.

But I had come to Predappio, where Mussolini was born, to witness the annual celebrations of the Duce's famous march on Rome. In reality, as was by now well known, he didn't take part in the march, preferring to go by train. But this didn't stop the faithful from showing up, and it certainly hadn't dissuaded the communist mayor from encouraging tourism, even building a large car park around the cemetery where Mussolini's remains were kept. I walked uphill among small, stooped *fascisti* wearing faded black shirts. It was dark in the crypt and cramped. Mussolini's coffin occupied the centre, flanked by what were said to be (an early doubt occurred to me here about the authenticity of exhibits) the boots and shirt he was wearing on 28 April 1945 when he was strung up by a meat hook in Piazzale Loreto, the main square of Milan. In death his wife Rachele had finally supplanted the faithful Clara Petacci, and she lay at the great man's feet. Dependants – a film-director son, another who had been an intrepid aviator – were dutifully clustered about. I attended a mass in honour of Mussolini's soul in the small village church, where I tried without much success to rebuke the priest. In the autumn sunlight the Duce's small band, now members of a new organization known as Fiamma Tricolore, went through their paces. No, it was true that Mussolini hadn't liked elections, but one couldn't say that they were much use anyhow. But the Duce wasn't an anti-Semite, and he gave good reasons to love Italy – something his successors had failed to achieve. He was a defender of socialist values against the ravages of liberal capitalism. Nothing in the struggles of the Third World would have seemed alien to him. I began to ask a moustached Central Committee member of Fiamma Tricolore whether this was the right way to describe a man who had bombed Abyssinian tribesmen – but this was futile, and I soon abandoned my efforts.

'Inside every anarchist,' the Duce had said in a rare moment of wit, 'a failed dictator is trying to get out.' We were used to asking whether Mussolini could return and, by the same measure, whether it was possible for those around us to become like him. Perhaps we should ask instead whether, given different circumstances, the Duce and his likes might have constructed themselves differently. I could imagine Mussolini as a third-rate movie star. He was a brilliantly unscrupulous journalist and I could certainly see him engineering the Benetton campaign. I had no way of knowing on what side he would have placed himself in the matter of Europe – probably he would have had it both ways, depending on the size of the subsidy reaching his party and his followers. And yet he would certainly have reserved the right to change his mind.

In his time Mussolini had built a grandiose square for his home town, surrounding it with the sort of bloated but elegant public architecture that proved to be his least obnoxious gift to Italy. Beyond the square, on each side of the street, rival *emporie* opened their doors. They sold busts in bronze or coated plastic, black shirts, ties, scarves, breeches, black fezzes, plastic helmets and pom-pom hats, modified cycle boots and leather trousers, bottles of wine, ashtrays, corkscrews, wallets. Local wines came labelled with insignia, cracker mottoes or stern images of the Duce's peanut head that made him look like the patriarch of an Italian Addams family. For those who had travelled far SS insignia were available, as well as models of open Mercedes cars in which a small figure with a moustache stood, raising his hand. Trade was brisk, and a proprietor explained to me that the Internet had been a boon, facilitating orders from far-off places like Japan and Nebraska. Perhaps I had wanted to buy a Mussolini watch but I found I couldn't.

I waited in the street to interview the communist mayor. Nothing like this was available in Germany, of course, where its existence would have provoked a near-collapse. But it also seemed appropriate to me that Mussolini had fetched up here in a kitsch emporium, for he was after all the great dictator of kitsch. Something in Italy (most likely the fact that images or costumes came piled up in such vigorous profusion, but possibly also the superior light) meant that it was easy to live with horrible or merely tasteless things. However, one could never tell how grateful one should be for such a gift. I would rather live in a looser, easier place like Italy, than in Germany, but I could also see the threat implied by the relativizing aspects of the new populism. Predappio showed that revisionism led, among other things, to participation in the market culture implied by the existence of pom-pom hats.

Everything went because nothing mattered very much. I was only half reassured by the mayor's protestations to the effect that the Duce was good for tourism, and that he planned anyhow to create a more serious centre for anti-fascist studies.

It was drizzling when I came to Austria, and the Trapp meadows were shrouded with ugly grey clouds. There were few banners in Linz, but I counted horn buttons, green billiard baize collars and *lederhosen*. *Dirndls* were worn in profusion, in reds, pinks and blues. Among the women as well as the men a certain stoutness appeared de rigueur – it showed that we were among serious folk for whom the tags of 'racist' or 'xenophobe' might be considered inappropriate. As a joke, and because he believed in his own self-parodying version of national kitsch, the beer correspondent of the left-wing Vienna newspaper *Der Standard* was wearing a pair of bright knee-length red socks with his lederhosen. We were talking about populism and food. I wondered why the *wurst* and beer were always better on the Far Right – and whether this indeed presaged a world of boring mainstream parties and dull, homogenized foodstuffs. He was telling me that we should start a campaign for the preservation of what he called European Basic Food: blood puddings, *leberkäse*, *boudin*. We would not be short of sponsors. At that moment the leader of the Freedom Party of Austria (FPÖ) came into the hall. Jörg Haider was accompanied by his handsome, stoutish wife and a wedge-shaped formation of bodyguards and aides. He seemed either to be about to start running or to have momentarily slowed down for our benefit. His smile had been laboured over for many years, and I saw how he raised his hand carefully to avoid any compromising position.

And yet it was the Leader's costume that astonished me. Last time we had met, he was wearing a Tory-blue suit and a blue tie, and we were sitting in a posh office at the Vienna Parliament fitted out with blue sofas and matching curtains. He told me how much he liked Mrs Thatcher. She had inspired him, not just with her policies, but by the way she never gave up the fight against her foes, pursuing dead orthodoxy until a lance could be stuck through its throat. However, Haider had jettisoned his suit for a brown, tight-fitting affair in cotton, which appeared to be kitted out with a great number of pockets and zippers. If so much as a wallet or a pen were inserted into a pocket the effect would be spoilt. He was also wearing an open-necked electric-blue shirt with a collar the dimensions of which implied reciprocal risk, or folly, or at its most charitable the desire to emulate Burt Reynolds playing an ageing porno king from the San Fernando Valley. Strangely, the effect was touching as much as ludicrous, and I began to unpack once again my ambivalent feelings towards the figure of Jörg Haider.

We moved backwards with the crowd. Haider was here at a special congress of the FPÖ which he had hijacked twelve years ago, transforming it from a sleepy, ineffectual opposition grouping to a subversive engine of his own. The occasion was a familiar story of corruption (made marginally less banal by the fact that the Leader appeared to have been aware of it) but this was a pretext for Haider's determination to change the character of his party, making it entirely subordinate to his own will. A new fully electronic system of voting was rigged up. With the aid of a device looking like an excessively cumbersome TV channel zapper, delegates could vote on anything presented to them. But they were being asked to vote for Haider – with their assistance he proposed to grant himself absolute power within the party, including the ability to hire and fire any of his candidates. A muted excitement gripped the bourgeois crowd around me.

They knew that they were about to do something reprehensible. Nonetheless, they were going to do it.

For foreigners Haider was the first interesting thing to have happened to Austria since Orson Welles went down the sewers – what he did, and whether he succeeded, would affect the rest of Europe. At one moment his success had seemed assured, but now his fortunes appeared to be less certain. Austrians were divided over whether he was a smart if reckless politician, prepared at last to modernize, or even blow apart, the carved up world of coalition politics in Austria, which had ensured that the same parties stiflingly remained in power since the last war; or whether he was indeed an heir to the Nazi tradition and an instance of the new Austrofascism. The word 'yuppie' came easily affixed to his sporty features, and he appeared to appeal to many neglected sections of Austrian society, including young women and men, the old, blue-collar workers. In the most recent elections for the European Parliament, he polled an astonishing 27 per cent of the vote, placing his party on a par with two ageing rivals. Despite mid-middle-age, Haider kept himself embarrassingly trim. He still referred to himself and his party as being somehow 'new', though it did appear that he wouldn't get enough votes to destroy the old system. And yet if he failed to overthrow the system where would that leave him? Those around him spoke of sudden attacks of black dog. It seemed as if all the running, preening and denouncing finally wasn't getting him anywhere. There were even rumours – I didn't take them seriously – to the effect that he might retire.

'He is dangerous,' the *Standard* man said loudly, as we counted vote after vote in Haider's favour, some of them reaching the sort of proportions demanded by the most exigent socialist-bloc dictators. Haider's danger, my mentor explained, came not from the quarter that one might have expected. It was his lack of consistent ideas that constituted the real problem. Haider just lined up with whatever appeared to be the mainstream current of protest. It wasn't clear whether he believed in many of the causes he espoused. However, that didn't preclude the exercise of an absolutist dogmatism. Haider wasn't a Nazi, and it wasn't clear whether he should be called a fascist. But those who voted for him would find themselves betrayed if he ever got to power. In some respects it could be said that the process of betrayal began earlier, at the very moment one encountered the configuration of buttons before us and decided to press H for Haider. I held the FPÖ device in my hand, pressing all the buttons in turn.

These days it seemed that politicians of all stripes throughout Europe didn't believe in very much, relying instead on polls and marketing. The Haider question – the Austrian one, to be sure – was whether a dictator could be animated by nothing more coherent than the fluctuations of opinion polls. In Vienna I experienced the unease I usually did. It was easy to dismiss the city as a relic, but something told me that we hadn't done with what Austria meant, and that in its apparent deadness it could supply a version of the European nightmare. Like the country, the city was mysteriously blocked, and it appeared as if little or nothing could be done about this. It felt like a large over-ornate cemetery to me, and I could identify with the spirit of antagonism that Haider appeared to tap with such effortlessness. There must be something to be done about the deadness of Austria. But I'd felt queasy the first time I met Haider, without knowing exactly what it was that produced this effect. His gentian-coloured eyes stared into me, but I couldn't see what, if anything, was behind them. At that time I was prepared to give him the benefit of the doubt on the Nazi question. It was true that Haider's parents were both middle-ranking Nazis, but that could be said of very many Austrians. Haider was an intelligent man, who had been an associate professor of law and who, unlike most European politicians, had bothered to keep up with the new currents of right-wing thought.[5] He travelled frequently to the United States, where he had taken part in the New York marathon and, somewhat less convincingly, hobnobbed with various minority associations. In his efforts to reassure, he had even gone so far as to address B'nai B'rith.

It must be possible for a man whose parents were Nazis to be a democrat – and this meant that his many assertions to the effect that there were 'no brown stains' among his followers were at least worth taking seriously. The Resistance Documentation Centre, which occupied a musty suite of rooms in a crumbling municipal building, had a long and honourable record of attempting to confront Austrians with their unwholesome past. The centre, as its director Wolfgang Neugebauer explained to me, had also examined Haider, and the latter had sued a number of times, causing the centre to airbrush the cover of an encyclopedia of the Extreme Right in which he was featured along with Nazi insignia. Grey-haired, dogged, Herr Neugebauer wouldn't be drawn on the question of the Haider sexiness. 'I'm not a woman and I can't know,' he said. But he was persistent, and he marshalled his evidence with a familiarity born of long dislike. It was clear to me that he hated Haider as a type of Austrianness – one that he would have wished to see eradicated many years previously – even as he disapproved of him profoundly as an individual and fallible politician. He told me that Haider was, if not a Nazi, at least 'a little dictator'. I mustn't be taken in by all the empty talk about America and democracy. This was Europe, after all, and he opened file after file in which Haider's dubious proposals – statements which were sufficiently ambiguous not always to merit retraction – were on record. But I learned that Haider had on occasions been less guarded. He was obliged to resign from the position of Governor of Carinthia after he had commended Hitler for his politics of full employment. Haider invariably spoke defensively when he mentioned the Nazi past, and it was as if he resented having to apologize for its existence – or disliked the fact that, with his background, he would always be reminded of it by his enemies. But he did return to the old music of Nazism, and this could be interpreted as stubbornness or opportunism, or both. In 1995 Haider addressed a meeting of Waffen SS veterans held in Krumpendorf, a small Austrian town. These were old men from all over Europe whose younger selves had chosen to serve Hitler. The speech Haider gave to them was a distressing mixture of wheedling apologetics and vengeful demagogy. Not content with praising the elder generation for their staunch performance in a tough time, alluding wholeheartedly to their 'values' which were worth conserving as part of the national history, Haider also attacked those whom he called 'the lefties of political correctness' for having wanted to bury the past.

It was a truly shameless performance – a conspicuous instance of having it every way at once. Just as unattractive was the style in which Haider approached the matter of foreigners. Austria could boast a grand if also catastrophe-ridden multiethnic past from the days of the Habsburg Empire, and the Vienna phone book was filled with Slav names. But the creation of post-imperial Austria and the murder of the large Jewish community had made the country predominantly German, ill at ease with the prospect of any ethnic re-dilution. Haider had havered over the matter of whether Austria should be re-annexed to Germany, until in the mid-1990s he appeared to settle for the conventionally xenophobe position of opposing the European Union on the grounds that it would, sooner or later, cause Austria to be swallowed up. Where Slav immigrants were concerned his views were tougher – he believed that they should not be there. Although foreigners made up less than 9 per cent of the population (somewhere around the European average) and only three in one hundred foreigners became Austrian each year, Haider warned – with what appeared to be surreal implausibility – of the dangers of the country going multicultural. Austrians required protection from the alien – they had a right, he repeated, to remain themselves. 'Austria', he declared, perhaps redundantly, given its treatment of foreigners, 'is not an immigrants' country'. In 1992, Haider sponsored a referendum on the question of what should be done with immigrants. One of the measures proposed was the creation of a separate apartheid-style school system for immigrants' children, ostensibly to enable them to learn German more rapidly. He also suggested the usual scheme of 'voluntary repatriation' for those who had already acquired passports. When booby traps were placed in Carinthia on signs telling gypsies to go home and letter bombs sent to prominent anti-racist campaigners, Haider explained that this was the work of foreign criminal elements. (Some of them, as it turned out, were not – in 1999, a middle-aged white chemist identified with an organization known as the Bavarian Liberation Front was found guilty of sending bombs through the post.) Responding to Haider's various initiatives in 1993 the government cravenly toughened the residency requirements applying to foreigners. The Ministry of the Interior even threatened to rescind the residency permit of any foreigner occupying less than 10 square metres. Foreigners were obliged to supply copious details of the apartments they inhabited, down to the window sizes and the plumbing. There was a ten-year waiting period for anyone wishing to take the momentous step of becoming an Austrian.

Austria, I reminded myself, was not alone in constituting a laboratory in which one might see the future through the survival of a less than appealing past. But it was also the place in Europe where this was most easily done. I could hang around waiting for Haider outside the Vienna Parliament where Adolf Hitler (if *Mein Kampf* was to be believed) had conceived his distaste for democracy. And I was also able to interview one of Haider's lieutenants in the fake-Gothic Rathaus where in 1895 the mayor of Vienna, Karl Lueger, had invented the idea of ethnic quotas in government, thus excluding Jews and Slavs. Haider and his party were complaining about the municipal subsidies given to those who were opening Chinese restaurants in Vienna, on the grounds that they were destroying traditional Austrian food. When I suggested to an aide that the campaign might be called 'The Last Schnitzel' I was surprised that he took it seriously.

Everywhere in the Vienna suburbs were huge glazed-eye posters of Jörg Haider, open-necked, white-collared, bearing the haunting slogan 'THIS MAN STANDS IN THE PATH OF THE MIGHTY'. Confused by this claim, I went to the premises of ORF – Austrian public television. There I watched Haider bungee jumping, rollerblading, rock climbing, downhill skiing, cross-country skiing, running, striding, falling into ditches or turning the wheel of his Porsche. I heard him describe himself – the term itself was, like Haider, some way beyond parody – as a 'lifestyle politician'. In one bizarre sequence, he was to be seen modelling sportswear sponsored by his own party. I noticed that his Puritan-maid white collar was even larger than usual. Instead of flirting with the camera, he seemed to glare fixedly, with a forlorn, disconnected expression. All this displaying of himself, coupled with so much movement, didn't give the rational, Leader-like impression that he wished to convey. He looked as if there was something that he desperately wished to hide.

And this is what he was like when I interviewed him – so much so that I was left dizzy. He didn't deny his positions; instead he moved sideways rapidly, implying that these questions might once have been important but that he preferred to leave them in the past. There was a future, and he was part of it – the youthfulness of his party was something he referred to persistently, as if that explained or even justified anything. When I suggested that plebiscites of the kind he appeared to solicit were not always compatible with democracy, he suggested that he and his followers would decide about that. They would not use their power irresponsibly. Everything to do with the Hitler past, every criticism of the positions he had taken with respect to foreigners was the work of his enemies. I was left with a grimace, a pair of blue eyes, and the sense that if emptiness might ever be called deep, this was how it would feel. A storm broke out as we talked, and Haider, abruptly unhappy, terminated the interview. It appeared that he had to go to the Parliament in order to vote on a motion connected with the identification of paedophiles released from prison.

Afterwards, I stood in the rain, wondering at what I had experienced. Haider might or might not come to power in Austria – only a few months after he was said to be finished, in the spring of 1999 he won 38 per cent of the vote in regional elections in his own Carinthia.

The Freedom Party entered into a new coalition with the People's Party in February 2000. After celebrating his fiftieth birthday on a mountaintop, with torches and yodelling, Haider remained half in the background, giving interviews in his native Carinthia. When a boycott was organized, he threatened the EU with retaliation. He flew to Canada in order to visit a Holocaust museum. He told journalists that Churchill had committed crimes against humanity. In one bizarre newspaper article, written for the *Daily Telegraph*, Haider compared himself to Tony Blair. Both men, he suggested, were free of the old ideological ballast, appealing to the young and socially mobile. Haider, it was suggested, was less tough on asylum-seekers than Blair. And of course they both wished to do something about paedophiles. But Haider had failed to anticipate the degree of hostility provoked by his presence in government. He appeared to be shaken by the large demonstrations that took place every night in Vienna. Although support for him and his policies rose throughout Austria, it was also evident that his many enemies would not, as he had perhaps hoped, get used to him. Haider resigned his post as head of the Freedom Party a month later. He said that he did not wish to make things difficult for his colleagues. Most Austrians assumed that this meant he would be back once he had found another way down the mountain.

Cleverer than Le Pen, Haider had known how to adapt his ideas to the present. One should not underestimate him, or make the mistake of concluding from his appearance that he was a futile figure, doomed to self-extinction. There was no reason why someone like him should not get elected Chancellor or Prime Minister in the future – and the future of Europe might well prove to accommodate a number of Haider-like figures, from Scotland to Calabria. For Haider understood many things about contemporary disaffection. Like the other populists he had been able to comprehend the depth of antagonism towards the new structures of international Europe, whether they were those of capitalism or bureaucracy. He also understood that racism, to be accepted in Europe, must be discreet, attaining a kind of normality. It must become no longer worth discussing at all, otherwise it would be rejected. What appeared to be an excess interest in clothing was in effect the old Austrian obsession with good taste updated. Finally, Haider also grasped that many Austrians, and indeed Europeans, were sick of politics. Ageing, though not always as gracefully as him, they wanted to be left alone in moderate prosperity. If they were to be led at all, it would only be by someone who possessed guile and sleight of hand. In that respect the interdiction placed on the politics of dangerous individualism in Austria had proved to be the perfect training ground for Haider. It had shown him how one must be charismatic and banal at the same time. And it had also demonstrated how changing one's mind was no disfavour in the new world of populist politics – so long as certain immovable pieties, those of race and identity, were adhered to.

We were nowhere near understanding the implications of the weakening of nation states which had afforded some sort of identity to their citizens for so long. In some instances, where people were indifferent or keen to trade in one not-so-loved brand of being for another, the effect might be benign. Those who had signed up for the European experiment, among whom I included myself, must hope that this would be the case. The sociologist Ernest Gellner used the phrase 'secondary cultural pluralism'[6] to describe the various *Braveheart*-style totemic local attachments – beer mats, football insignia, half-dead or exhumed languages, lost sovereignties reclaimed only in appearance – of the new Europe middle class. But it was possible already to anticipate the existence of an injured sense of identity. Never quite able to seize power, not able to do much, the proponents of such views would nonetheless be in a position to spoil or disrupt. Many of them (I included Haider within this category) were not democrats or not wholeheartedly so. They would gain from the identification of 'Europe' with the failings of democracy. They would say, rightly perhaps, that the arrogant super-structure of 'Brussels' was a sham, and that they were hindered in their efforts to point this out by any number of defective institutions. They would feed off impatience with meaningless procedures. If the foreigners in their midst proved more acceptable to Europeans (not that this was likely) they would find other ways of dramatizing the predic-ament of small people dominated by forces they couldn't control. Though they wouldn't always say so, it would be clear to those who voted for them that democracy itself was at fault. Alas, I understood that it was already too late to discuss such groups, or people, as a hypothesis. They were already there, among us, working their malign way.

'Strong views weakly held' was how the historian A. J. P. Taylor had characterized what he considered to be his own frivolity. He meant to disassociate himself from sober-suited (and, it was implied, less than competent) colleagues. In the event, Taylor wasn't in the least frivolous; but he understood the power of stupidity. His astute analyses of international affairs didn't hide from him the perception that the power of hatred rested on indifference or delusion, in particular among those who called themselves democrats. And evasions were still prominent in contemporary Europe. Indeed they were what electorates required of their politicians – in poll after poll Europeans revealed themselves to be indifferent about the quality of democracy available to them, even while reviling their politicians for their failure to provide anything better. It was easy to say that Haider and his like fed off the widely available store of hatred in Europe, but the truth was that they were also made possible by our own failures. Meanwhile, it was the wardrobe that stuck in my memory. Convenient as this might have been for the rest of us, in particular those who called themselves anti-fascists, it didn't seem likely to me that fascism would return to Europe wearing brown trousers and a toothbrush moustache. Instead, we would find ourselves with something like Jörg Haider and his strange variety of open-collared leisurewear.

# THE BLACK GUIDE

'But between the day and night
The choice is free to all; and light
Falls equally on black and white.'
W. H. Auden, 'Negroes'[1]

Often, while I was with those I called the fascists, I see-sawed
between nausea and despair. This wasn't merely, or even
primarily, because I didn't like meeting those in whose company I found myself and didn't especially enjoy so protracted
an encounter with the enemy. It was also a result of what
I conceived to be the difficulty, finally, of knowing how
important they were. If they weren't important, I was wasting
my time on curiosities, and I had inadvertently become an
antiquarian of sorts, as well as an atrocity tourist, trailing
around Europe in search of items from the grubby or horrific
past. I knew journalists or writers who did this for a living,
and I had told myself (perhaps a little priggishly) that cultural
beachcoming and objets trouvés weren't for me. However,
this was among the most difficult assignments of my life, and
I couldn't quite explain why; indeed the only way I could
respond to this was to say that at some point I would
consider my serial encounters with fascists to be over, and it
would be when I knew there was nothing left for me to

discover. But the trouble was that I didn't know how or when to stop. And I was now certain that 'fascism' was bad for the health – that I could guarantee from my own crankiness. Who could ever have imagined that it wasn't harmful?

Sometimes I felt like a cartoon figure, running as hard as I could away from or towards something. I hoped I would finally run off a cliff, coming to rest God knows where, anywhere so long as it was many leagues away from those in whose indifferent, hate-filled presence I reluctantly found myself. The trouble was that it hadn't occurred to me just how simple and wholly predictable (and how immovable, too, resisting even the equivalent of dynamite) the racist *discours* was. It was possible to write lengthy, energetic books about the lives of the great fascists, but that didn't mean that one wouldn't have been terminally, poisonously bored in their presence, loathing their table talk; or would have failed to find them as ridiculous as their suburban lineal descendants. The more I watched videos of Hitler and Mussolini, the more I became convinced of this. Like many awful things, racism, or race hate, was both relatively easy to identify and, finally, unfathomable. It was banal in the oldest, truest sense, because it was everywhere. People had written many books about it too, and well-funded libraries existed to hold these volumes. Each year the temperature of racism was taken in copious, mostly misleading polls. The industry of race relations ground on even when people had begun to doubt its efficacy. But seeing racists was a different matter to registering their existence, and among friends a sense of muted surprise or even outrage attended my own efforts. Why would anyone bother to see so many dreadful people?

In 1995, I went for the first time for many years to Vienna, a city that had frightened me when I first attempted to learn German there as an adolescent. Searching for the Far Right, I found myself drawn not to its contemporary practitioners, but to the heritage of fear and hatred in the quiet city. You could sign up for many tours in Vienna, going down the sewers in search of the Third Man, or setting out towards the Alps to the uplifting sounds of the Trapp family. But there was one tour which was not advertised, or indeed available, and it was perhaps the most important one: The Adolf Hitler Guided Tour. One rainy day I found several of the slums which Hitler had occupied as a teenager. The best-preserved was near the Central Station, and it was abandoned, though adjoining apartments were, appropriately, frequented by Slav hookers who slid in and out of their décolletages as they negotiated the narrow stairs. The young Hitler's neighbourhood was little changed – it was possible to buy porn at the kiosk where, it is said, Hitler acquired the anti-Semitic magazine *Ostara*, the work of a crazed former Cistercian monk who called himself Jörg Lanz von Liebenfels.

The teenage Hitler's most prized magazine came filled with pop-culture fantasies according to which a Nordic race of blue-eyed blondes would take over the world, crushing socialism and feminism, sterilizing the mentally handicapped, and otherwise disposing of those considered to be of inferior race, such as the Jews. Nowadays one could find these ideas on Internet web pages romantically called Stormfront or White Aryan. They were everywhere, as they had been in early twentieth-century Vienna. Among historians, however, and not just Austrian ones, the role of Vienna in encouraging Hitler's anti-Semitism was a matter of dispute. Twenty years ago, the connection was taken for granted; there was no reason to doubt Hitler's own account in *Mein Kampf* of how he first met 'caftan-wearers' in Vienna, and became sick to his stomach at the sight of them. But Hitler, it turned out, knew some Jews; insofar as he was capable of any relationships, he appeared to have tolerated their presence, even doing business with them. *Mein Kampf* was a work of propaganda, written some thirteen years later, after Hitler's traumatic war experiences, and at a time when he wished to present himself as a serious anti-Semitic politician. It now seemed possible to talk of an early or ur-Hitler preceding the one we knew so well. This insecure, hopeless adolescent wasn't the full-blown anti-Semite of 1919, advocating first the deportation and then the liquidation of European Jews, but a hater of a more recognizable kind. At this stage he merely admired contemporary anti-Semitic politicians. The desire to emulate their efforts, or supersede them, was yet to come. This, it occurred to me, was a very Austrian trait, and it made me wonder what would have occurred to Hitler had it not been for the Great War. Perhaps he would have remained a genteel anti-Semite. Perhaps he would have gone on painting mountains and street scenes.

I came back to Vienna in 1998 to find that Hitler's apartment was in the process of being yuppified. Building materials were stacked everywhere, and a van belonging to an Adolf Grubner was parked outside the window. By now I had met so many people like the early Hitler. They were badly educated but certain in their ideas. They were young, many of them, with no women around them. It seemed hard for them to make any contact with the world. Some aspect of death or readiness for extinction clung to the young militants in whose midst I found myself, as indeed it had to Hitler. What Sebastian Haffner, one of Hitler's most perceptive biographers, called 'an empty life and hence one which, though certainly not happy, was strangely lightweight, and lightly discarded' could be filled only by the overwhelming presence of an idea.[2] It didn't matter that the idea had been tried, and failed, or was in other respects stupid or wholly reprehensible. Among the young militants no importance was attached to the 'real' Hitler. What they wanted was someone of their own from history, an ultimate deviant to whom all their frustrations could be attached. They had made Hitler into the sort of comic-book creation which the real Führer had enjoyed as an adolescent.

That summer, too, I visited Hitler's Eagle's Nest, near Berchtesgaden, close to the Austrian border. You got there by bus these days, swaying precipitously around the hair-pin bends. The tea house where poor Neville Chamberlain misguidedly abased himself had been turned into a restaurant where pork and dumplings were served as the dish of the day. Middle-aged climbers adjusted their gear for hikes to further peaks, while their pets struggled with magpies for cast-off crusts. This placid scene struck me as a nice metaphor, illustrating the degree to which we had little to fear from any precise simulation of the European past. I was overcome with a sudden access of good feelings. All we had to do was believe in ourselves and act decently. If we became genuine European citizens (I began to elaborate on this idea) we would find our own ways of finishing with racism. When I said this to my French colleagues, however, I was roundly criticized for my light-headedness. It seemed that I was ignorant, and that I was unaware of ideology. Nothing could be quite so simple. Nothing *should* be so simple. As we drove down again, swaying queasily around the bends, they suggested that it wasn't enough merely to want everyone to be better democrats. All over Europe there were enemies. The implication was that special measures to combat the foe were still required. We argued vigorously and, at the end, out of exhaustion, I half accepted their criticisms. Perhaps the circumstances of classical fascism had indeed gone. But the hatred still remained, seeking expression; and we did have to find ways of containing, if not overcoming it.

And yet I wondered about this once I was off Hitler's mountain. A spirit of mild bourgeois worry surrounded the subject of race hate, deadening the reality which it claimed so earnestly to be animating. The catastrophe of mid-twentieth-century European civilization ensured, rightly, that there would always be an audience who responded to warnings to the effect that the awfulness might in time return. However, the anti-fascist prescriptions were far from convincing. Sometimes it seemed as if the purpose of such organizations as SOS Racism was not to eradicate the phenomenon, but – as the title implied – save it, like a whale or a rare baboon. I was wary of so much voyeurism mixed with reprobation evident in the many sober-minded films about Swedish or Swiss skinheads. Were they the victims of the deficiencies of the Welfare State? Did they shave their hair to look ugly? Did anyone care? It was hard to think that a single one of the many bloody-minded specimens whom I had met might have been converted by such well-meaning efforts, just as it was difficult to imagine young frontists taking seriously the spectacle of actresses and film-makers encamped outside a church filled with *sans-papiers*.

I was certain, too, that petty or indeed intensive gaggings of offenders against what had become canons of politeness were not the answer. Censorship might not be a serious problem for Europeans, but it was nonetheless an embarrassing one. So much high-minded interdiction appeared foolish, and it was a holdover from post-war sackcloth. I was embarrassed to see so many ex-Trotskyist protagonists from 1968 exercising power in order to deny constitutional rights to their opponents. In Germany the phenomenon of left-liberal censorship was especially distressing, allowing as it did the clamps on consciousness which permitted the well-meaning to stay locked into a false seriousness about every aspect of the world. Sometimes it seemed that the German Left was engaged in a permanent project of self-censorship under the guise of blocking out the Nazi remnant. How else could one explain the bizarre reluctance of the German Greens in 1999 to countenance action against the atrocities of Slobodan Milošević on the grounds that, because of their own dangerous past, Germans should be disqualified from war?

Liberalism had become something of a dirty word among many Europeans. It meant the erosion of welfare cultures and the power of American capitalism. Although Europe was said to be a liberal society, it contained precious few genuine liberals. I returned to what Isaiah Berlin had written: 'Everything is what it is: Liberty is liberty, not equality or fairness or justice or culture, or human happiness or a quiet conscience.' The trouble was that, for Europeans, liberty appeared to have declined in importance relative to other things. Censorship was ultimately an expression of self-mistrust – it implied, if indeed it meant anything, that some sort of renewed outbreak of nastiness was feared. But so sophisticated a place as Europe shouldn't endlessly be seen to lack confidence in itself because of its stained past. Although there was more censorship in Europe than twenty years ago, it was exercised in a spirit of self-defeat. It was part of a system of correctness whereby Europeans, decade after decade, were treated as wayward children. It would last, certainly (many cases would be argued, and impassioned pleas would be made, to the effect that it should be retained), but the observance would be increasingly perfunctory. It would not survive the introduction of the new aids to freedom of expression such as the Internet, nor indeed the lack of boundaries of the Europe in which we all lived. And I would be glad when it was over, even if the consequences were occasionally painful. For we would never truly know what those whom we reproved actually believed if we persisted in our demands that they speak in a language that accorded with our own prejudices.

I now believed that the worst wouldn't come from those who mimicked or conserved the outrage of the past. A deviant, anti-democratic popular culture, disturbing to our sensibilities, nauseating in its cruelty or historical incompetence, wasn't what we ultimately had to fear. Instead, we must look for the face of evasion. We had to be prepared for the appearance of many comforting lies, coming from those who assured us that they were, appearances to the contrary, democratic politicians with our interests at heart. By now I had met so many people like this: able to fish in the same murk as their clumsier, more overt associates, their power came from the ability to deny that this was what they were doing. It was the difference between the mad dog Le Pen and his smoother Mr Bean rival Mégret, or between Haider and the neo-Nazis.

In 1998, British newspapers reprinted the text of Enoch Powell's infamous Birmingham 'rivers of blood' speech on its thirtieth anniversary. 'We must be mad, literally mad,'[3] is how Powell described the arrival each year in grey Britain of Caribbean or Indian immigrants. 'It is like watching a nation busily engaged in heaping up its funeral pile.' Like his successors, Powell affected not to be a racist – he had been touched by the memory of the Raj, having served in India, and he explained that Indians were, for the most part, more intelligent than the white Britons whom he addressed. Jews were above ordinary intelligence, too. It was the difference of national or ethnic cultures that Powell – again, like his successors – wished to conserve. If the word had been current he, too, would have reviled the idea of multiculturalism.

Powell's speech caused his disgrace within the Tory Party. But it was also the beginning of the acknowledgement of white working-class resistance to immigration. In that respect the Powellite crusade wasn't wholly in vain. Powell alluded to a Tiber foaming with blood in accents that must have been far away from those of his listeners, and which I had never encountered in my own travels. However, it wasn't his dated classical scholar fustian or his inordinate (and less than accurate) affirmations of imminent disaster that kept my attention. I was interested in the pensioner he claimed to have discovered in his Wolverhampton constituency:

> She is becoming afraid to go out. Windows are broken. She finds excreta pushed through her letter box. When she goes to the shops, she is followed by children, charming wide-grinning piccaninnies. They cannot speak English but one word they know. 'Racialist,' they chant.[4]

At the time the press had demanded to meet this old lady, without success. Powell's official biographer fared no better in his efforts – he was told that her name had been lodged with a solicitor, with instructions that it should never be made public; and, bizarrely, he appeared to accept this. But I felt that I had already met this old lady many times. She hadn't died; indeed she was part of a large unhappy European family of the persecuted and righteously embittered. Nephews and nieces of hers popped up in Jörg Haider's speeches, to denounce Serb or Slovenian swindlers unmasked in Carinthian benefits offices, but it was in Le Pen's inspired ramblings that she attained her apotheosis:

Think of the old lady, whose flat is broken into and whose fingers are broken, or who is made to swallow detergent, to know where her savings are hidden . . .

In our country, pity the widow and the orphan, for their lot will never be a happy one. And pity the poor, the millions of poor of this country for they are the first victims since they can never leave the slums in which they are lodged, and it is they whose task it is to assure the moral security and balance of the bourgeois society whose members of course live so far away while preaching the virtues of tolerance . . .[5]

A feature of such rhetorical outbursts was the lavish disregard for the claims of literal truth. The Seine might indeed catch rhetorical fire, or the Thames foam again with bitterness – or there again, they might placidly flow towards the indifferent sea. Recently, the bodies tipped into rivers or harbours had been those of Arabs killed by marauding white gangs. But there would always be European politicians holding these views and people ready to listen to them. It didn't matter whether the interlopers actually forced detergent down throats, raped or murdered the old ladies. The point was that they boasted 'names that weren't French'. Whether the old lady really existed or not didn't matter – as Le Pen himself might have said, it was *un détail*, not something worthy of consideration within the larger scope of things.

I wondered whether it wasn't the fact that my protagonists were so far beyond rational argument that left me drained and angry after each abortive confrontation. 'HOW TO INTERVIEW A FASCIST', a latter diary entry read, in parody of Emily Post. I concluded that it was a question of waiting and needling; sooner or later, they broke under pressure, revealing themselves. But I acknowledged that derision, too, had its place. About the dictators, W. H. Auden had written sombrely in 1939, and with a sense of shared responsibility:

> I and the public know
> What all schoolchildren learn
> Those to whom evil is done
> Do evil in return[6]

Such impeccable sentiments now seemed dated to me. Those whom I had met were not always victims, and their leaders often did well from the culture of self-aggrandizing paranoia. They operated a lucrative racket in victimhood. Even allowing for their provenance from a bar in New York at the outbreak of World War Two, Auden's sentiments reeked of falseness and easy, hand-wringing resignation. For there were different ways of not giving the last word to hate peddlers. Our age came overloaded with fake seriousness as well as conspicuous vulgarity; and, given the choice, I preferred humour to portentousness or moral posturing. In 1932, the front page of a Munich newspaper came adorned with a photocomposite picture of Hitler in top hat and wedding tails, posed (this latter detail would now be considered offensive) with a black bride.[7] 'DOES HITLER HAVE MONGOLIAN BLOOD?' ran the caption, and its author Fritz Gerlich pursued the notion by using the 'racial science' of Nazi quacks against Hitler himself, concluding by means of photographic close-ups just how poorly Hitler measured up to his own racial criteria. Alas, Gerlich's humour didn't save him, and he was rapidly removed from the scene, murdered in Dachau. However, among anti-racist campaigners I missed his spirit, and that of his luckier Hollywood exile contemporary Ernst Lubitsch, for whom the elegiac recitation of absurd and touching Jewish names in the 1942 comic masterpiece *To Be or Not to be*, one after another, anticipated what Hitler would do within months to the Jews of Central Europe.

I had started, reporter-style, with the simple object of knowing enemies. There they were, before me now, sitting like grinning guignols. As Saul Bellow remarked about the dead, I didn't need to visit them; they would come to find me. Although this had not been my primary objective, by now I did know more about what motivated them. 'I suppose one must either abolish unemployment – or abolish Le Pen,' the historian Pierre Vidal-Naquet had said to me, sighing. What I didn't know was how that could be accomplished or, if it proved impossible (which was more than likely), how one might ensure that the ideas opposing Le Pen and those like him were so significant or attractive that all of us need no longer fear the seepage of poison.

For the fascists preyed on the inadequacies of what Karl Popper had called the Open Society. Never anxious to pre-serve democracy, because it threatened their project, they were careful to emphasize its shortcomings. If they spoke long and loudly enough on this theme, it was reasoned, people would listen, as they had done in the past. In our time democracy in Europe was stronger, to be sure; but one might also enumerate its failings. Many institutions (the EU itself was surely one of them) were comprehensively blocked, and could be called democratic only in a formal, straitened sense. The idea that democracy was a creation of individual citizens, and could be sustained only by their vigilance and civic participation, had sadly fallen into neglect. It could also be said, sadly once more, but in a spirit of realism, that many Europeans these days were not so overwhelmingly interested in the practice of democracy after all. The sense of relief with which they had greeted the opportunity to rebuild their shattered civilization had, by and large, been replaced by the sense that an unreasonable degree of good fortune came with the European package. Most Europeans accepted consumer capitalism because it worked for them. They would tolerate minorities as long as they caused no problems. What remained of the Welfare State would be kept going as long as no sacrifices were required. Towards democracy itself, they held pretty much the same views. But the feeblest aspect of European democratic practices, as the fascists had understood, could be perceived in the treatment of those considered to be foreigners. No one in Europe knew how many of them should be admitted. No one really knew why they were there, other than to do things which most Europeans would rather not do. And no one was certain how much freedom should be allowed to these interlopers. There was nothing new about these attitudes, but this didn't make them less threatening.

'I was Europe's last chance,' Hitler remarked in his testament, dictated shortly before he killed himself. In 1945, following the failure of fascist 'experiments', the settled minorities of Central Europe had been destroyed through deportation and gassing. There were additional forced movements of refugees when Germans were expelled from Poland or the Sudetenland – millions of Europeans were shifted around the map, fetching up in places they wouldn't have anticipated. The creation of an Eastern socialist bloc, inaccessible behind its frontiers, ensured that the 'unlucky' Europeans – Czechs, Slovaks, Ruthenians, Bulgars, Slovenes – would have to live among their own kind. Much of the old liberal project of protecting minorities through the practice of self-determination, which animated the 1919 Treaties, had in effect been abandoned, though no one said so. Although the war had been fought in the name of internationalist solidarity, and against what we now call 'cleansing', abruptly, not in the way anyone might have wished, Europe was a place where nation states held jurisdiction over one ethnic stock. Between them, Stalin and Hitler had created a more or less stable Europe composed mostly of states in which Europeans of similar ethnic backgrounds lived. Just as Ireland was for the Irish, Poland was Polish and indeed Germany (as few Europeans would now regret) definitively German. The same was true of Tito's Yugoslavia, where only a bare illusion of ethnic harmony, encouraged by the usual gross propaganda about brotherhood, concealed the realities of separatism.

It was in this context, of a Europe that had failed in its dealings with minorities, tragically and comprehensively, but appeared to have been given yet another chance, that the new foreigners from outside Europe were to arrive. When the experiment of mass immigration began in the 1950s, encouraged by labour shortages and population decline, it was assumed without forethought and for no reason in particular that no one would stay.[8] 'Immigration on a large scale', suggested the 1948 British Royal Commission on Population, 'could only be welcomed without reserve if the immigrants were of good human stock and were not prevented by their religion or race from inter-marrying.' Yet the practices of liberal capitalism and the insatiable demand for labour to make up for the millions killed, or to man rapidly growing factories, made such nice discriminations impossible. Immigrants were needed, and they were given some sort of welcome, albeit grudging. However, except in Britain, where the newcomers possessed British citizenship as a consequence of the newly created Commonwealth, it was not assumed that they would stay. In 1964 Der Spiegel presented Armando Rodriguez, the millionth gastarbeiter to arrive in Germany with a motorbike but not a passport. Migrant workers were housed in barracks or in the decaying centres of cities. Entrances to parks in Switzerland carried the signs: 'No entry for dogs and Italians.' Boarding houses in Britain were labelled: 'No Blacks, Irish or Dogs.'

When the long post-war boom finally came to a close at some time in the early 1970s, the liberal immigration policies ended, too. Whether businesses had sought them out, as they did in France, going to the *bled* in search of labour; or operated a licence system, as Germany did in relation to Turkey; or merely not hindered their arrival, as was the laissez-faire British habit, the reaction among the representatives of European states was similar. They were frightened of adverse response from their own native populations, who saw themselves cheated of the jobs that were rightfully theirs, and they took fright, suddenly. In 1968, the basis of British citizenship was changed, from the Empire, where it had previously been rooted, back to the mother country. To be British it now became necessary to have a *British* parent. Germany's 1965 'Foreigner's Act', gave the state powers to expel immigrant workers on any grounds. During the 1970s and 1980s both Germany and France initiated schemes designed to make it easier for foreigners to return home. 'The Federal Republic is not an immigrant country,' the German Federal Commission reported in 1977. 'Germany is a place of residence for foreigners who will eventually return home voluntarily.' In France the Constitutional Court blocked the more extreme of these 'go back home' provisions, granting the right to stay to those who didn't have passports and thus over-ruling politicians. Such moves were hailed by legal experts as early milestones along a road on which in Europe, as in the US, matters of citizenship would be decided by courts, and these would take precedence over the whims of politicians. But the effect was not to make the immigrants wanted. Nor did it render comprehensible to voters the attempts to settle those who were there and now brought their families to live with them. Instead it seemed as if the French elite had been reluctant to accept the 'guests' and had done so only under duress, pressured by legal considerations that had little or nothing to do with the 'real', and thus legitimate, sources of popular feelings. It could be said, therefore, that in voting against immigration, and creating the Far Right, Europeans were merely reflecting the lack of resolution of their elites, who hadn't specially wanted this enormous influx of foreigners and, once they were there, didn't know what to do with them.

Just as damagingly, this confusion undermined the provisions that were made for the foreigners. Whether they were housed in ghettoes often built for them, as in France, or carefully dispersed through the population, as they were in Germany, or merely, in what had become the British way, left to fend for themselves, the idea of their contingent, rootless state persisted. If it was easy to change the basis of nationality, it could be changed again. If the immigrants were indeed commodities in the labour market (the basis on which their presence had been rendered acceptable) they should be treated as such. But if they were no longer migrants or visitors, or indeed foreigners, having by default become citizens, something had gone wrong; and they should also go before it was too late. Hatred fed off the mistrust of elites that came with lack of work, or indeed (as members of the populist right became convinced) lack of democracy. It flourished amid the evolution of grudges and mass discontent; and it took hold in the idea of a giant, consuming conspiracy directed against the old, and 'real', peoples of Europe. The creation of an even more distant, supranational 'Europe' augmented it, granting respectability to this fantasy. This was how movements like the Front National came to exercise the hold they did. And yet it was no good changing the law, as the right-of-centre government in France did in the early 1990s, in response to the Front's demands, qualifying the old notion that it was enough to be born in France with the idea that one must have a French parent or choose to be French. These measures were not enough – all they achieved was the precipitate demand that more should be done, and that all repatriation of those called, insultingly, *Français de fraîche date* (FFD) should now take place, along with the *sans-papiers*, the illegal workers.

But there was also good reason for so much official timidity among those whose job it was to make such decisions. Even if one didn't accept that Europe was a tribal place, dominated by the poison of ethnic memory, it could often seem so. It was difficult to get Europeans to accept foreigners in their midst. It was all but impossible to envision a Europe filled with foreigners, and altered by their presence. Portions of Europe had once accommodated sizeable foreign populations only to extinguish their memory, when the old graveyards crumbled from neglect or the unattended plaques conveniently fell off the walls. In Europe churches became supermarkets or mosques, and the bricks from synagogues were used as millstones. Where history was recreated, it was often falsehood. Tastelessly, the struggle to obliterate or appropriate went on, as if the past were a wrecker's yard. Foreigner hatred was an old European theme, far more significant than such baubles as the Euro or harmonized taxes. It was still a subject about which open argument was difficult.

In early 2000, the UN published a report suggesting that Europe would require 150 million extra workers within the next twenty-five years. Germany alone would need to import half a million foreigners each year. Not all of these could be found in the poorer regions of the EU. Where would they come from? How would they be greeted? Would their presence give rise to new Le Pens and Haiders?[9] The question of how Europeans saw the foreigners in their midst was the most significant one of our time. It determined the sort of Europe we all chose to inhabit – when additional atrocities on the scale of the Kosovo war occurred, a civilized Europe would be required to offer asylum. We needed to understand what, if anything, foreignness meant to Europeans. It was the most important question, surely, for us all, because it defined the only frontier left of any significance. Only by deciding rationally about such matters as citizenship and belonging would we Europeans finally know or understand who we were. One of the claims of Europe to importance lay in its espousal of the universalist vision of humanity based on rights. Common sense indicated that such claims could not be taken seriously in a place where race hate still prevailed, and where citizenship, once granted, wasn't taken seriously. The freedoms granted to native Europeans – not just to travel without passports, but to work in different EU countries and, in most cases, to vote in local elections in countries where they were not citizens – made such contradictions more absurd. One might imagine as a hypothesis the respective fates of two Turks from the same village, one going to France, where he became a French citizen, and was tormented by the FN; the other fetching up in Germany, where he was taunted by neo-Nazis, and never ultimately became German. Why was it so hard to secure asylum in liberal Britain and so much easier in liberal Germany? Why should it be necessary, once due application was made, to wait ten years in order to become an Austrian when the same process took less than a year in France?

Century after century, tribes or religious minorities had travelled back and forth across Europe. Who remembered now that in the mid-eighteenth century half of the Berlin population consisted of Protestant immigrants from France, persecuted in their country of origin and accepted happily by Frederick the Great? The real story of foreigners in Europe was a complicated one, not easily adapted to populist slogans. It was marked by failure, but there were successes too – and not necessarily in the places where one might have expected to find them.

Depending on where they ended up in Europe, foreigners were either required to integrate or allowed to make their way in a climate of indifference and apathy. In the Netherlands, immigrant cultures were added on to the national structure according to which separate 'pillars' – Protestantism, Catholicism, Women's Rights, and Labour – were formally guaranteed autonomy. Muslim separatism was successfully reduced to the level of the problems posed by the Dutch fundamentalist sects who insisted, in violation of national laws, that women, being inferior, should not vote in their internal proceedings. But the result, I was told, was not wholly successful. Many of those for whom 'cultural' funds were available refused to take them, preferring to be thought of as Dutch. 'Those who cause least problems are thought to be most integrated,' a Dutch friend explained. In Britain there were still, from time to time, riots. Visitors could claim that fifty-odd years of migrations had merely effected the integration of formerly foreign Indians, Pakistanis and West Indians within the British nexus of class and frustration.[10]

Indian or West Indian friends warned me away from the question of race or race attitudes in Britain. They wanted to be British and not to inhabit a place where their own identity was pored over by outsiders. If they made films, or were journalists, they were often sick of the ethnic specialism assigned to them, and which, their own intense efforts notwithstanding, they found hard to shed. Discussions about race had a tendency to vanish, like so much else in Britain, into the intensively particular. Yes, after all, one could point to the abuses, not always recorded in British newspapers, particularly if the victims didn't conform to editors' views of who should legitimately be drawn to the public's attention. And one could recall the stubborn placing of racial attacks on a par with those in 'racist' Germany or higher than those recorded by French police forces. But such indices were at best misleading. Was it really the case that Britain, as a Dutch sociologist had alleged, was more racially violent than Le Pen's France?

Of course there was racism in Britain, and of course Britons were racists – but these were banal remarks, capable only of rehashing the obvious on talk-radio shows in which racists, despite the many legal provisions restricting their utterances, were still present to heap up abuse. It was as if the periodic, half-hearted study of 'race', dependent on the recycling of stereotypes, or the recounting of misleading statistics, had ended by generating its own inheritance of misleading half-truths from which it was difficult, if not impossible, to escape.

In 1982, I was responsible for a television show in which the young writer Salman Rushdie was given a half-hour of airtime to talk about British racism. He removed his glasses, glaring at the camera. 'Britain is not South Africa,' he began. 'I am reliably informed of that.' And then he went on, minute by minute, to itemize the shortcomings of the Pink Race, and the craven attitudes of representatives of the British liberal state. He suggested that the progressive denial of rights to large minorities under threat in the former Empire (the problem of the Hong Kong Chinese had not then arisen or been disgracefully evaded; nor had Britain yet perfected the policy towards asylum-seekers which placed it among the meanest European nations) was a scandal. And he ended by reminding his viewers that they were the real problem – not the foreigners but them. 'When Gandhi was asked what he thought of British civilization, he said: "It would be a good idea,"' Rushdie concluded, bowing out with what shocked audiences mistakenly took to be a sneer, but which was in reality stage fright. The performance would not have been thinkable in any other European country at the time, or even perhaps since outside the Netherlands and Scandinavia; and it caused much offence. There were those who thought the young author was exaggerating or merely trying to draw attention to himself. Others, perhaps more pertinently, resented the way he referred to himself and other Indians as 'blacks'. The outburst elicited a number of complaints from anti-racist organizations, though I was glad to see that these were rejected by the broadcasting authorities. I wasn't repentant about the piece nor, I was glad to find out, was the author. Nothing was gained by the smothering of such matters; and Rushdie had been correct in suggesting that politeness was no weapon against hatred.

But I was intrigued to see that he, too, now believed that things had changed in Britain. Racism was indeed banal, and there was no special evidence to the effect that the Pink Race enjoyed the presence of foreigners any more than twenty years previously. And yet, in London particularly, a rough and ready multiculturalism had taken root. When in spring 1999 the city appeared to be threatened by an outbreak of vicious nail bombings, there was not even a vestigial sense that the victims didn't belong in Britain or (an attitude that might somehow have been perceptible twenty-odd years previously) 'had it coming to them'. The phrase 'live and let live', with no equivalent in German or French, had been annexed by such characters as Grant in *EastEnders* and given general currency. It represented the way in which English people, in particular, who were routinely declared to have no identity or one that somehow needed reclamation from the jumble of nationalities of the British Isles, liked to see themselves. Originally the territory of 'protest' writing or film-making, race mixing was now depicted, more simply, as what went on in Britain. Curry houses and British blacks playing football seemed more to represent contemporary Britain than the costume dramas made by the BBC. In Mike Leigh's remarkable film *Secrets and Lies* the white family ended by accepting, grudgingly, to be sure, their long-lost black sibling given away for adoption. The relationship between the suburban whites, preoccupied by their barbecues, new cars and en-suite bathrooms, and their sharply professional newly found black daughter, cousin or niece wasn't either comfortable or successful. But that was the point of Leigh's modern British fable, giving to the film its unsentimental sense of the present.

'I am only a lodger, and hardly that,'[11] the freed slave Ignatius Sancho wrote about Britain in 1780. In 1990, the same unease was present in Hanif Kureishi's *The Buddha of Suburbia*, but so was the more modern idea that one might belong and not belong at the same time:

> I am often considered to be a funny kind of Englishman, a new breed as it were, having emerged from two old histories. But I don't care – Englishman I am (though not proud of it), from the South London suburbs and going somewhere. Perhaps it is the odd mixture of continents and blood, of here and there, of belonging and not, that makes me restless and easily bored.[12]

I couldn't imagine lines like these, assured as well as impertinent in their familiarity, coming from any other part of Europe. Nowhere else would you be encouraged to treat the presumed gifts of 'integration' with such lightness, or milk for so many jokes the numerous absurdities implied by the quest for assimilation. In Britain you could at once be so-British and not-British; nowhere else was the equivalent even the remotest possibility.

Britain had been lucky, of course, helped by a common language, minority religions to which the secular majority displayed the greatest indifference, and the totemic extravaganza of British life implied by the existence of a monarch at her happiest amidst crowds of straw-skirted dancers and officials wearing funny hats. But the confected nature of British national identity – the way in which the usual magic properties of places or moments came mixed with pious memories of collective needs, and the mysterious manner, given the colony-grabbing past, in which both of these had come to seem more important than the fiction of race – had also helped. Despite the weather and the landladies, Britain had also found a way of allowing foreigners to tolerate, or even occasionally enjoy, the prospect of being in some sort of new home. This was not, so far as I could see, the case in much of the rest of Europe.

In 1947 George Orwell was sitting in a draughty Scottish hotel when he heard two businessmen talking about the Polish workers drafted in to deal with the labour shortages in the mines. The younger businessman suggested that the Poles should be sent home. Orwell was aghast, seeing in such remarks 'the contemporary equivalent of anti-Semitism':

> The race hatred and mass delusions which are part of our
> times might be less bad in their effects if they were not

reinforced by ignorance. If in the years before the war, for instance, the facts about the persecution of Jews in Germany had been better known, the subjective popular feeling against Jews would not have been less, but the actual treatment of Jewish refugees would have been better. The refusal to allow refugees into this country would have been branded as disgraceful. The average man would still have felt a grudge against the refugees, but more lives would have been saved.[13]

Post-war Europe was supposed to guarantee that ignorance could no longer be an excuse for indifference. In this respect, it had succeeded remarkably well. We Europeans now knew more about what went on around us than we might have done in the 1930s. There were certainly fewer 'mass delusions' in Europe. The disposition to look after the victims of catastrophe wasn't always lacking. All we needed to acquire, it seemed, was a more intense sense of solidarity or, if that proved impossible, a more developed idea of the degree to which, in certain instances and given due warning, *difference* wasn't always dangerous or indeed reprehensible. We needed to discover a sense of Europeanness that wasn't dependent on the old and by now artificial boundaries of national cultures. In order to be Europeans we had to acquire the habit of accepting foreignness. It was as simple as that – but then of course I realized that it wasn't.

Sitting in a portside cafe in Toulon, while I waited to hear more from the frontists about the impossibility of living with foreigners, I came across Voltaire's 1727 account of the Stock Exchange floor in London:

> You will see there representatives of all nations gathered together for the benefit of mankind. Jew, Muslim and Christian deal with each other as if they shared a common faith, and they only call infidels those who are bankrupt . . . at the

end of these peaceful and free assemblies, some go to the synagogue, others go to drink; this man is off to be baptized in a huge vat in the name of the Father, Son and Holy Ghost; that one is going to have his son circumcised and have mumbled over the child Hebrew words that he doesn't understand; these others here are going to their church where they will wait for God's inspiration, hat on head, and they are all happy.[14]

Voltaire didn't know about, or chose to ignore, the treatment meted out to Catholics, particularly if they were Irish, in eighteenth-century Britain. He loved Britain – as later French sages would later discover America – unwaspishly, without discrimination and with a passion he never experienced at home. Yet Voltaire's London did accommodate a degree of what we would now call multiculturalism; and I was struck by how much difficulty the notion still presented to many Europeans. In every Far Right speech I sat through in France or Germany allusion was made to the American or Anglo-Saxon enemy. 'Melting-pot' (the last syllable was pronounced '*pott . . .*' with a stage snake hiss, by Le Pen) or 'patch*work*' sounded much worse in French, as did the omnipresent '*multi-culti*' in German. But it was never clear to me exactly what the words meant to Europeans.

In America, multiculturalism was nowadays used mainly in the context of education. It applied to the notion that the old, simple hierarchy of values derived from the predominantly white society no longer applied, and that schools or universities should strive to give their pupils some sort of identity, however vestigial, deriving from the competing cultures from which they had come. Multiculturalism struck at the pretensions of Eurocentrism in America. In a way that Voltaire would instantly have understood, and perhaps even approved of, the idea had been applied to non-ethnic minorities, including gays and lesbians. It posed the problem of whether bilingual education facilitated integration. More profoundly, it asked the question of whether integration was any more possible or indeed desirable. For cultural conservatives, such as Robert Bork, multiculturalism was a comforting lie designed to smother the troubling paradoxes of a contemporary America in which few any more admitted to holding views in common, or even got on with each other:

> The United States now faces the question of how far a culture can stretch to accommodate more and more ethnic groups and religions and still remain recognizable as a culture rather than an agglomeration of cultures. Which leads to the further question: Can a national identity, something resembling a national community, be maintained when cultural unity is destroyed?[15]

One could argue about whether America had indeed come to this (I doubted that it had, though it might well do within a few decades), but such fears were not likely to assume even vaguely material form in Europe. Those whom I talked to might suggest that the identity of France or Germany was endangered, but this was clearly not the case, by any measurable criteria. Germany, France, the Netherlands or Britain might contain sizeable foreign populations, but they would never be overwhelmed by foreignness. Quite possibly, a European multiculturalism would ultimately exist, but it would never be the same as the American one. This was because European national cultures, pre-existing the nation state and painstakingly built up over hundreds of years, were so different from each other; and because these differences, ultimately, were their raison d'être, even in what we might end by calling, perhaps reluctantly if we were

British, a federal Europe. They would not mysteriously fade away.

At the beginning of 1999, the new red and green coalition attempted to alter the nationality laws in Germany. There was nothing new about the idea of finally removing the old definition of Germanness, enacted as long ago as 1913 and long ago discredited by history, whereby the only true Germans were blood ones. Indeed the change had been discussed for many years. Most civilized Germans, it seemed, were embarrassed by the anomaly whereby the remaining Germans who were descendants of those who had settled in Russia centuries before became citizens the day they arrived, while Turks were obliged to wait for many years. Many Turks had never become German because this meant that they would have to abandon their Turkish passports, thus losing the right to return home if they ever wanted to. More than a million of these German Turks, who had businesses and houses, paying their taxes and behaving like good Germans, were anomalously regarded as foreigners. It was to them, primarily, that the new legislation was addressed; and they would be allowed to keep their Turkish passport while becoming Germans. To the Greens this was a small recompense for the indignity to which they had been subjected for so long. But the legislation was opposed not just by the Far Right – one might have assumed this would be the case – but by supposedly more moderate parties, too. It seemed that the idea of dual citizenship bothered many Germans. They believed it wasn't appropriate – that one should either be German or something else, and that one couldn't be both. Over a million German citizens signed a petition to this effect.

In London I met one of the two German Green Members of Parliament who were of Turkish origins. Cem Özdemir was dressed impeccably, and he spoke the sort of business-school English of Eurocrats or international consultants. Mockery had become his way of dealing with difficult or embarrassing situations and he explained that his parents shared this predicament. They had lived in Germany since the early 1960s. His father was prosperous, and thought of himself as German. But he knew his parents wouldn't choose to be German rather than Turkish – his parents would have lived most of their lives in a country where they remained foreigners. But then Özdemir began to talk about the anomalies in his own life. On trains, even when he went first class, he was the only person in a crowded carriage whose passport was examined. This happened even when he took out the German equivalent of Hansard, or the *Frankfurter Allegemeine*, or folded his jacket neatly over his knees like the good German businessman he had nearly become. It seemed that there was nothing a Turk could do which would make him appear as serious as a real German. Insurance companies didn't return his calls – they were not legally required to, though they couldn't refuse him a policy. At airports he was often asked how long he was staying in Germany, even when he used the diplomatic passport which was his right as a member of parliament. When he took his seat in the parliament building, he could be seen on television each day, behind the bulk of Helmut Kohl. People called his office to complain or ask whether his presence was necessary without any apparent consciousness of what they were doing. 'Can't they find someone German?' they asked. It would take time to remedy these deficiencies. He implied that it would take a very long time.

In France, somewhere near the German border, I attended the annual celebrations at a half-derelict château belonging to a friend. The local socialist mayor was there, the teacher and all the village dignitaries. Before fifty of us sat down to dinner, we were entertained by a dance troupe from the nearby town. They were well-scrubbed teenagers, eager to do well, and they performed in pink or grey jumpsuits. Some were Arabs, some were blacks, some French white. The music, of course, came from America. Like so much in Europe to do with race or culture, the effect was contrived, freighted with good intentions but nonetheless unbearably light. And yet the episode told me that something close to multiculturalism could be anticipated in contemporary Europe. The real question now was whether it was successful or not – and whether Europeans were prepared to allow it to work its own way. It wasn't enough for French rappers to copy American originals, passing the result off as native dissent. Benetton's giant, vacant hoardings wouldn't convince Europeans that they lived in a place where good things could be shared with the hitherto feared or despised alien. We needed something better – and something more recognizably European. Despite the abolition of formal frontiers, walls still surrounded Europeans, marking them off from each other. Until the walls were pulled down multiculturalism would remain a matter of dance performances and football teams. I remembered what I had argued over in Berchtesgaden with my French colleagues. Of course, the alteration of 'attitudes' – it was a refrain of Blairism and the Third Way touted as an alternative to the restructuring of society which no longer seemed plausible – wasn't by itself enough. Of course the word 'culture', having been appropriated by management consultants, had become more or less unusable. You could neither change attitudes from the top down, by diktat, nor was it possible to rely alone on programmes of public education. If it could be instilled at all, tolerance of The Other (I admired the high-sounding French expression) wouldn't occur rapidly. Nor would the habit of rubbing along (a pertinent, low-level English expression) take hold instantly. But I had been right to suggest that this was what really counted in Europe, and not just the formal, written-down definitions of democracy, with which our ageing as well as supposedly new institutions were festooned.

I had changed, through exposure to so much hatred. How had I changed? I was more in favour of what Europe was becoming than I had been. There was much that was less than satisfactory about the hasty attempts of European politicians to tell themselves that they weren't like Jörg Haider – and the boycott of Austria in early 2000 never lost its air of opportunism. Whether we liked it or not, the preservation of Europe had become a European issue. The lack of frontiers now meant that such matters concerned all of us, as Europeans; and it was no longer appropriate, in this context at least, to guard against intervening in the affairs of other countries. Nonetheless such interventions should perhaps not be a daily occurence, and they must be grounded in legal procedure. The French word for an interdiction, given under the Constitution and designed to retain order, was *garde fou* – the wall or moat at the edge of an asylum designed to keep the inmates inside. Europeans didn't require protection from ideas nor indeed from themselves. But it would be appropriate to create a single document guaranteeing democratic freedoms throughout the new Europe or interdicting their destruction. This would dispose of the notion that anyone coming to power would find it possible to destroy the legal rights of a minority without being expelled from the Union. Laws or declarations couldn't by themselves ensure that abuses wouldn't happen. They might prohibit the sort of quasi-legal coup engineered by Hitler, but they could never ensure that it would never happen. However, they would make it more difficult to sustain the pretensions of those, like

Mégret or Haider, who tried to create separate mini-republics of hatred from the town halls or villages they controlled, with the affirmation that such practices were desirable or legal. Guarantees of individual or minority rights existed in national constitutions and they were enshrined in the European Court of Human Rights, to which all European states were signatories. However, I felt that something stronger was needed. It might even be part of a European Constitution, though there were those – in Britain particularly – who would protest. Of course, we would have to wait – everything in Europe took longer than expected – but it would be worth it, because a Europe without the guarantee of rights was nothing at all.

Like so many Europeans I had been shocked, most of all, by the wars following the collapse of Yugoslavia, in Croatia, in Bosnia and later in Kosovo, without understanding exactly what Europe could reasonably have done to forestall or minimize the catastrophe. Beginning as an attempt to carve up what remained of the old Federal Republic presided over by Tito, the conflict had come to remind Europeans of the awful mid-century past. But the atrocities were happening in the Europe of our time – they were *ours*. What we now called ethnic cleansing had begun as a simple, highly effective set of contemporary prescriptions. You took a village by force, burning the houses so that the inhabitants couldn't return. Then you separated the women and children from the young men. The women and children were placed on tractors or buses. The men were either encouraged to try to escape and then shot – or they were driven to a shed or an open field and killed one by one. These actions were repeated throughout Yugoslavia, mostly, but not uniquely, performed by Serbs against Muslims. Depending on no technology other than the cast-off weapons of the old socialist bloc arsenal, they were difficult to anticipate or prevent. It was also not easy to identify, capture and punish the perpetrators. These were the truly shaming episodes of our time.

But they had made me take seriously the idea of Europeanness. Now it was the question of what Europe was *for* that had come to bother me. If it wasn't about democracy or failed to be so, if it just subsisted vaguely around the question of money (and I found I resented the time and effort spent on the standardization of banknotes, remaining wary of a union that really existed only through the medium of corporate mergers), then the place, alas, wasn't for me. But I now came to see being European as a continual battle of sorts. It was possible, I believed, to envisage the liberal idea of Europe mattering both at home and in the rest of the world. It was possible – but only if Europeans believed in themselves. For that to happen Europeans would need to establish, beyond possible doubt, their own civilization of rights. And in that struggle the way they decided to treat the alien, whether in their midst or not, was of fundamental importance. They (or we) could no longer rely on declarations or get Americans to stand in, criticizing them for belligerence when things got tough. In this sense, admittedly remote from the noise of Brussels, the European hour had come.

Four years after the worst post-war ethnic killing on European soil, I wanted to see what had happened in Srebrenica, the remote town where, in the summer of 1995, over seven thousand Muslims were taken out and killed. I flew to Sarajevo and four hours later found myself in the territory of the Republika Srpska, the Serb heartland of Bosnia. In the Hotel Fontana in Bratunać, there were pinkish stained tablecloths and a surplus of waiters with moustaches and soiled napkins served *slivowitz* and harsh peppermint tea with the consistency of primitive mouthwash. Smoke surrounded the dais on which the small orchestra played loudly. Around them and to the back of the room sat Serb families. The band leader bowed in every direction, called out, and one by one the children came forward. They were dressed in elaborate, red or puce spangled outfits. Some of them sported the sort of trouser suits favoured by child groups like the Osmonds twenty-five years ago. Others wore what looked like minia-ture bridal gowns or the kind of expensive get up favoured by over-eager hookers in the old monster hotels of socialist Europe. They were extravagantly made up. They sang tune-lessly, but everyone applauded loudly when they were fin-ished. I realized that this was the only time I had seen Serbs *en famille*, smiling, not toting guns or adjusting the wide belts they wore around compendious guts.

But the Hotel Fontana was where, in the days prior to 12 July 1995, General Ratko Mladić organized his massacre. He wished to clear Srebrenica, designated as a 'safe area' by the UN, of its Muslim population. To that end he assembled a small army of Serb soldiers, some artillery pieces and more than seventy buses. Mladić and his troops encountered no opposition from the Dutch troops whose job it was to protect the town. It seemed that Mladić now believed that he could do whatever he wished to those whom he had captured. Quickly, the Muslim men were separated from their women. They were taken off to sheds or football fields, where they were murdered. Their bodies were dumped in mass graves throughout the countryside. Those who escaped and tried to cross the mountains into Muslim territory were also killed. There were only a handful of survivors.

Only a portion of the bodies, indeed, had by now been identified or even found, perhaps fewer than half of those who were murdered, and I learnt that the remains of some were stacked in refrigerated trailers parked in an abandoned factory. I went to the neighbouring town of Tuzla, a Stalinist industrial city turned military-and-aid entrepôt, where I sat in a crowded viewing room belonging to the local television station. Here I watched a videotape shot by a Serb camera-man and later smuggled to the West. It was the everyday banality of what had occurred that was striking. Here were the Dutch troops wearing berets and shorts, looking not like soldiers but the organizers of a downmarket Club Med, busy with bits of paper, shouting and remonstrating. Here were the soon-to-be killers and, by their side, the victims, skinny, poorly dressed, panicking – you could see fear or resignation in their faces. The Muslim women sat silently in the buses. They knew what was going to happen – how could they not know? One piece of the film showed guns firing in the summer haze over what seemed to be a car radio, and you could hear the Serb rock music in the after echo of the blasts. There were black portions in the film – atrocious things which someone had seen fit to edit. A man called out for his son, who had gone to hide in the hills. He was made to do this under gunpoint by the Serb soldiers. 'It's all right,' he repeated, as if his teenage son had merely strayed beyond a perimeter of a holiday beach, 'it's safe here' – and you could see from his face that he knew that when the son did finally come both of them would be murdered, as indeed it appeared they were.

Next day I met the woman who had been married to this man and who had lost both her sons in Srebrenica. Sitting in her small, neat living room I realized that I would never, no matter how many books or films I read, or wrote, or watched, or made, understand the full extent of her pain, or what caused humans to commit such acts. For it appeared that Mladić had been proud of his work. Stout, shovel-faced, beaming with pleasure, the General was photographed walking in triumph down the streets of Srebrenica surrounded by his officers. With the baffled, beaten Dutch, he was imperious or, more surprisingly, brusquely pedagogical. He knew the sort of world he wanted, and it was a better as well as a more realistic one than theirs. In the compound at Potočari, a crumbling factory made over to the Dutch which he now regarded as his own, he delivered lectures to those whom he had humiliated and, by implication, to the shallow, heedless West itself, whose envoys now stood at his pleasure. Muslims bred like rats, and they started wars. They would occupy Holland within three years if no one did anything to stop them. When one Dutch soldier interrupted the General, pointing out that in Holland people of different races lived together and that they had done so for many years, Mladić brushed him aside. It didn't matter, he said, these ideas didn't matter at all. He would do what needed to be done.[16] There was no point in arguing with Mladić, and the Dutchman fell silent. He could scarcely have comforted himself with the notion that scenes such as this one had been enacted many times before, and all over Europe.

It was snowing in Srebrenica and there was no noise in the town's main street. From time to time a cart went by, pulled by a mangy horse, carrying nothing. In better times, Srebrenica had been a spa town, and then it had been subjected to the kind of rural industrialization project beloved of communist planners. The town's pretensions were never fulfilled and now shelling and looting had destroyed it. At its centre, the Town Hall, built at the beginning of the century, during the Austrian occupation, was shuttered. There were boards around the abandoned cultural centre and the shopping mall. One store sold pitiful bright polyester jerseys and tracksuit bottoms. Evacuated of its original Serb population before it had been turned by the UN into a safe area, cleansed of its Muslims, Srebrenica had been resettled after the Dayton Agreement with Serb refugees from the suburbs of Sarajevo. It seemed that they had been rushed from their homes, often leaving most of their possessions behind. They had gone to a town and a piece of the country which they didn't know, and which, in its present state, offered them scant livelihood. Aid had been withheld pending some demonstrable form of political progress (it was an American stipulation, the work of a diligent senator from New Jersey, anxious that Serbs shouldn't seem to draw profit from aggression), and these abandoned, trodden on people were now angry and resentful. It was they – many of them were cultured folk, in their former lives philosophy teachers or ballet amateurs – who went listlessly about the streets in search of firewood, or climbed eight floors to their high-rise flats without water or light.

Walking up and down the main street, stamping in the bitter cold, it would have been hard to imagine any place more derelict in Europe – or one of which the prospects appeared less promising. But appearances were in this instance deceptive. Each day a small American patrol from the nearby base visited Srebrenica. They gave sweets to the children and chatted through their interpreter. One floor of the otherwise boarded up hotel had been turned over to the OCSE – the ponderously named Organization for Co-operation and Security in Europe. Here we met the Irishman and the American whose task it was somehow to construct a laboratory capable of creating the circumstances in which democracy could thrive. Equipped with email, laptop and mission statements, energetic and fresh-faced, Larry Sampler gave me an insight into what it must have been like suddenly to find oneself in charge of a piece of Germany in 1945 filled with guilty secrets and what were then known, with a tinge of resignation, as displaced persons.

The task of re-education, he conceded, was formidable; but it was an important aspect of the Dayton accords, agreed to by all parties. To be seen to espouse democracy, the reluctant inhabitants of Srebrenica must now hold town meetings. At present they were stalled over the matter of national anthems, and each side was in the habit of walking out when the other's tune was played. But reparation for the act of ethnic cleansing also required something deeper, and this was the resettlement of at least a few Muslim families in the town. Sampler didn't pretend that, speaking personally as an educated American, he would advise them to settle there. In his view any family of Muslims wishing to settle here would be remiss in their duties as parents, if not insane – and not just because there was no work. He explained that the town held no prospects for these new 'foreigners'. Both the Cyrillic alphabet and the Orthodox religious education would be offensive to them, and the new 'revisionist' history of Bosnia-Herzgovina (compulsory for any school receiving aid) was not yet complete. These struck me as among the less important reasons for not returning, but Sampler was surely correct in his gloomy assessment. Nonetheless he was also right to insist that what he called the international community must give refugees the choice of returning or not. New houses could be built (the contract was thought to be about to go to Norway, whose wooden houses furnished sports villages, or South Korea, with much experience in prefab construction for US bases) or indeed old ones restored. At the end something – not much, admittedly – might remain of the old, recently ruined, multi-ethnic society of Bosnia. For this was the reason, as he reminded us, that so much money and effort was being spent in this awful place. It was why he felt good about being here and didn't want to leave to complete his dissertation on the media, race and ethnicity. 'They must be able to choose, even if they say no,' he repeated.

Others I knew became depressed in Bosnia. What appeared to be the useful, pleasure-giving side of what they did each day – taking notes, writing things up – vanished amid so much hatred and indifference; and they felt vaguely guilty. But my own training, I could now see, had proved useful. I felt abruptly grounded coming here, pulled to earth, and in the end it wasn't so bad a feeling. There was life of a sort, and even meaning on the blighted periphery. All the more or less airy speculations entertained by Europeans in Brussels were absent here. Bosnia wasn't Europe, to be sure, but it was a part of Europe. You could not only fly here easily, you could also, being here, in the cold and proximity to suffering, understand bits of the European past. It was to avoid the re-emergence of places like Srebrenica that the new Europe was created more than forty years ago. In Bosnia the often ludicrous confections whereby civilization idly entertained itself appeared to vanish. It was as if a screen was suddenly lifted, showing instead of brightly painted dioramas or special effects, a forlorn collection of bones and rags. The lesson was this – no point in worrying what might, or could, happen when it had already occurred here. One must simply stop it happening again. If it did happen, as in Kosovo, Europeans must be prepared to do more than pick up the pieces. If necessary, they must be prepared to defend whatever it was they believed in. And one must not rely on the work of others to install human rights. 'I was too late,' the appalling protagonist of Camus' *The Fall* explained when he failed to jump in the Seine on the way back from dinner in order to rescue a would-be suicide. 'One is always too late.' This was the old European story of cynicism or apathy, and one must somehow hope that it could be altered.

But I was also to be comprehensively surprised here. At a town meeting held in the local school Larry Sampler alluded to the 'old politics' holding back the pace of transformation. He and his Irish partner were engaged in what appeared to be a feud with blowhard nationalists. Threats had repeatedly been issued, and gifts of scotch or *slivowitz* hadn't caused them to be withdrawn. In order to install democracy, it had been necessary to debar one recently elected participant on the grounds that he was stirring up hatred. I hadn't come all this way to see another hate-peddler, but on impulse I decided to visit one of these old politicians. Of course, I had to wait a while, sitting in cafes, watching videos of Courtney Love; but I realized that it had been worth it as soon as I walked into the smallish office, stacked with tapes.

A girl with dark, combed-out hair and a tight-fitting black denim trouser suit busied herself with the recording equipment, hesitating between an old scratched video of a Tom Cruise movie and some Serb folk songs. Because Srebrenica was in a deep valley, and thus didn't receive conventional broadcast signals, the town was totally dependent on its local radio and television service. Momcilo Cvetinović was the owner of the local station. He was a squat man, with a moustache and the cowlick-covered flat brow made notorious by Serb leaders whom English or Scottish political romantics such as Fitzroy Maclean found so appealing. His creased leather jacket and mud-caked boots gave him the air of an early Bolshevik. But it wasn't these individual items of clothing, or indeed his physical appearance, that made me feel we had met already. I knew exactly what he was going to say before he opened his mouth. In the same way as one might acquire a black belt, a certificate enabling one to spot dry rot or an expertise in double accounting, I knew how to spot fascists. I could tell them at six paces or a hundred, and I didn't require DNA sampling. I could pick them out from crowds or in group photographs, and by now surely I could smell them, too.

My new acquaintance talked about his principled squabbles with the agents of democracy. *They* believed that they could eject him from his position at the television station. However, they would shortly learn that he owned the equipment. Most of the town – over 70 per cent, it turned out – had voted for him, and now he was being illegally removed. His sullen whine lingered over the tobacco smoke, wrapping itself around the relics of Eastern bloc kitsch with which the room was furnished. Obduracy was his marker, to be placed everywhere around him, donated with great generosity to those in whose presence he found himself; and he believed, simply, that being Serb was being right about the world. It was astonishing – I might have been listening to Le Pen or Haider, Bossi or Mégret. I could have been in any of the cramped, loveless and joyless places I had seen throughout Europe, in Toulon, Antwerp, Cotbuss or Greve. Even when Cvetinović alluded to the massacre, with the observation that it hadn't been quite real, much had been exaggerated by the West and the Muslims, and that killings anyhow happened in all wars, I wasn't specially surprised. This was what they had said to me, each of them. It was how they replied when you asked them those sort of questions. And I realized that, for me at least, it was time to stop seeing these people.

For the fascists were surely bound to lose. They were, I was convinced, like old movies now. They might return to us, but it would be without ever really coming back. My hunch was that we would never again see what might be termed as a real fascist government taking power in Europe and doing its worst. Of course, there might be dubious figures capable of manipulating the past, and there might be fascist noises made. Of course, the hatreds that had made fascism possible would persist. And perhaps our own weakness, or their lack of scruples, would allow the creation of various attenuated forms of hatred, almost as sordid as their originals. But the real thing? I didn't think so. Or at least I hoped not. But as I walked through the deadened streets of Srebrenica, I reminded myself again (one should do this often, I told myself, and I didn't care how banal it sounded) that the only real hindrance lay in each of us.

# NOTES

## INTRODUCTION

1 Umberto Eco, *The Guardian*, 19 August 1995.
2 *International Herald Tribune*, 14 July 1995.
3 The periodicals, books and magazines devoted to the phenomenon are too numerous to cite. Not all of them are accurate. Among many conspiracy school surveys of the Far Right, the most readable as well as the most lurid is *The Beast Reawakens*, Martin Lee (Little, Brown, London, 1997). More cautious, and perhaps more reliable, surveys include: *Fascism*, Roger Eatwell (Chatto and Windus, London, 1995); *Fascism, Past, Present, Future*, Walter Laqueur (New York, Oxford University Press, 1996); *Extrémismes en Europe*, Jean-Yves Camus ed. (CERA, Editions L'Aube, Paris, 1997); *Les héritiers du Troisième Reich*, Patrick Moreau (Seuil, Paris, 1994); *L'Extreme Droite en Europe*, *Pouvoirs* 87 (Seuil, Paris, 1998).

## LOOKING FOR THE FASCISTS

1 *Bagatelles pour un massacre* was a success when it was published by Editions Denoël in 1937. The publishing details (as with much else regarding Céline's appalling career) are to be found in *Céline*, Philippe Alméras (Robert Laffont, Paris, 1994).
2 Enzo Siciliano, *Pasolini* (Random House, New York, 1982), p. 325. For the fullest account of Pasolini's views see Barth David Schwartz, *Pasolini Requiem* (Pantheon, New York, 1992).

# NOTES

3   *As I Please*, 24 March 1944, reprinted in George Orwell, *The Collected Essays, Journalism and Letters* (Penguin Books, London, 1970), vol. 3, pp. 135–9.

4   Eugen Weber, *The Hollow Years* (Sinclair-Stevenson, London, 1995), p. 119.

5   Pierre Drieu la Rochelle, *Journal 1939–45* (NRF, Paris, 1992), p. 302.

6   Alméras, p. 183.

7   Louis-Ferdinand Céline, *Bagatelles pour un massacre* (Editions Denoël, Paris, 1937), p. 145.

8   Quoted in Alméras, p. 290.

9   T. W. Adorno et al., *The Authoritarian Personality* (Norton and Co., New York, 1982), pp. 11ff.

10  Adorno et al., p. 64.

11  Alberto Moravia, *The Conformist* (G. F. Flammarion, Paris, 1985), p. 114.

12  Nicholas Mosley, *The Rules of the Game/Beyond the Pale* (Dalkey Archive, Elmwood Park, Illinois, 1991), p. 571.

13  Patrick Leigh-Fermor, *A Time of Gifts* (Penguin Books, London, 1977), p. 43.

14  Maurice Bardèche, *Qu'est-ce que le fascisme?* (Pythéas, 1995), p. 162.

15  François Furet and Ernst Nolte, *Fascisme et communisme* (Plon, Paris, 1998), p. 15, pp. 50–51.

16  Richard J. Golsan ed., *Fascism's Return* (University of Nebraska Press, Lincoln, 1998), p. 142.

17  Simone de Beauvoir, *Beloved Chicago Man: Letters to Nelson Algren* (Gollancz, London, 1998). p. 35.

18  Quoted in Mark Mazower, *Dark Continent: Europe's Twentieth Century* (Allen Lane, London, 1998), p. 16.

19  Jean-Paul Sartre, *Réflexions sur la question Juive* (Gallimard, Paris, 1955), p. 10.

20  Mathieu Lindon, *Le procès de Jean-Marie Le Pen* (P.O.L., Paris, 1998), p. 135.

21  1965 speech to the International Catholic Association for radio and TV, Rome. Quoted in Michael Tracey, *Hugh Greene: A Variety of Lives* (Bodley Head, London, 1983), p. 243.

22  Isaiah Berlin, *The Proper Study of Mankind: an Anthology of Essays* (Chatto and Windus, London, 1997), p. 197.

## FÜHRERS OF NOTHING

1  Jeffrey Herf, *Divided Memory: The Nazi Past in the Two Germanys* (Harvard University Press, Cambridge, Mass., 1997), p. 205.
2  Alexandra Richie, *Faust's Metropolis* (HarperCollins, London, 1998), p. 735.
3  Herf, p. 168.
4  Orwell, vol. 3, p. 456.
5  Lee, p. 274.
6  Ingo Hasselbach, *Führer-Ex* (Chatto and Windus, London, 1996), p. 298.
7  VFS report, 1996.
8  Ruud Koopmans, *A Burning Question: Explaining the Rise of Racist and Extreme Right Wing Violence in Western Europe* (Wissenchaftszentrum Berlin Für Sozialforschung, WZB, 1995), p. 12.
9  VFS report, 1996.

## LIES IN OUR TIME

1  Deborah Lipstadt, *Denying the Holocaust, the Growing Assault on Truth and Memory* (The Free Press, New York, 1993), p. 172.
2  Lipstadt, p. 181.
3  Muriel Spark, *Collected Fiction* (Houghton Mifflin, New York, 1995), p. 300.
4  Primo Levi, *If This is a Man . . .* (Abacus, London, 1987), p. 66.
5  Primo Levi, *The Drowned and the Saved* (Abacus, London, 1988), p. 11.
6  Apart from Deborah Lipstadt's work on denial, which deals primarily with its American proponents, the best work on the subject is by Pierre Vidal-Naquet. *Les assassins de la mémoire* (La Découverte, Paris, 1987) is a collection of his polemical essays. *Qui sont les assassins de la mémoire?* is reprinted in *Réflexions sur le génocide tome III* (La Découverte, Paris, 1995).

Another essay, *The Future of a Negation* by Alain Finkelraut, is published by the University of Nebraska, 1998. There are many polemical tracts by 'deniers' – these can nowadays be found on the Internet.

7  Lipstadt, p. 2.

8  Eric Delcourt, *La police de la pensée contre le révisionnisme* (Diffusion R. H. R., Paris, 1994). Delcourt is a lawyer who has defended many deniers.

9  John Stuart Mill, *On Liberty* (Penguin Books, London, 1974), p. 68.

10  Vidal-Naquet, p. 9.

11  Vidal-Naquet, p. 103.

12  Chomsky's defence is reprinted in full in a collection of texts by Robert Faurisson, *Mémoire en défense* (La Vieille Taupe, Paris, 1980), p. ix.

13  *Le Monde*, 1 September 1998.

14  Émile Zola, *J'accuse* (Éditions Complexe, Paris), pp. 26 and 113. Zola's 1898 appearance was given cover treatment in the mainly anti-Dreyfusard tabloid press of the day.

15  Robert Faurisson, *Vérité historique ou vérité politique* (La Vieille Taupe, Paris, 1996), p. 95.

16  Faurisson, *Vérité historique*, p. 96.

17  Georges Pompidou, *Anthologie de la poésie Française* (Hachette, Paris, 1961), p. 405.

18  Vidal-Naquet, p. 11.

19  *Le Monde*, 29 December 1978. Faurisson's own account of his troubles appears to be scrupulously accurate.

20  Kremer's testimony (and Faurisson's annotations) are reprinted in *Mémoire et défense*, pp. 109–148.

21  Faurisson, *Vérité historique*, p. 193.

22  Martin Gilbert, *Auschwitz and the Allies* (Michael Joseph, London, 1981), p. 262.

23  Arthur Koestler, *The Yogi and the Commissar* (Danube edition, London, 1965), p. 90.

24  Céline, p. 1.

25  Gilbert, p. 309. The story of the lost photograph and its recuper-

ation is also told in Norman Davies, *Europe* (Oxford University Press, Oxford, 1996), p. 1026.

## HOW TO KILL AN ARAB

1 '*Moi, Khaled Kelkal*', *Le Monde*, 7 October 1995. All subsequent quotations from the Dietmar Loch interview are taken from the newspaper transcription.
2 *Haut conseil à l'intégration.* Quoted in Emmanuel Todd, *Le destin des immigrés* (Seuil, Paris, 1994), p. 125.
3 CSA survey of French attitudes, 24 November to 6 December 1997. Reprinted in *Le Monde*, 16 September 1998.
4 Albert Camus, *L'Étranger* (NRF, Paris, 1942). *Le premier homme* (Gallimard, Paris, 1995).

## NOTHING IS THE SAME

1 Hugo Young, *One of Us* (Macmillan, London, 1989), p. 233.
2 E. J. B. Rose, *Colour and Citizenship* (Oxford University Press, London, 1969), p. 608.
3 *The Times*, 2 March 1968.
4 Quoted by Nick Cohen, *New Statesman*, 26 January 1999.
5 John Upton, *The Times*, 14 July 1999.
6 Passages from the Lawrence report are taken from the on-line version, with no page numbers.

## TO THE FRONT AND BACK

1 Although there are many books about the Front, relatively few authors have exposed themselves personally to the frontists. Exceptions are: Michel Samson, *Le Front aux affaires* (Calmann-Lévy, Paris, 1997), which describes scandal-ridden Toulon; Mark Hunter, *Un American au Front* (Stock, Paris, 1997), which conveys exactly the right note of baffled fury. An early effort to infiltrate the FN is Anne Vincent's *Au Front* (Gallimard, Paris, 1987). Of the many sociological or psephological surveys the most acute is Pascale Perrineau, *Le symptôme Le Pen* (Fayard, Paris, 1997).

2 Maryse Souchard and others, *Le Pen: les mots* (Le Monde Éditions, Paris, 1997), pp. 163ff.

3 Speech of September 1990, quoted in Souchard, p. 166.

4 Martine Aubry and Olivier Duhamel, *Le petit dictionnaire pour lutter contre l'Extrème Droite* (Seuil, Paris, 1995), pp. 16 and 198.

5 The most exhaustive (and also the most entertaining) is Gilles Bresson and Christian Lionet, *Le Pen* (Seuil, Paris, 1994).

6 Bresson and Lionet, pp. 315 and 333.

7 Quoted in Souchard, p. 31.

8 *Libération*, 9 February 1998.

9 Michael R. Marrus and Robert O. Paxton, *Vichy et les Juifs* (Calmann-Lévy, Paris, 1981), pp. 17–18.

10 The best account of Mégret's career is in Michael Darmon and Romain Rosso's *L'après Le Pen* (Seuil, Paris, 1998).

11 This was prescribed in the FN manifesto, drawn up under Mégret's supervision.

12 Perrineau, p. 150 and 165.

13 Marcel Ophuls, *The Sorrow and the Pity* (screenplay) (Outerbridge and Lazard, New York, 1972). Also Henry Rousso, *Le syndrome de Vichy* (Seuil, Paris, 1990).

14 Samson, pp. 116 and 124.

## THE NEW LOST TRIBES OF EUROPE

1 See Hugo Young, *This Blessed Plot* (Macmillan, London, 1998), for an extended examination of 'Euroscepticism'.

2 Orwell, vol. 2, 1940–43, p. 41.

3 see *Pouvoirs*, pp. 22ff.

4 For the history of the Blok see Rinke van den Brink, *L'Internationale de la haine* (Editions Luc Pire, Brussels, 1997) and Hugo Gijsels, *Le Vlaams Blok* (Luc Pire, Brussels, 1993). For the parallel activities of the French-speaking Belgian Far Right see Manuel Abramowicz, *Les rats noirs* (Editions Luc Pire, Brussels, 1996).

5 For biographical details see Melanie Sully, *The Haider Phenomenon* (Columbia University Press, New York, 1997), pp. 57ff.

# NOTES

6 Ernest Gellner, *Nations and Nationalism* (Blackwell, Oxford, 1983), pp. 39–52, 119.

## THE BLACK GUIDE

1 W. H. Auden, from 'Negroes', *The English Auden* (Faber and Faber, London, 1977) p. 293.
2 Sebastian Haffner, *The Meaning of Hitler* (Phoenix Books, London, 1997), p. 4.
3 Powell's speech reprinted in *New Statesman*, 17 April 1998.
4 For some background to the speech see Simon Heffer, *Like the Roman* (Weidenfeld and Nicolson, London, 1998), pp. 460 and 468.
5 Le Pen's speech in Assembly elections, spring 1997, author's translation.
6 W. H. Auden, *The English Auden*, 1 September 1959, p. 245.
7 Ron Rosenbaum, *Explaining Hitler* (Macmillan, London, 1998), p. 157.
8 Mazower, pp. 326ff.
9 *International Herald Tribune*, 9 January 2000.
10 Todd, p. 205.
11 Quoted in Caryl Phillips, *Extravagant Strangers* (Faber and Faber, London, 1997), pp. 6–7.
12 Hanif Kureishi, *The Buddha of Suburbia* (Faber and Faber, London, 1990), p. 3.
13 Orwell, *As I Please*, 24 January 1947, *Collected Essays*, vol. 4, p. 314.
14 Voltaire, *Lettres philosophiques* (Flammarion, Paris, 1964), p. 47.
15 Robert Bork, *Slouching Towards Gomorrah* (HarperCollins, New York, 1996), p. 298.
16 David Rohde, *Endgame* (Westview Press, New York, 1997), p. 222.